Off The Beaten Track
ITALY

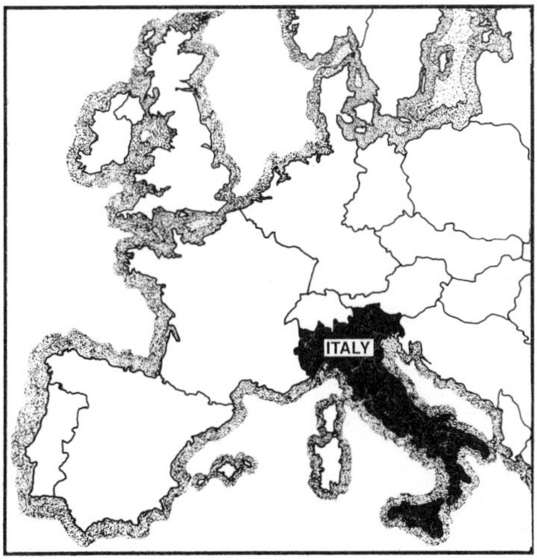

OFF THE BEATEN TRACK
ITALY

MPC

British Library Cataloguing in Publication Data:
Whitney, Phil
Italy.
1. Italy - visitor's guides
I. Title II. Sale, Richard, 1946-
III. Woodyatt, Nancy III. Collins, Martin, *1941* - V. Series
914.5'04928

Published by:
Moorland Publishing Co Ltd,
Moor Farm Road,
Ashbourne,
Derbyshire
DE6 1HD
England

ISBN 0 86190 234 3 (paperback)
ISBN 0 86190 227 0 (hardback)

Colour origination by:
Quad Repro Ltd, Pinxton, Notts

Printed in the UK by:
Butler and Tanner Ltd, Frome, Somerset

Cover photograph:
Sorrento (*Photobank International*)

Colour illustrations have been supplied as follows:
Veneto; Father Alessandro Berlincioni. *Sesto-Sexten*; Bolzano Provincial Tourist Office. *Pampeago; Val di Cembra; Lake Tenno; Lake Molveno*; Foto Flavio Faganello. *Church, Antagnod; Châtillon; Val di Cogne; Villa Monastero; Piazza Vecchia; Trento; Malcesine; Sperlonga;* Italian State Tourist Office. *Backstreet, Umbria*; Chiara Piovanelli. *Lucca*; R. Scholes. *Elba; Orvieto Cathedral; Gaeta; Avellino; Sculptures, Gaeta*; Strawberry Media. *Selinunte*; Guido Picchetti (Strawberry Media). *Bagnara Calabra; Tropea; Scilla; Tindari*; N. Woodyatt.

Black & White illustrations have been supplied as follows:
Father Alessandro Berlincioni pp13, 165; Foto Flavio Faganello (Trento) pp79, 87, 89, 81; Italian State Tourist Office pp17, 21, 55, 57, 59, 63, 83, 181, 183, 185, 199, 203, 209, 211, 212-13, 221, 223, 231, 243, 246, 247, 249, 251, 263, 267, 298; Latina Provincial Tourist Board p235; Mariacarla Penzo p135; Provincial Tourist Office (Novara) pp73, 75; R. Sale pp33, 35, 51; Strawberry Media pp105, 121, 233, 262, 300, 304; B. Schwartz (Strawberry Media) pp19, 126, 163; M. H. Sedge (Strawberry Media) p103; R. Wickley (Strawberry Media) p292; Tiziano Panini pp95, 99, 147, 157, 187; P. Whitney pp161, 179; P. and L. Whitney p259; N. Woodyatt pp284, 285, 287, 290, 294.

Note on Maps
The maps for each chapter, while comprehensive, are not designed to be used as route maps, but locate the main towns, villages and places of interest.

Contents

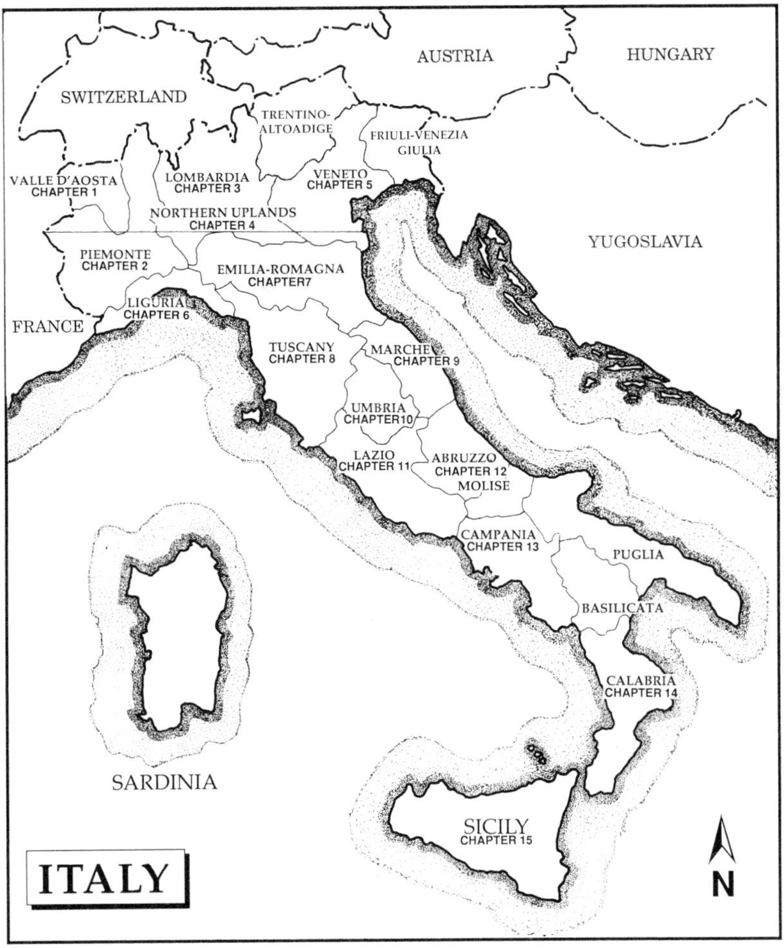
AUSTRIA
HUNGARY
SWITZERLAND
TRENTINO-ALTOADIGE
FRIULI-VENEZIA GIULIA
VALLE D'AOSTA
CHAPTER 1
LOMBARDIA
CHAPTER 3
VENETO
CHAPTER 5
NORTHERN UPLANDS
CHAPTER 4
YUGOSLAVIA
PIEMONTE
CHAPTER 2
EMILIA-ROMAGNA
CHAPTER7
LIGURIA
CHAPTER 6
FRANCE
TUSCANY
CHAPTER 8
MARCHE
CHAPTER 9
UMBRIA
CHAPTER10
LAZIO
CHAPTER 11
ABRUZZO
CHAPTER 12
MOLISE
CAMPANIA
CHAPTER 13
PUGLIA
BASILICATA
CALABRIA
CHAPTER 14
SARDINIA
SICILY
CHAPTER 15
ITALY
N

Introduction

Western Europe is a continent of great diversity, well visited not just by travellers from other parts of the globe but by the inhabitants of its own member countries. Within the year-round processes of trade and commerce, but more particularly during the holiday season, there is a great surging interchange of nationalities as one country's familiar attractions are left behind for those of another.

It is true that frontiers are blurred by ever quicker travel and communications, and that the sharing of cultures, made possible by an increasingly sophisticated media network, brings us closer in all senses to our neighbours. Yet essential differences do exist, differences which lure us abroad on our annual migrations in search of new horizons, fresh sights, sounds and smells, discovery of unknown landscapes and people.

Countless resorts have evolved for those among us who simply crave sun, sea and the reassuring press of humanity. There are, too, established tourist 'sights' with which a country or region has become associated and to which clings, all too often, a suffocating shroud — the manifestations of mass tourism in the form of crowds and entrance charges, the destruction of authentic atmosphere, cynical exploitation. Whilst this is by no means typical of all well known tourist attractions, it is familiar enough to act as a disincentive for those of more independent spirit who value personal discovery above prescribed experience and who would rather avoid the human conveyor belt of queues, traffic jams and packed accommodation.

It is for such travellers that this guidebook has been written. In its pages, no more than passing mention is made of the famous, the well documented, the already glowingly described — other guidebooks will satisfy the appetite for such orthodox tourist information. Instead, the reader is taken if not to unknown then to relatively unvisited places — literally 'off the beaten track'. Through the specialist knowledge of the authors, visitors using this guidebook are assured of gaining insights into the country's heartland whose heritage lies largely untouched by the tourist industry. Occasionally the reader is urged simply to take a sideways step from a site of renowned tourist interest to find one perhaps less sensational, certainly less frequented but often of equivalent fascination.

From wild, scantily populated countryside whose footpaths and byways are best navigated by careful map reading, to negotiating the side streets of towns and cities, travelling 'off the beaten track' can be rather more demanding than following in the footsteps of countless thousands before you. The way may be less clear, more adventurous and individualistic, but opportunities do emerge for real discovery in an age of increasing dissatisfaction with the passive predictability of conventional holidaymaking. With greater emphasis on exploring 'off the beaten track', the essence of Italy is more likely to be unearthed and its true flavours relished to the full.

Martin Collins

1 • The Valle d'Aosta

To the casual observer, Italy is a land of sun and sights, Adriatic and Mediterranean beaches, Venice and the ruins of Pompeii. Mountains are usually thought of secondly, in the form of the sculpted limestone of the Dolomites. But, whereas the northern slopes of the Alps are more famous and sometimes more dramatic, these mountains are shared between France, Switzerland and Austria. The whole of the southern slopes of the Alps are to be found in Italy, from the Occidental Alps to the west (where the alpine chain turns southward and heads for the Mediterranean, taking the border between France and Italy with it) to the Julian Alps to the east, where Italy meets Yugoslavia.

In the west, Italy shares the summit of Mont Blanc (calling it Monte Bianco) with France and the summit of the Matterhorn (calling it the Cervino) with Switzerland, with much high, cold, permanently snow-covered land between. As the Alps decrease in height, the pre-alpine peaks, up to 8,000ft, tumble down from them towards the Lombardy Plain, enclosing as they do, some of Europe's finest holiday lakes. Further east the Dolomites begin to rise, reaching some of their grandest heights close to the Austrian border.

This closeness to foreign borders has also meant that the northern uplands have seen, at very close hand, the struggles for domination both of the uplands themselves, and of Italy. Italy has been a unified country only since the wars of the Risorgimento in the second half of the nineteenth century, a little over 100 years. Prior to that the alpine regions saw overlords who spoke Spanish, German and French, and though no pockets of Spanish speakers now remain, there are several areas where French or German is still the first or equal first language of the locals.

One such area of bilingualism is the region of the Valle d'Aosta, the first region viewed by many tourists as they cross the Alps via the Great St Bernard Pass, the Little St Bernard Pass, or the Mont Blanc and Great St Bernard Tunnels.

The Valle d'Aosta is a roughly rectangular shaped region covering an area of approximately 1,260sq miles. The 'valley' is really the valley of the Dora Baltea river from its origin in the many streams running off Mont Blanc down to Pont St Martin where the mountains, which until then form the valley sides, open out. Of the two sides, the higher is the northern one, formed by the Pennine Alps separating the Valle d'Aosta from Switzerland. This chain begins with Mont Blanc, Europe's highest mountain, at the head of the region, then continues with the Grand Combin, the Matterhorn and finally Monte Rosa, Europe's second highest mountain.

A main road and a motorway follow the course of the river as far as Aosta before dividing into the three roads which connect the valley with France and Switzerland; the Mont Blanc Tunnel, the Great St Bernard Tunnel (and Pass) (Col du Grand-St-Bernard or Gran San Bernardo), and the Little St Bernard Pass (Col du Petit St Bernard or Piccolo San Bernardo) (the two passes are only open in summer while the tunnels are open all the year round). The nearest international airports are Milan and Turin, in Italy, and Lausanne in Switzerland. Most of the region's towns, beginning with Aosta, are situated along the Dora Baltéa river, while the others, almost without exception, are sited in the side valleys formed by the tributary rivers.

Since the opening up of the two tunnels linking the valley with France and Switzerland made it an important link between northern and southern Europe, the valley has rapidly developed into one of Europe's most important tourist centres. During the peak winter season the main ski centres at the heads of the main and tributary valleys become very crowded, although there are many smaller skiing stations which tend to attract local custom rather than the bulk of the tourists. Some of the higher ski resorts offer skiing all the year round and these logically remain busy even during the summer months. These months, particularly July and August when the Italian schools are on holiday, also attract a large number of walkers, although the resorts are never anywhere near as crowded as the seaside towns in Italy. Even the less important centres in the Dora Baltéa valley are the starting points for footpaths leading up into the mountains and their foothills while, for the more experienced walker, there are tracks connecting most of the tributary valleys. Only the easiest of these tracks ever get busy, while the more arduous ones and the real alpine footpaths are much less frequented.

The best periods to visit the region are May-June and September-October, avoiding the main holiday period while at the same time missing the snowfalls which at times render much of the valley

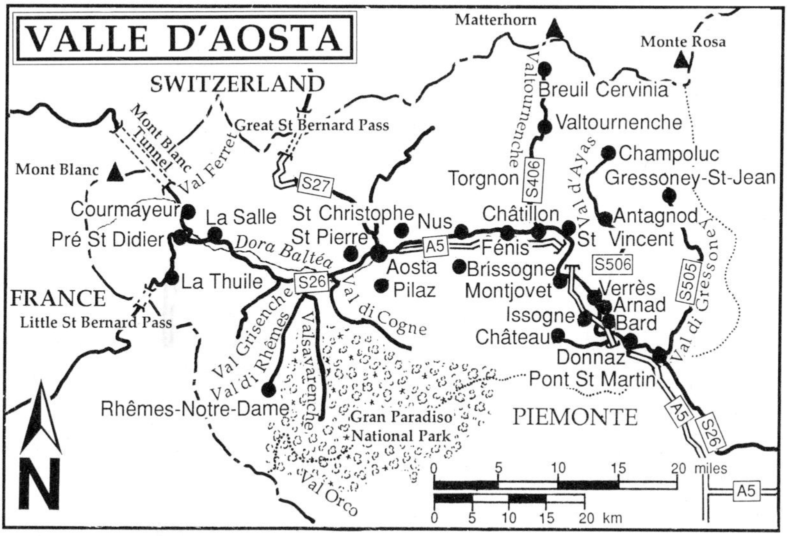

inaccessible. The climate in these months is usually mild with very little rainfall. In fact, so little rain falls that the small amount of agriculture which contributes to the economy of the valley depends to a large extent on irrigation schemes.

Culturally, the Valle d'Aosta is half Italian and half French, a fact which is officially recognized by the Italian constitution which has designated the valley as an autonomous region with a separate administrative structure. The French and Italian languages are used side by side in official documents and on road signs while the region's own dialect, which has strong historical connections with Provençal French continues to be widely used, particularly in the more remote areas.

From Roman times the valley has been important, the Great and Little St Bernard Passes breaking the alpine chain on each side of Mont Blanc and offering ways out of, and equally importantly, into Italy. As a result, from Roman times the valley was heavily fortified, and it still has an amazing succession of castles strung out along its length, castles too often missed by the visitor as he or she sweeps through on the A5 *autostrada*. Only in 1869 was Aosta incorporated into Italy, having been for a long time part of Savoia and, for a short time, French. The French-speaking valley inhabitants were suspicious of moves to 'Italianise' them and separatist rumblings were quelled only with the granting of autonomous status in 1948.

Artistically and architecturally the region has been often influenced by its neighbours although these influences have frequently taken some time to make themselves felt. The traditional indigenous art form of the valley is woodcarving and the pride of the valley are the mainly baroque wooden altars which are to be seen in almost all the region's churches.

Courmayeur, at the head of the main Aosta valley, is a renowned mountain and skiing centre. From here one of the great alpine journeys is made by cableway to Chamonix, taking the cablecar from Courmayeur to the Aiguille du Midi at 12,610ft — with a stupendous view of Mont Blanc — and descending on the French cableway. This is hardly off-the-beaten-track, but it does offer an unusual day out. Elsewhere, Courmayeur itself has little to offer the tourist looking to avoid the mass, but do find the time to visit the little Museo Alpino — across from the church — where there is an interesting collection of alpine bric-à-brac, together with a poignant collection of memorabilia of alpine guides who died in the mountains.

Courmayeur can become busy if the weather is good and it is often best to continue down the valley to **Pré St Didier**, a pleasant, small, thermal and mountain resort from where an impressive *orrido* (gorge) can be reached in half an hour, or for the more adventurous, the summit of Mont Crammont (9,977ft) can be reached in about 4 hours, an ascent for which the reward is another marvellous view of Mont Blanc.

Two-and-a-half miles east of Pré St Didier at the mouth of the Little St Bernard valley is **Morgex**, with its fine seventeenth-century parish church and the tower of the Castello d'Archet, said to date from the tenth or eleventh century.

Also from Courmayeur, a couple of good excursions follow the two valleys that form the cross-beam of the 'T'-shaped valleys at the head of the main Aosta valley. The main valley, the upright of the 'T', runs past Courmayeur to **Entrèves**, where the lower station of the Aiguille du Midi/Chamonix cableway is situated. From Entrèves the **Val Ferret** runs north-east, a road following it as far as Arnouvaz, at the bottom of the Triolet glacier. After Planpincieux the valley widens out, the broad floor of open meadows being easily accessible and offering fine walks with good views to the Grandes Jorasses, the shapely bulk on the Italian-French border. The walk up to the Col Ferret at 8,310ft is comfortably accomplished, allow 3 hours from the road end; the Col represents the border between Italy and Switzerland. The view in all directions is excellent, but the eye is drawn to the phenomenal view along the 'T' top bar, the Val Ferret, and the Val Veny beyond Entrèves, the view of this last valley stretching all the way to the Col de la Seigne at its head.

Mountain peaks of the Valle d'Aosta

The **Val Veny** is also worth a visit. Go to the twin lakes of Combal and Miage, separated by about 330ft of mountain, but worlds apart, **Lac Combal**, the lower lake, is formed behind a moraine dam, the debris having been brought down by the Miage glacier. Near it are lush meadows, a contrast to the wild surroundings of **Lac Miage**, ringed by peaks and rugged terrain, and close to the Miage glacier itself.

Each of these valleys are taken by a well signed footpath, which leads on to explore the better scenic areas of the Aosta region. Val Ferret is followed by using Alta Via 1, Val Veny by using Alta Via 2. Each of the routes is quite superb. Alta Via 1 crosses all the northern valleys, to finish about 45 miles away at Gressoney-St-Jean, while Alta Via 2, about the same length, takes the southern side of Valle d'Aosta going through the Gran Paradiso National Park to finish at Champorcher on a side road from the main valley. Each route is through a fantastic wonderland of natural scenery, with good opportunities to see many of the high-level alpine animals. The paths are not easy, several sections requiring mountaineering experience and equipment — most especially the route through the Planaval Pass on Alta Via 2, which requires real climbing. Moving down the valley, sections of the two walks will be used to explore little visited areas, but committed walkers should seriously consider completing one or other of the routes.

A very worthwhile section of Alta Via 2 starts at La Thuile in the next side valley, the one which leads to the Little St Bernard Pass. The road to the pass is very pretty, particularly towards the top where Lac Verney lies in a meadow-surrounded hollow ringed by snow-capped peaks. Here it is possible to be quite alone with the scenery.

La Thuile is an old mining town (mining for anthracite) a pretty place, well positioned among trees and meadows and from which Alta Via 2 leads off, at first along the little road to La Joux then following the river that drains the Rutor glacier. On the river there are three fine waterfalls, after the third of which the path turns uphill towards the lakes of Glacie, Bas and Haut. Beyond Lac d'en Haut is the glacier and the skilled climbing section of the route, but there is no need to walk that far. Indeed it is only really necessary to go as far as Lac du Glacie — allow about 3 hours — from which the view is remarkably impressive, and there is also a good chance of seeing marmots and chamois, and the elegant black grouse.

On down the main valley, be sure to find time to visit the church at **La Salle**. In it there are two statues of the Madonna, one from the thirteenth century and another from the fourteenth, the latter believed to have been based on Oropa's *Black Madonna*. Two other statuettes are even more remarkable, representing Mary Magdalen and St John and thought to represent some of the finest Flemish work of the fifteenth and sixteenth centuries. The figures are very stylised, but are beautifully crafted. Also worthy of a visit are the nearby castles of Avise, Blonay, Cré and Arvier, the latter three in ruins.

The next side valley is the **Val Grisenche** which holds a very large reservoir, the Lago di Beauregard, which has a track all along one shoreline. The valley is almost closed near where it leaves the main valley, the remote castle of Montmayeur dominating both valley and view, with a backdrop of some very wild country. The valley head is dominated by the Rutor glacier and there are some small hotels catering for skiers, mountaineers and walkers.

Two side valleys lead off from **Introd**, but go to the village itself to see the castle and church, huddled together and extremely picturesque. Do visit the church to see the beautiful wooden panels thought to be among the finest examples of this fifteenth-century Aostan art.

Beyond, the **Val di Rhêmes** is a fine, straight valley with an excellent village, **Rhêmes-Notre-Dame** towards its head, dominated by the fine peak of Granta Parci, an 11,110ft peak. The village is a fine centre for walks, the best is along the waymarked path to Lac Retaud, hidden among the trees. For the more adventurous, Alta Via 2 can be followed eastwards to the Col di Entrelor, a round trip of about 3 hours and involving about 1,500ft of climbing. The compensations are magnificent views, and the chance of seeing some of the alpine fauna.

The neighbouring **Valsavarenche** is also crossed by Alta Via 2, and is another fine, secluded valley. Indeed, it is probably the most unspoilt of all the valleys, lying deep in the Gran Paradiso National Park, where several species of deer can be seen grazing by the roadside. The Valsavarenche is the only valley which fully penetrates the park, and the section of Alta Via 2, going west, is about the finest walk anywhere in the park. It climbs to the Orvieille hut — once a royal hunting lodge for the kings of Italy — and then continues past Lac Djouan and Lac Noir to the Col di Entrelor already visited on the route from Val di Rhêmes. The walk — allow about 4 hours — passes the known haunts of ibex, and also traverses in front of the chain of high peaks which forms the divide between Aosta and Piemonte.

The **Gran Paradiso National Park** was established in 1922 — exactly half a century after the world's first, Yellowstone in America — and protected within its 225sq miles are about 20 species of animals and 200 species of birds. In reality, because the park joins France's Vanoise National Park, the protected area is about 400sq miles. It is patrolled constantly by a corps of keepers and there are heavy on-the-spot fines for those who break the rules of the park. Besides picking flowers, disturbing animals and lighting fires, camping without written permission from the park authorities is also prohibited. For those who respect the rules the park is a real natural treasure house with many well marked paths and an information centre at Rhêmes-Notre-Dame.

The ibex is the park's foremost animal, and is its symbol, but there are also chamois and marmots, mountain hares as well as others. Ironically, it was in the Valsavarenche, in 1914, that the last lynx was killed, so there are no longer any of that most elusive of felines. Included in the bird population are the golden eagle, Tengmalm's owl, black woodpecker and snow finch. Those especially wanting to see ibex and chamois can visit the park in May or early June, when, as the snow thaws, fresh grass springs up in the lower valley slopes, the animals come down to eat and it is then possible to see them from the road. Alternatively, later in summer when the upper slopes offer food, the animals come out from the mid-slope woodland and can be seen above the 6,500ft contour. The best time for viewing is early morning when they are feeding.

Those interested in the plant life of the park should make a point of going to the Paradisa, an alpine garden in **Valnontey**, a side valley from the Val di Cogne, the next southern-going valley along the main Aosta valley. This garden is certainly off-the-beaten-track, but is well worth the visit to see the trees, shrubs and, in season, flowers of the park, laid out in surroundings so natural it is difficult to believe that it is the work of man. As Val di Cogne leaves the main valley, look out for the castle in **Aymavilles**, a fourteenth-century building renovated in the eighteenth as a manorial house, and very elegant with its contrasting stone colours.

The **Val di Cogne** rises into the Gran Paradiso group from St Pierre and its ease of access, great natural beauty and the high plain around Cogne which has been greatly exploited by the tourist industry make it one of the most popular tourist resorts in the Valle d'Aosta.

Further down the main valley, just before Aosta, is the village of **St Pierre** with its two fine castles. The older of these, which dates from the twelfth century and houses council offices, was restored in the last century and now has the appearance of a castle in one of Hans Christian Anderson's fairy tales. This castle dominates the village while the other, Castello di Sarriod della Tour, just to the east of the town, is little changed from its original fourteenth-century appearance and is used to house art exhibitions. Still closer to Aosta is the battlemented Castello di Sarre restructured in 1710 from the remains of the original thirteenth-century castle. The castle was bought in 1869 by Vittorio Emanuele II and from then until 1945 it was the royal hunting lodge. The central hall is decorated with 1,987 pairs of antlers!

Aosta itself is a city of contrasts, apparently modern and yet with an enviable collection of Roman and medieval remains; the capital of one of the most famous tourist regions in the world and yet usually quiet and peaceful.

Not for nothing is the town referred to as the 'Rome of the Alps'; even the name is Roman, derived from *Augusta Praetoria*, and too frequently the splendours are side-stepped. Of the Roman town, a perfect rectangle 792 x 625yd, the surrounding wall, with twenty towers, is still largely intact, though most of the present towers were built in the thirteenth and fourteenth centuries on the original foundations. Of these, the Bramafon complex — more castle than tower — is about the best. It is situated in the southern wall, towards the south-west corner. The Roman praetorian gate, at the centre of the western wall, is good, but it, too, has an added tower, here since the twelfth century. In the north-eastern corner, the Roman theatre has

The Roman theatre at Aosta

only a section of its stage wall remaining, but that section — 72ft high — is very impressive. In the wall, towards the north-western corner, the barracks of Challant house a new museum due to open in 1988.

A short way along the road outside the Porta Pretoria is a magnificent archway, the Arch of Augustus, built there both to honour Caesar Augustus and to commemorate his victory over the Salatians. Still further along the same road is a 20ft-long Roman bridge which has outlived the river it was built by the Romans to span. The remains of the amphitheatre which could originally house 20,000 spectators can be visited in the grounds of the thirteenth-century convent of Santa Caterina (with the permission of the nuns) although the scarcity of the remains make it less interesting than the convent itself with its fine Romanesque bell tower.

Also in the town, and well worth a visit, is the monumental complex of Sant' Orso, with a fine twelfth-century campanile. Inside is a remarkable series of eleventh-century frescoes, some magnificent artwork, and a beautifully roofed, arcaded twelfth-century cloister.

The church itself was built in various phases, the oldest part dating from the end of the tenth century. The crypt is original while the majority of the building dates from the fourteenth century although much of the carved wood decoration is Renaissance and baroque. Also worthy of a visit is the adjacent Priorato built at the end of the fifteenth century as the prior's residence. At 10 Via Sant' Orso behind the Priorato is the town's archaeological museum, the most prized exhibit in which is a small silver bust of Jove found during excavations on the Little St Bernard Pass.

Despite the importance of Sant' Orso it is not the city's most important religious complex; that honour belongs to the fine cathedral in Piazza Giovanni XXIII. Founded in the eleventh century, the cathedral, which has two medieval bell towers, was restored and altered in the fifteenth and sixteenth centuries to its present form, with the exception of the neo-classical façade added in the nineteenth century. The most interesting part of the cathedral is the presbytery where the fifteenth-century carved wooden choir stalls look over a large twelfth-century mosaic. The fifteenth-century cloister contrasts with other parts of the complex as it is partially Gothic in style. Next to the cathedral, excavations have brought to light much of the Roman forum while the nearby archdeacon's residence is built over a Roman temple.

A pleasant walk which begins from the city along a track beginning near the Roman bridge takes the visitor up to the Castello Duca degli Abruzzi with its small alpine museum and then to the pleasant village of **St Christophe** on the banks of the Dora with a fine view over the city.

Fairly easy alpine walks which can be taken from near Aosta in summer are: Monte Fallere, on a track which leaves the pleasant minor road between Ville sur Sarre and Vetan on a large grassy saddle to the right of the road, and, to the Becca di Viou on a track beginning 3 miles along the road to St Christophe. Various other

Fénis castle

walks can be undertaken from **Pilaz**, a modern ski resort to the south of Aosta reached either by an 11-mile-long tortuous mountain road or much more easily by cablecar from near Aosta station.

The Great St Bernard valley which links the Valle d'Aosta with Switzerland has not been greatly developed by the tourist industry, although there is at times a fairly heavy flow of traffic heading for or coming from the tunnel. There are some ski-runs however and a variety of walks and climbs about which more detailed information can be obtained from the Association of Alpine Guides in Valpelline and Ollomont. In good weather the best route between the valley and Switzerland is not through the tunnel but over the pass which not only saves money but takes in some of the best alpine scenery as well.

Five miles east of Aosta on the northern side of the valley is the fine Castello di Quarto which was built towards the end of the twelfth century and added to regularly over the next two centuries. Facing the castle on the other side of the valley is the village of **Brissogne** with another ruined castle. From here, it is possible to walk up to a group of small lakes on the side of Mont' Emilius.

Nus, another 2 miles down the valley, is a pleasant old village situated at the entrance to the valley of St Barthelémy which can be penetrated by car as far as **Lignan**, and then on foot. A number of interesting footpaths begin from Lignan, particularly the one to the sanctuary of Cuney, built in the seventeenth century by the Dominicans of Nus and rebuilt in 1869. Expert climbers can venture onto Monte Faroma from Lignan. A mile from Nus is the small village of **Fénis** where there is one of the most magnificent medieval fortresses in the whole of Italy, a glorious mixture of square and circular towers and embattled walls, the embattlements being the delightful fish-tails so familiar to those who have visited the Italian Lakes. The castle was started in the mid-fourteenth century, but was added to and rebuilt until the late fifteenth century. Within the outer wall there is an astonishing courtyard with circular steps rising to a beautifully frescoed gallery. The frescoes — the proverbs are in old French — are early fifteenth century, rather formal, but compelling because of their situation. Fénis stands at the mouth of the **Val Clavalité**, a very beautiful valley, not accessed by road, which has, at its head, the mountain Tersiva, a snow-capped pyramidal peak maintaining the beauty of the valley it dominates.

The ruined medieval castle of **Cly** was abandoned in the sixteenth century, but the chapel still shows traces of the original thirteenth-century frescoes. It can be visited by leaving the main road at Chambave towards St Denis, from where a minor road leads directly to the spur where the dramatic ruins dominate the valley.

Continuing on the same minor road will eventually bring the visitor into the **Valtournenche** more usually entered from **Châtillon**, a pleasant little town from where the castles of Challant and Ussel are also easily reached. The first of these contains frescoes dating from 1502 in its chapel, while the second is particularly interesting as it represents a transitional period in castle architecture in the valley — retaining some aspects of the castle-fortress style while others bear more relation to the later concept of the castle as primarily being a noble residence and only secondarily a stronghold. The Valtournenche is one of the most beautiful and as a result most visited of alpine valleys throughout the year.

At the valley's head is the peak known by Italians as Cervino, but more commonly known to English speakers as the **Matterhorn**. Seen across Lac Bleu, just south of the valley-head village of Breuil-Cervinia, the Matterhorn is certainly impressive, but has nothing like the grace it displays to visitors to Zermatt on the other side of the border. Few entering Valtournenche will want to miss the peak, but go also to **Torgnon**, set on the western side of the valley close to where it leaves the main valley, and there visit the small parish church museum. Here, there is a very rare fourteenth-century wooden *Christ on the Cross*, a brutal, yet moving carving, a series of

Val d'Ayas

early sixteenth-century woodcarvings of the Madonna and saints, delightfully painted, and other fine works. The church itself has a huge crucifix, again German and sixteenth century, and again quite unremitting in its portrayal of blood and pain.

Montjovet, a little further down the main valley, is divided into several small villages including one composed almost entirely of small fifteenth- and sixteenth-century houses. This village stands below the rocky outcrop where the ruins of the eleventh-century castle can be seen with their original tower. Near the outcrop, the Romanesque church of San Germano and traces of the original Roman road and bridge are also of great interest.

The next northward leading valley is **Val d'Ayas**, a wide, lush valley, justifiably popular with many visitors who leave the A5, and reached over the Colle di Joux from St Vincent or on the SS506 which leaves the main valley at Verrès. The floor of the valley is meadowland, at first, offering some fine walking near the river. Further up, a road leads off westward to **St Vincent**, crossing the Colle di Joux and going through a section of excellent conifer forest with endless opportunities for picnicking. Further on again is **Antagnod**, a well positioned village whose church contains some fine medieval embroidery. Higher again are a series of pretty villages, each a fine centre for walking, with the glaciers and peaks of Monte Rosa as a background to all views. From **St Jacques**, a fine section of Alta Via

1 goes along the eastern side of the valley, through the woods, passing Souzun, Crest and Cuneaz to wilder country on the flank of Testa Grigia, where it is possible to see marmots. Nearer **Crest**, the summit above the route can be climbed — it lies at 5,075ft, 760ft above Crest and due north of it — for an excellent view into Val d'Ayas. Nearer the start of the valley, visit **Graines** or, rather, its castle, set in an impressive position on a rocky outcrop. It is a very early castle, eleventh century, and of a type known as primitive, its walls encircling the outcrop's top. Within the walls the tower remains more or less intact, but all the other buildings are ruinous. One still identifiable ruin is the chapel, and such was the defensive intent that even it has walls 3ft thick!

Near to where Val d'Ayas meets Valle d'Aosta, and for precisely that reason, is a castle. Unlike the elegance of Fénis, Verrès is a solid, imposing bulk. Built in the late fourteenth century it is recognised as the pinnacle of late Gothic castle architecture, and not just in Italy, but in Europe as a whole. At first glance, its size — some of the walls are sheer for about 100ft — and apparent austerity of design, suggest a war engine pure and simple. But look closer, at the chimneys, the windows and the arches: there can be found some delightful touches, Verrès having been home to the Challant family, as well as being a fortress.

In **Verrès** itself the early sixteenth-century parish church with its ogival doorway is worth a visit, as is the adjacent monastery. The carved stonework around the doorway is of particular interest.

Built by Giorgio di Challant in the late fifteenth century, **Issogne** castle, which represents a fusion of Gothic and Renaissance architectural ideas, was bought by a painter at the end of the last century and carefully restored — both inside and out — to its original condition and then donated to the state. Here, too, stands the beautiful wrought-iron pomegranate fountain, dating from about 1500, but, for all its weaving of delicate patterns, it is as bold a piece as was ever produced by modern art when it 'discovered' iron.

Near Issogne is **Arnad**, a pleasant village with an excellently restored church. It is a fine building, a huddle of stone parts, half-circles, projecting eaves, a half-dome here, a connecting roof there, essentially eleventh century, but with a fine fifteenth-century portal whose elegant rising columns writhe together at their high point like snakes or — and more likely — like tree trunks. The odd garret apparently has a fine set of early fifteenth-century frescoes, but these are not, sadly, on view at present.

Beyond Arnad, the old valley road is confined by the Bard Gorge, while the A5 tunnels its way past. There, at the constriction, be sure to see the castle.

The fortress of **Bard** which stands high over the town of the same name, was built at the beginning of the eleventh century and then restored after being demilitarized by Napoleon. The town itself has many houses dating back to the medieval period, some of which were later joined together with arches to make larger houses. Bard is definitely off-the-beaten-track, though there are intentions to restore it, and the work associated with this may restrict access. But go anyway to marvel at the fortifications working their way up the hill, and to wonder that Napoleon once walked an army through the gorge at night, without being noticed from this spot!

From Bard, a fine, though short, valley, the **Val Champorcher**, leads off west. Alta Via 2 finishes — or starts — at **Château**, the main village, and a fine piece of walking is the section from the village to **Lago Miserin**, a very picturesque lake. The walk is through fine woodland and past several waterfalls before wild, open country is reached. Here, look out for marmots. The walk to the lake takes about $3^1/_2$ hours, though this can be shortened to about $1^1/_2$ if the road, an old mule track, is taken to Dondena. This is, however, at the expense of the wooded section. It is probably best to visit Val Champorcher during the week as it tends to get very busy at weekends.

A large number of footpaths begin from **Dondena** at the head of the valley — many of them fairly easy going. The summits of the Delà, Moussaillon and the Cima Beccher mountains can all be reached in a couple of hours without much difficulty while the 5-hour ascent of the Rosa dei Banchi should only be attempted by the more experienced. Another walk for the experienced is known as the Finestra di Champorcher which after 7 or 8 hours reaches the head of the Val di Cogne.

Back in the main valley the next small village is **Donnaz** where the woodcarvings of the choir-stalls, the pulpit and the confessionals in the parish church of San Pietro in Vincoli are exceptional, as are the remains of the Roman consular road which cuts through the rock for a distance of about 240yd and at one point is spanned by an arch carved out when the road was built.

The last Aosta side valley is the **Val di Gressoney**. The valley is largely inhabited by the Walser, a people who came from Switzerland in the Middle Ages, and who still speak an ancient German dialect. There are, however, even odder linguistic pockets. **Gaby**, a pretty village, has a population of Provençal speakers — a French dialect — despite being situated between Issime and Gressoney, two strongly Walser districts. At **Issime**, the valley becomes very narrow at the Guillemore ravine, a fine place to visit with a waterfall and water-shaped rock hollows. Be sure, too, to go to the parish church at Issime, for the frescoed façade, a sixteenth-century *Last Supper*, and an amazing seventeenth-century baroque altar, which cannot easily be described, but should under no circumstances be missed. At the head of the valley, chair-lifts take visitors onto the flanks of Monte Rosa. From the top of one, going onto the east side of the valley, an excellent walk, with views to Monte Rosa, leads to Lago Gabiet, a fine mountain lake. It is also possible to walk to the foot of the Lys glacier flowing down from Monte Rosa. This is a fascinating trip, but unless you are very experienced and have good equipment you should not venture onto the glacier; be content with a first-hand view.

During the week outside the main holiday periods **Gressoney-St-Jean** and **Gressoney-la-Trinité** are both ideal centres either for walking or for winter sports.

At the foot of the Val di Gressoney is **Pont St Martin**, known as the gateway to the Valle d'Aosta. Despite the presence of the nearby ruined twelfth-century castle, the main attraction of Pont St Martin is the first-century BC, perfectly conserved Roman bridge from which the town takes its name. The bridge carried the main road to Aosta until 1831 when a new bridge was built alongside. The bridge is over 100ft long, 75ft high and 17ft wide. While in the vicinity of Pont St Martin it is worth taking the small road to **Perloz** where the church of San Salvatore boasts an impressive *Last Judgement* frescoed in 1676 by local artists.

Further Information
— The Valle d'Aosta —

The information given in the 'Further Information' sections of each chapter is as up-to-date as possible but opening times do change and visitors are advised to check before departing. Information is arranged alphabetically where possible.

Tourist Information Offices

Aosta Town Office
Ufficio Informazioni Turistiche
Piazza Chanoux 8
Aosta
☎ (0165) 35655/40526

Aosta Regional Tourist Office
EPT
Narbonne Square
Aosta
☎ (0165) 303725

Towns with Alpine Guide Centres
Aosta; Breuil-Cervinia; Champoluc; Cogne; Courmayeur; Gressoney-St Jean; La Thuile; La Trinité; Ollomont; Rhêmes-Notre-Dame; Valgrisenche; Valpelline; Valsavarenche; Valtournenche.

Museums and other Places of Interest

Aosta
Museum of the Cathedral Treasure
Open: winter, Tuesday-Sunday 3-5.45pm, summer (April to September) Sunday 3-5.45pm, Tuesday-Saturday 10am-12noon and 3-5pm.

Sant' Orso
Open: daily except Monday 9.30am-12noon, 2-6.30pm (Closing at 5.30pm Saturday and Sunday).

Courmayeur
Museo Alpino Duca degli Abruzzi
Open: Tuesday-Sunday 9am-12.30pm and 3.30-7pm.

Fénis
Castle
Open: daily except Tuesday 9am-12noon, 2-5pm (6pm in summer).

Gignod
Museo di Arte Sacra
Near church
Open: every day 8am-6pm.

Issogne
Castle
Open: daily except Monday 9am-12noon, 2-5pm (6pm in summer).

St Nicolas
Musée Cerlogne
Open: July-August 9am-12noon and 3-6pm.

Centre d'Etudes Franco-Provençales
Open: Monday-Saturday 8.30am-12noon and 2-4.30pm.

St Pierre
Castle and Natural Science Museum
Open: May-September, Wednesday-Monday 9am-12noon and 3-7pm.

Castello di Sarriod della Tour and Archaeological Museum
Open: May-October, Tuesday-Sunday, 9.30am-12noon and 3-7pm.

Sarre
Castle
Open: June, Saturday and Sunday, July-September 10-11am and 2.30-4.30pm (Closed Tuesday).

Valnontey
Paradisa Alpine Garden
Open: daily June-the first snows of winter, 9am-dusk.

Verrès
Castle
Open: March-November 9.30am-12noon and 2-4.30pm, December-February 9.30-11.30am and 2-4pm.

2 • Piemonte

With the exception of the Valle d'Aosta, Piemonte or the upper Padana valley and the mountains which enclose it, occupy the whole of the north-western corner of Italy. More than 40 per cent of the 9,800sq miles which go to make up the region is mountainous while another 30 per cent is hilly. The north-western and southern limits are defined by the western arch of the Alps and include Europe's highest mountains while the eastern border is formed by Lago Maggiore and the Ticino river. The alpine landscape was mainly modelled by the glaciers during the last Ice Age and their exacerbation of the natural breaks in the range allows the Alps to be subdivided into four separate sections: the Alpi Marittime, characterised by many small lakes and dense woods of chestnuts which divide Piemonte from Liguria; the Alpi Cozie which extend from the valley to the west of Monte Argentera to Moncenisio (included in this range are three of the most important ways of access to the region; the Fréjus Tunnel, the Moncenisio Pass and the Monginevro Pass); the Alpi Graie which extend from the Moncenisio Pass to the Colle Ferret, dominated by Mont Blanc and the Gran Paradiso; and finally after the Valle d'Aosta, the Alpi Pennine, which include the Matterhorn and Monte Rosa. The hills at the foot of the mountains are formed of alluvial deposits, while the other two hilly areas around Torino and Monferrato were originally islands in the Padana Sea. One characteristic which unites all the hilly areas however is the cultivation of vines. Parts of the Piemontese plain are very fertile and intensively cultivated with fruit and vines, but others are formed of hard red clay and parts are still uncultivated although the tapping of the many underground water courses for irrigation has led to improvements since the last war.

The climate in the region is variable, as both continental and maritime influences are felt with the anticyclones which sweep down from Siberia during the winter, giving way first to the damp currents from the Atlantic and then either to the dry heat from the

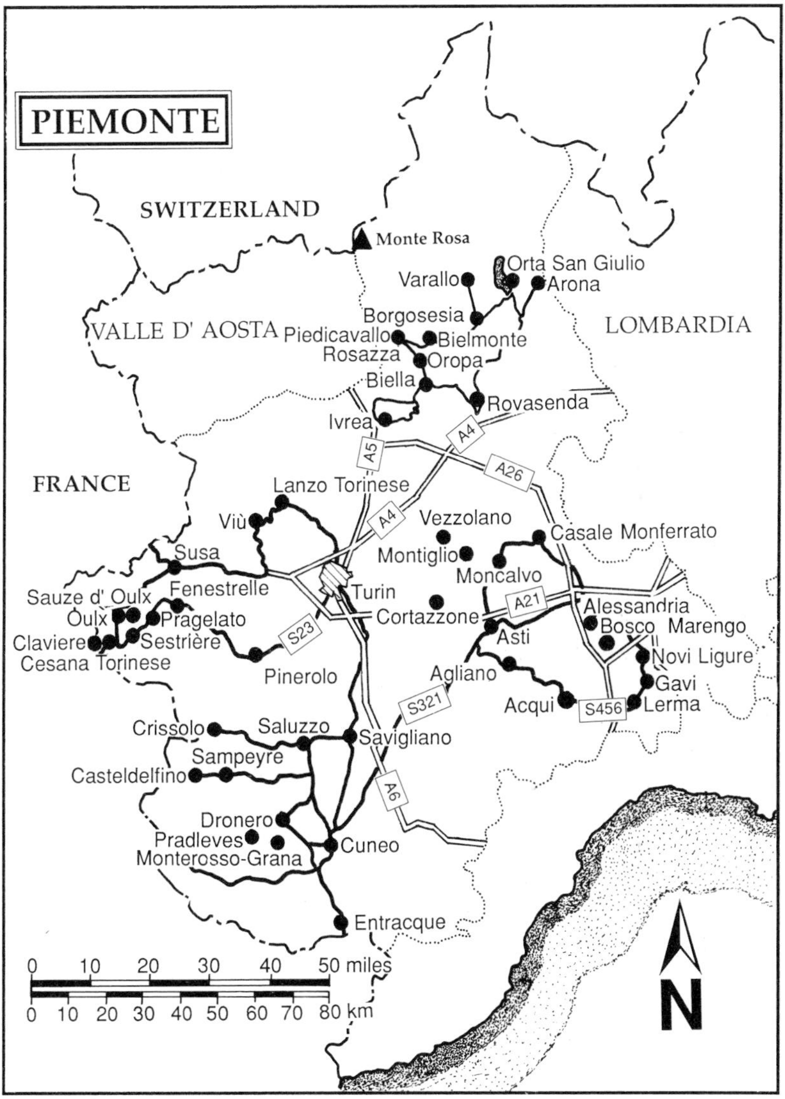

Sahara or the damp heat which blows up from the Azores.

A variety of vegetation is present which is particularly rich around the shores of Lago Maggiore, while perhaps the most striking sight to the non-specialist is the alpine carnation which only grows at altitude. The Gran Paradiso was made a National Park in 1922 in order to protect wildlife and within the park, as mentioned in Chapter 1, the visitor may well see many rare species.

Although the Duke of Piemonte became the King of Italy when the country was united in the 1860s, Piemonte had only been a recognisable political entity since the end of the sixteenth century and several times the House of Savoy had been faced with virtual ruin before Fortune lifted them to the throne of Italy. The few years for which Turin was the nation's capital (before this function was taken over by Florence and then by Rome) therefore left very little mark on the region, which alongside its industrial face can still show another which is essentially a human one, faithful to its own traditions.

This chapter contains four major excursions from the towns of Turin, Cuneo, Alessandria and Biella. Visitors intending to go long-distance walking or mountaineering in the areas mentioned here should provide themselves with detailed maps and suitable equipment.

Being in the north-west corner of Italy the region can be reached from the channel ports in a day's drive. Alternatively there is a small international airport in Turin and larger, better served ones at Milan and Genoa.

Excursions from Turin

Follow the Stura valley northwards from Turin to **Lanzo Torinese** where the old centre still has a typical medieval look with narrow, twisting streets crossed by a succession of arches. Of exceptional interest is the Ponte del Diavolo (Devil's Bridge) built in 1378. The bridge is well over 100ft long and arches up more than 50ft from the two squat solid towers which support the ends.

Cross back to the south bank of the river and follow it along into the Valle di Viu, a beautiful valley where the road climbs up until it eventually reaches the small Lago Malciaussia and a mountain shelter, just before the border with France. **Viu** itself is situated low down in the valley among thick chestnut woods, and is a popular centre for summer mountain holidays. One of the finest walks from Viu is the 3-hour ascent of the Via di Calcante to the north of the town.

Just after Viu, a steep mountain road leads up and over the mountains which separate the valley from the Valle di Susa which culminates in the Mont Cenis Pass. Follow the valley steadily upwards until the pleasant town of **Susa** where the road forks for Mont Cenis in one direction and the Monginevro Pass in the other. This important strategic position earned Susa the name 'Key to Italy' in the past. Although the bulk of the buildings date from the medieval period or later, the underlying structure of the town is Roman. A small amphitheatre, excavated in 1957, can be seen near the thirteenth-century basilica of San Francesco founded by Beatrice, wife of Tommaso I di Savoia at the request of the saint himself. The town's castle has undergone many restoration programmes over the century which have cost it much of its originality but it is still well worth visiting for its civic museum.

Twenty minutes' walk from the town are the ruins of the Brunetta fort built in 1708 then dismantled by Napoleon in 1797. Another short walk takes the visitor to the ex-church of San Saturnino where some remains of an earlier pagan temple can still be seen. Many other more taxing mountain walks also start from Susa; a large-scale local map is to be recommended.

Continuing up the valley, the next town of interest is **Oulx** where several old churches and other buildings of interest can be seen, particularly in the Alto Borgo, the oldest part of the town. High up above Oulx at almost 5,000ft is Sauze d'Oulx which is made up of mainly modern buildings which have thrived with the growth of the winter sports industry. The ski-runs here are some of the finest in Piemonte.

After Oulx the road passes up through the wild rocky gorge of Soubras before widening out at the village of **Cesana Torinese,** another popular winter sports resort where the Susa and Chisone valleys join together before the Monginevro Pass. The village was the home of Cézanne's family and the artist himself spent much of his life here. Nearby **Claviere** was one of the first Italian towns to develop as a ski-resort although its effectiveness was reduced after the last war when the border was moved and affected the ski-slopes.

Begin the descent of the Chisone valley, dropping down steeply into **Sestriere** which boasts almost 50 miles of ski-runs of varying lengths and difficulties. The peaks of several of the mountains around Sestriere can be reached both on foot or by cablecar by the less energetic. **Pragelato,** lower down the valley, has many of the same facilities as Sestriere, but also the advantage of having many fewer visitors. It is also an extremely attractive group of hamlets where, in summer, the visitor can walk in the shade of fine evergreen woods and also find a magnificent range of alpine flora. Eight miles further down the valley another resort, **Fenestrelle** has an extremely interesting 'Museum of the Mountain', which not only relates to the history and traditions of the local people, but also has sections devoted to the flowers and minerals of the area. Just below Fenestrelle are the remains of one of the largest groups of fortresses in Europe — the Forte di Fenestrelle, which includes the ruins of the eighteenth-century Forte San Carlo, an important prison during the Napoleonic and Risorgimento periods.

Pinerolo, situated where the valley meets the plain, was, for centuries, an impregnable French fortress until, faced with the impossibility of keeping their supply lines open in times of siege, the French themselves pulled down the defences at the end of the seventeenth century. With the removal of the defensive walls progress has gradually over-run the old centre, but the fifteenth-century *Duomo* with its magnificent tripartite Gothic façade and the elegant late Gothic church of San Maurizio which overlooks the town from the public gardens on top of a hill are sights which will always be worth seeing.

Excursions from Biella

It is quite possible that the view from your hotel window in **Biella** will take in, at some point, a cotton mill. Do not complain about this as the Biellese are justifiably proud of their textile industry which has been one of the most important in the world for several centuries. The industrial archaeologist is sure to enjoy him or herself in Biella and fortunately there are enough buildings of interest to keep the art lover happy as well. The primitive-looking Romanesque baptistry, which dates from the tenth century, is a case in point, the walls including fragments of Roman masonry such as the pagan sculpture of the *amorini* (sculpted cherubs) above the west door. The *Duomo* itself is a poor eighteenth-century re-creation of the original but the 175ft-high bell tower was originally part of the ninth-century castle of Biella. Two other churches which should be visited in Biella are the Renaissance churches of San Giacomo and particularly San Sebastiano where the carved choir-stalls are very fine examples. The civic museum has been stocked mainly by bequests from local collectors and as a result contains a great variety of exhibits from fragments of Roman masonry to delicate pieces of porcelain and Murano glassware.

Leave Biella on the SS144 and begin the 8-mile climb to the village of **Oropa** where the sanctuary is one of the oldest and most important of those dedicated to the Virgin Mary. The sanctuary is now a vast complex of churches and chapels, the construction of which began at the beginning of the eighteenth century. The sanctuary's origins, however, date back to AD369 when Sant' Eusebio, while fleeing from persecution in Vercelli, hid a wooden crucifix, which had been carved by St Luke, in the rocks. The basilica incorporates the primitive chapel which originally stood on the site and where traces of thirteenth-century frescoes can be seen on the walls. A chair-lift from Oropa takes you up to the small Lago Mucrone, from where it is possible to walk higher up the mountain of the same name or, in winter, to ski down it.

Proceed northwards from Oropa on the narrow unmetalled road which climbs over Monte Tovo to **Rosazza** and **Piedicavallo**, pleasant villages which offer numerous possibilities to walkers. Take the scenic SS232 which climbs gradually up out of the valley as far as the small resort of **Bielmonte** which offers a variety of shortish ski-runs and is to be recommended particularly on weekdays just outside the main season.

Continue on the same road which continues through fine scenery high up on the side of the mountains for several miles, then turn left and head up the left bank of the Sésia river to **Varallo**. A popular mountain resort, Varallo has a temperate climate the whole year round as well as considerable beauty, both man-made and natural. The hills immediately around the town are thickly wooded which adds to the pleasant atmosphere, while just slightly further up the valley are the bare slopes of Monte Rosa where it is possible to ski all year round. The town boasts a large art gallery and a small but interesting museum with a well furnished ornithological section. The buildings most visitors wish to see, however, are the Cappella della Madonna di Loreto (a gracious Renaissance construction a mile outside the centre, with lively frescoes painted by some of the finest northern Italian artists of the period) and the large religious complex known as the Sacro Monte. The Sacro Monte was begun in the fifteenth century when a Franciscan monk returned from a pilgrimage to the Holy Land and decided to recreate the buildings he had seen there. After his death however the theme of the Sacro Monte was changed by Borromeo to portray artistically and architecturally the story of Redemption as part of the ideological battle of the Counter Reformation. As a result the central basilica, Nuova Gerusalemme, is decorated with over 800 statues and 4,000 frescoed figures. The Sacro Monte can be reached in 20 minutes on foot, with a $2^1/_2$-mile drive, or most easily of all, by a 2-minute ride on the funicular railway.

After Varallo, drop down the valley again, although this time on the opposite bank, as far as **Borgosesia**. If time allows, stop for a while in **Quarona** where the old church of San Giovanni sul Monte has gradually been built up over the last 2,000 years from what was once probably a Roman barracks. Turn left at Borgosesia and climb over the hills to Lago d'Orta. Turn left along the shore of the lake, which is one of the lesser known of the Italian lakes, follow the road around the top end of the lake and down the other side as far as **Orta San Giulio**. Orta San Giulio is a very picturesque little town on a small peninsula facing the Isle of San Giulio. The most interesting building in the town is the Palazzo della Comunità which, like the parish church of Santa Maria Assunta, dates from the Renaissance. Like Varallo, Orta has its own Sacro Monte among the beech and pines of the hill immediately to the south-east of the town. The 376 terracotta statues which decorate the seventeenth-century sanctuary illustrate scenes from the life of St Francis. The Isle of San Giulio, which is also dominated by an important church, is also well worth visiting for its general atmosphere of charm and peacefulness. A regular ferry service of small boats runs throughout the year.

Continue along the shore of the lake to its southern extremity and then take the second turn on the left along the minor road which leads to **Arona**, 7 miles away on the shore of Lago Maggiore. The town is a pleasant old town with some particularly fine churches. The ruined castle was once one of the most powerful in the area being the seat of the Borromeo family and birthplace of the famous cardinal, San Carlo Borromeo. The castle was reduced to its present state on the orders of Napoleon in 1800 owing to its strategic importance in the hands of an enemy. Two miles outside the town, high on the hill overlooking the lake, is a magnificent statue of the saint erected in the late seventeenth century. The statue, which is 68ft high, is hollow inside and it is possible to climb up as far as the head.

From Arona follow the SS142 back towards Biella as far as Gattinara and then take the left fork to visit the fine castle at **Rovasenda**. Parts of the castle date from the fifteenth century but the majority, including the formidable square keep, date from the first half of the thirteenth. The other castle in the village is a folly, having been built in the old feudal style in the first years of this century. From Rovasenda, the centre of Biella is soon reached, being little over 10 miles away on good straight roads.

Another, shorter excursion from Biella is to **Ivrea** 18 miles to the south-west, although much closer in a straight line. Take the SS338 over the long ridge of high ground known as the Serra, which separates the provinces of Vercelli and Turin. Although nowadays the name Ivrea is immediately associated with modern technology, being the home of Olivetti, there is much of historical interest in the town which was once a Roman city. The most interesting part of the town is the area where the cathedral and the castle are situated,

Church at Antagnod, Aosta

Panoramic view of Châtillon, Aosta

Winter in the Val di Cogne

Lakeside, Orta San Giulio

which was once the Roman acropolis. The cathedral has had pieces added on and rebuilt over the centuries, but the crypt and the two towers at the rear still remain from the original ninth-century cathedral. Behind the cathedral, beyond the remains of the twelfth-century cloisters, stands the solid, rectangular fourteenth-century castle. Of the four cylindrical towers which reinforce the corners of the castle, one is shorter than the others, having been badly damaged by a gunpowder explosion in 1676. The town's civic museum is divided into two sections; one which is devoted to local traditions and folklore, and the other, more general, collection which is, however, particularly notable for its oriental section consisting of items brought back by missionaries and explorers. At the beginning of the main road leading to Vercelli, the remains of a late imperial Roman amphitheatre can be seen. During the excavations of the amphitheatre the remains of several Pompeian-style frescoes have been found. Several small lakes are situated among the hills immediately to the north of Ivrea, which offer opportunities for several pleasant, but not too strenuous walks.

Excursions from Alessandria

From its formation in the twelfth century until the late nineteenth century **Alessandria** was one of the most heavily fortified towns in northern Italy. Since then, however, much new industry has been established and the city has expanded rapidly in all directions. The old city walls have been replaced by an inner ring-road and only a few of the older buildings remain to testify to Alessandria's glorious past. For all that, it is a fairly pleasant city and an ideal base from which to see the surrounding area. Not being an important centre for tourism the hotels and restaurants tend to be more realistically priced than in many other places.

Three miles south of the city is the Villa Marengo, built in 1847 on the spot where Napoleon won one of his greatest battles in 1800. Inside the villa is a museum dedicated to the campaign of 1800 which culminated in the Battle of Marengo. Another interesting building not far from Alessandria is the late Renaissance church of Santa Croce in the village of **Bosco Marengo**. The church was built on the orders of Pius V, a native of the village, and of the many excellent works of art produced in the church, the finest is undoubtedly the green marble sculpted mausoleum which holds his body.

From Bosco Marengo, take the main road towards Novi Ligure, and then either fork right after about a mile towards Basaluzzo and

Painted façade, Orta San Giulio

then follow the Lemme river along to Gavi, or alternatively continue to Novi Ligure and then take the narrow road over the mountains to reach Gavi. Completely unspoilt, **Gavi** gives an idea of what many of the Ligurian towns just over the mountains would be like were it not for the high level of rural depopulation there. The twelfth-century church of San Giacomo was given a baroque facelift at the beginning of the eighteenth century but since then has fortunately been restored to its original medieval form. The other particularly noteworthy building in the town is the fortress on the hill overlooking the northern end of the town. The fortress was built by the Genoans in the sixteenth century, although part of a castle which had already stood on the site for 400 years was incorporated.

From Gavi, head south-west towards Ovada as far as the pleasant village of **Lerma**. The sixteenth-century Spinola castle has an unusual triangular courtyard, although the most interesting part of the village is that which clings to the steep slope beneath the castle and the parish church. The little houses here have changed little over several hundreds of years and as the hillside is too steep for motorised transport, the atmosphere is almost unique. The small hotel by the square at the northern end of the town is the centre of the village's social life and also provides excellent food at very reasonable prices in its restaurant. When deciding on your wine make sure you choose the local Dolcetto.

Drop down out of the hills, over the motorway, through Ovada and take the main road for **Acqui Terme**, an important spa town on the banks of the Bormida river. Originally the capital of one of the most important Ligurian tribes, the town became an important Roman centre and much later, in the thirteenth century, the capital of Alto Monferrato. The seventeenth-century Castello dei Paleologhi, which replaced an earlier ruined one, contains a fine archaeological museum with much of the Roman material found in local excavations. Parts of the *Duomo*, which has an exquisite marble portal, date from the eleventh century, while the San Pietro basilica is even older, having been restored in the tenth century. The apse is certainly the oldest part of the basilica although no-one is sure just how old it is.

Follow the Bormida Millesimo westwards for 10 miles to Bubbio and then turn right and climb out of the valley and across the Belbo valley to the small old town of **Agliano** which is situated high up between the Tiglione and Nizza valleys. The town is quiet and pleasant with some claim to being a minor spa resort, its main claim to fame, however, rests on the quality of its wine.

Fourteen miles further to the north is **Asti** which, apart from being the most famous producer of *spumante* (sparkling wine), is also a town of great historical interest. During the medieval period, Asti was known as the 'city of the hundred towers' for the large number of defensive tower houses which were built by important families in the city. Most have been demolished but several can still be seen at various points in the city, although most have been reduced in height.

There is much fine Gothic architecture in Asti, particularly the religious architecture, although the finest building of all is the squat octagonal baptistry of San Piero which dates from the early twelfth century. There are several interesting museums and art galleries in the town but the most interesting of all is that dedicated to the poet and playwright Vittorio Alfieri in the house where he was born and spent much of his life. As in Siena, Asti's traditional festival is celebrated with the Palio, a bare-back horse race preceded by a procession in medieval costume. The Palio takes place in September.

Follow the SS10 westwards as far as Baldichieri then turn right and head northwards to **Cortazzone**. This quiet village has a predominantly rustic character although the imposing castle on top of the hill shows that it was once far more important. The castle was rebuilt in the last century after having been badly damaged by the French, but parts of the original twelfth-century defensive wall and a tower of the same period can still be seen.

Six miles of undulating twisting minor roads bring you to the sanctuary of Colle Don Bosco, the birthplace of San Giovanni Bosco, which, after his death, was turned into a sanctuary dedicated to his memory. Another more important religious building is encountered another 6 miles to the north. The abbey of Vezzolano which is reputed to have been founded by Charlemagne, was extremely rich and powerful during the medieval period and contains many fine works of art as well as being an outstanding example of Romanesque-Gothic architecture.

The village of **Montiglio**, 10 miles to the east, is a very attractive place, an ideal stopping point which is almost entirely tourist-free. As usual, the village is built on a hill surmounted by a fine fifteenth-century castle. The streets which lead up to the castle are typically medieval, narrow and winding with lots of character. The chapel of Sant' Andrea in the grounds of the castle contains the largest cycle of fourteenth-century frescoes to have survived in Piemonte.

Moving eastwards again, the hills are particularly picturesque and if time allows, it is well worth sticking to the minor roads as much as possible, at least as far as **Moncalvo**. This busy little town is surrounded by the vineyards which provide its main source of income, and have done so for many centuries. Evidence of this can be seen in the late thirteenth-century church of San Francesco where one of the Gothic capitals which supports the church is decorated with scenes depicting the grape harvest.

Head north on the main road and then turn right in Cereseto for **Rossignano Monferrato**. During the Middle Ages, the castle of Rossignano, which stands high on a rocky promontory, was one of the most formidable in the whole of the Monferrato. The remains of the castle can still be seen within a park at the highest point of the town. Most of the churches in the town owe more to seventeenth- and eighteenth-century restorations than to their medieval origins but many of the privately owned buildings are still largely unchanged since that period, as is the street plan.

Another town to have undergone much restoration in the baroque period is **Casale Monferrato**, although there is still much of great interest here. The *Duomo* is an architectural hybrid: consecrated in 1107, the cathedral was badly damaged by fire a century later and repaired by the superimposition of Gothic repair work. By the middle of the last century the *Duomo* was in a dangerous condition and was only saved from demolition by a restoration which added baroque elements to the Gothic and the original Romanesque. One of the most interesting of the baroque *palazzi* in the town is the Palazzo Gozzano di Treville which houses a music academy and the civic museum. The building was designed by G.B. Scapitta, one of the leading Piemontese baroque architects, but building was completed by his nephew Vincenzo who introduced some neo-classical elements, particularly the façade. A Jewish museum is situated above the late sixteenth-century synagogue, just off the Via Alessandria. At the time the synagogue was built, Casale had a large Jewish population and the area around the building was a ghetto. Other important buildings include the sixteenth-century civic tower, built on eleventh-century foundations after the original building had burnt down, and the squat, rectangular moated Castello dei Paleologhi which, for the last 200 years, has been used only as a military warehouse.

Finally, to return to Alessandria do not follow the direct main road all the way as it lacks any real interest. Turn off the road to the right at San Germano, 3 miles south of Casale, and then pass through Terrugia, Frassinello and Vignale before turning eastwards and crossing the steep sided Grana valley, passing through the attractive but virtually unknown village of Lu, and eventually rejoining the main road at San Salvatore, 5 miles to the north of Alessandria.

Excursions from Cuneo

The oldest part of **Cuneo** is situated on the tip of the peninsula separating the rivers Stura and Gesso while the town becomes progressively newer as one moves back along the peninsula. With the exception of the ex-church of San Francesco, which is a fine Gothic building, almost all the noteworthy monuments in Cuneo date from the seventeenth and eighteenth centuries. Many times in its history the city has undergone long sieges and bombardments which have led to a fairly constant replacement of existing buildings. The ex-church of San Francesco, which has recently been restored after having been reduced to a variety of other uses, was for centuries the centre of civic life, burial-place of the most illustrious citizens, and display case for the military standards gained in battle, as well as a place of worship. Of the more modern churches the most interesting is Sant' Ambrogio which, despite having urgent need of restoration, is still an excellent example of the best of baroque decorative architecture.

Fifteen miles to the south-west of Cuneo, along good quality roads, is **Entracque**, an attractive old village in a wide pleasant valley which is an ideal starting place for many walks. The area to the south and west of the village constitutes the Argentera National Park where a series of clearly marked footpaths link together the several mountain shelters and the various peaks.

Return towards Cuneo as far as Valdieri then turn left up the steep mountain road with many hairpins which separates the Gesso from the Stura valley. Cross the Stura at Demonte and climb out of the valley on the other side. Do not take this road in bad weather or with a very low car as there is quite a long stretch where the road is little more than a rough track at almost 8,000ft above sea level. After the eighteenth-century sanctuary of San Magno the road is asphalted again as it begins to drop down the Grana valley. Part way down is the pleasant little village of **Pradleves** which over the last few years has developed some catering facilities for the walkers and climbers who frequent the valley, without becoming touristy. It is therefore to be recommended as a place to eat and take a quiet stroll through the surrounding chestnut trees. **Monterosso Grana**, 2 miles further down the valley shares many of the characteristics of Pradleves although it tends to be a little busier in the main holiday periods.

After Monterosso, turn left at the signpost for Montemale and cross over the range of hills separating the Grana from the Maira valley. The road drops down to the valley at **Dronero** where the fine Romanesque sanctuary of San Costanzo sul Monte is to be found on the slopes of Monte San Bernardo. Despite being in a poor state of conservation, the church (particularly the rear section), is an almost textbook example of twelfth-century Romanesque architecture.

With the exception of one or two centres in the upper valley, the Val di Maira has been virtually unscathed by the tourist industry despite being one of the most attractive valleys in the region. There are many woods and numerous side valleys which are impressively wild and unspoilt. Climb the valley until 2 miles after Stroppo and then take the right turn up the Elva valley where the road passes through several tunnels before reaching Elva itself and bearing eastwards towards Sampeyre.

Sampeyre is quite a thriving little town in the summer season and attracts many winter sports enthusiasts too in the peak winter season. Perhaps the most interesting feature of the town is the ethnographical museum in the town's junior school (*Scuola Media*) which is dedicated to the traditions of the many groups of Provençal origins who established colonies in the surrounding valleys. At **Casteldelfino**, 6 miles higher up the valley, the local dialect is still basically Provençal, while in several of the outlying hamlets, Provençal dress traditions are also maintained.

Head down the valley from Sampeyre to Venasca and turn left in the town towards Saluzzo. One mile before Saluzzo, at San Lazzaro turn left again into the upper Po valley and for 5 miles drive along the side of the river. Should you wish to ski continue up to **Crissolo** at the head of the valley, which is also the starting point for trips into the Monviso group, otherwise cross the river to **Revello**. Possibly founded by the Romans, Revello is a town rich in historical interest. The most interesting part of the town is the Piazza della Collegiata which is surrounded by fourteenth- and fifteenth-century buildings, the finest of which is the Collegiata church itself with its tripartite terracotta Gothic façade. The fine marble portal was added later during the Renaissance.

Next to the Piazza della Collegiata is Piazza Denin, the town's central square, where the eighteenth-century town hall and orphanage incorporate parts of the Palazzo Marchionale which previously stood on the site and which was the summer residence of Ludovico II, Marquis of Saluzzo. The most important of the surviving parts is the Marchionale chapel which contains several fine fifteenth-century frescoes including a *Last Supper* by the school of Leonardo da Vinci.

Saluzzo was a major cultural centre from the fourteenth to the sixteenth century and the historic centre of the town which dates mainly from that period is an excellent testimony of this. Essentially the centre consists of a harmonious mixture of small houses and noble *palazzi* which gradually lead one up through picturesque streets to the castle. A particularly fine *palazzo* is the Casa Cavassa built in the early fifteenth century for a cadet branch of the ruling family and which is now a museum, having been restored to recreate its original Renaissance atmosphere. Another building which must be visited is the Burgundy-Gothic church of San Giovanni. Although built in the fourteenth century the most important part, the apse, was only completed at the beginning of the sixteenth. The finest work of art in the apse is the mausoleum of Ludovico II, but the fine choir stalls and the overall use of a finely balanced play of light and shade should not be missed. The original castle no longer exists, having been replaced by the present one which served as a prison in 1825. A much more impressive castle is to be seen at **Manta,** $2^1/_2$ miles to the south of the town. Built in the fourteenth century by Tommaso III, the castle was transformed into an elegant dwelling by his illegitimate son Valerano. The most important of these alterations was the commissioning of a series of frescoes which depict scenes from the chivalrous romance *Le Chevalier Errant* written by Tommaso at the beginning of the fifteenth century. The frescoes, which are in an excellent state of conservation, are some of the finest surviving examples of the international Gothic.

Eight miles to the east of Saluzzo, **Savigliano** is another town with an interesting historical centre. Particularly worth visiting is the abbey of San Piero dei Cassinesi which, although most of the present building dates from the late sixteenth century, was actually founded in 585. Nearby is the ex-monastery of San Francesco which, as well as having a fine sixteenth-century cloister, is now the site of the civic museum. The contents include an archaeological collection, a gallery of Piemontese paintings, the pharmacy of the former Ospedale dell' Annunziata and casts of important works by local sculptors. From Savigliano the SS20 leads directly back to Cuneo.

Further Information
— Piemonte —

Airports

Turin
Caselle Internazionale
☎ (011) 5778361

Tourist Information Offices

Piemonte is divided into six provinces each of which has its own tourist board.

Province of Alessandria
Ente Provinciale per il Turismo
Via Savona 26
Alessandria
☎ (0131) 51021

Province of Asti
Ente Provinciale per il Turismo
Piazza Alfieri 34
Asti
☎ (0141) 50357

Province of Cuneo
Ente Provinciale per il Turismo
Corso Nizza 17
Cuneo
☎ (0171) 68015

Province of Novara
Ente Provinciale per il Turismo
Corso Cavour 2
Novara
☎ (0321) 23398

Province of Torino (Turin)
Ente Provinciale per il Turismo
Via Roma 222
Turin
☎ (011) 535181

Province of Vercelli
Ente Provinciale per il Turismo
Viale Garibaldi 90
Vercelli
☎ (0161) 64361

Museums and Other Places of Interest

This information is arranged alphabetically by town. Opening times have been given where available but do tend to change fairly regularly. Museums without opening times are temporarily closed for restoration at the time of writing or have erratic opening hours.

Acqui Terme
Museo Civico Archeologico
Castello dei Paleologhi
☎ (0144) 57555

Open: Wednesday, Thursday and Saturday 9am-12noon and 4-7pm, Sunday 9.30am-12noon. Prior notice recommended.

Alagna Valsesia
Museo Walser
☎ (0163) 91326
Open: mid-August every day; July Saturday and Sunday, other months by appointment.

Alba
Museo Civico
Via Paruzza 1/a
Open: Tuesday-Saturday 9am-12noon, Thursday and Saturday also 3-6pm.

Alessandria
Museo Civico e Pinacoteca
☎ (0131) 54681
Via Parma
Open: Tuesday-Friday 9-12noon and 2.45-6pm, and Monday pm, prior notice.

Alpino
Museo dell'Ombrello (Umbrellas)
Gignese
Open: April-September, Tuesday-Sunday 10am-12noon and 3-6pm.

Arona
Museo Città di Arona
Piazza de Filippi
Open: Saturday 9-11pm and Sunday 10am-12noon.

San Carlone
Statue/Tower of Borromeo
Open: 8am-12noon and 2-6pm. Closed November and Wednesdays in winter.

Asti
Mostra Permanente della Resistenza
Synagogue
Via Ottolenghi 8
☎ (0141) 32439
Open: Sunday-Friday 9am-12noon. Prior notice.

Museo del Risorgimento e Pinacoteca
Corso Alfieri 357
Open: Tuesday-Saturday 9am-12noon and 3-6pm, Sunday 10am-12noon.

Palazzo Alfieri Museum
Corso Alfieri 375
Open: Tuesday-Friday 10-12am and 3.30-5.30pm, Saturday and Sunday 10am-12noon.

Museo Archeologico
Ex-church of San Pietro in Consavia
Open: Tuesday-Saturday 9am-12noon and 3-6pm, Sunday 10am-12noon.

Bardonecchia
Museo Civico
Open: July-August Sunday and holidays 10am-12.30pm.

Barolo
Castle
Open: Friday-Wednesday 10am-12.30pm and 3-6pm.

Borgosesia
Museo del Folklore Valsesiano
Via Manifattura 10
☎ (0163) 22205
Open: Saturday 9am-12noon and 3-6pm, Sunday 3-6pm, other days by appointment.

Museo di Paleontologia e Paletnologia
Via Sesone 10

Isola Borromeo
Palazzo Borromeo
Isola Bella
Open: mid-March-end October, 9am-12noon and 1.30-5pm.

Botanical Gardens
Isola Madre
Open: as above.

Bra
Museo Civico
Via Craveri 15
Open: Tuesday-Sunday 3-6pm.

Carmagnola
Museo Civico di Storia Naturale
Piazza Sant' Agostino
Open: Saturday 4-6pm, prior notice recommended.

Casale Monferrato
Musei Civici
Via Cavour

Museo Israelitico
Synagogue
Vicolo Salomone Olper 44
Open: Sunday 10am-12noon and 3-5pm.

Cherasco
Museo G.B. Adriani
Scuola Media
Open: 1st Sunday of month 10.30am-12noon.

Chieri
Museo Civico
Via Palazzo di Città 10
☎ (011) 9470048
Open: Give prior notice.

Chiomonte
Galleria d'Arte
Via Vittorio Emanuele 75
Open: on request, ask in *Municipio.*

Cisterna d'Asti
Museo delle Arti e Mestieri di Un Tempo
Open: 3-6pm or ☎ (0141) 979118.

Cuneo
Museo del Pane e della Panificazione
Lungostura 24 Maggio 3

Domodossola
Archaeological Museum
Palazzo Silva

Frabosa Soprana
Grotta di Bossea Caves
Bossea ($4^1/_2$ miles)
Open: 10am-12noon and 2-6pm.

Ivrea
Museo Civico 'P.A.Garda'
Piazza Ottinetti 18
Open: Tuesday-Friday 9.30am-12noon and 3-6.30pm, Saturday closing 5.30pm.

Marengo
Villa Marengo
Museo della Battaglia
Open: October-May Tuesday-Saturday 2.30-5.30pm, Sunday 10am-12noon and 2.30-5.30pm, June-September Tuesday-Saturday 4-7pm, Sunday 9.30am-12noon and 4-7pm.

Monterosso Grana
Museo Etnografico Coumboscuro
Santa Lucia
☎ (0171) 98771
Open: 8am-12noon and 2-6pm, prior notice.

Nizza Monferrato
Wine Museum
Stabilimento Vinicolo Bersano
Piazza Dante
☎ (0141) 721273
Open: April-September Monday-Friday 9-11am and 3-5pm, Saturday and Sunday am only by appointment.

Novara
Museo Civico
Broletto
Open: Tuesday-Sunday 10am-12noon and 3-6pm.

Musei di Etnografia & Storia Naturale
Via G. Ferrari 13

Ovada
Museo Geologico
La Costa
☎ (0143) 80937
Open: by appointment.

Pinerolo
Museo d'Arte Preistorica
Viale Giolitti 1
Open: Saturday 3-7pm.

Museo Nazionale dell'Arma di Cavalleria
Viale Giolitti 5
Open: 9-11.15am and 3-5.15pm, closed Sunday pm Monday and Thursday.

Collezione Civica d'Arte
Piazza Vittorio Veneto 8
Mineralogical Collection
Corso Piave 7
Open: 10am-12noon and 3-6.30pm, 2nd Sunday of month.

Romagnano Sesia
Museo Storico Etnografico della Bassa Valsesia
Open: May-September Saturday 10am-12noon, other times ☎ (0163) 833483.

Sacra di San Michele
Abbey
Open: winter 9am-12noon and 2-5pm, summer 9am-12noon and 2-7pm.

Saluzzo
Casa Cavassa
☎ (0175) 87822
Open: April-September 9am-12noon and 3-6pm, other months 9am-12.15pm and 2-5.15pm.

Castello di Manta
$2^1/_2$ miles SE from Saluzzo
Open: Tuesday-Sunday 10am-12.30pm and 2.30-5pm, give prior notice.

Sampeyre
Museo Civico
Scuola Media
Open: most days in summer.

Santena
Castello dei Cavour
Open: Tuesday-Sunday 9am-12noon and 2-5pm.

Santhia
Galleria d'Arte Moderna
Via de Rege Como 7
Open: Monday-Saturday 4-7pm, Sunday 10am-12noon, closed August.

Savigliano
Museo Civico
Via San Francesco 9
Monday and Wednesday-Friday 9am-12noon, weekend 3-7pm except last Saturday and Sunday in month.

Serralunga d'Alba
Castle
Open: Tuesday-Sunday summer 9am-12noon and 2.30-7pm, winter 9am-12noon and 2-5pm.

Stresa
Centro Studi Rosminiani

Villa Ducale
Lungolago
Open: Monday-Friday 8.30am-12noon and 2.30-6..30pm. Closed August.

Villa Pallavicino
Corso Italia
Open: mid-March-early November 8.30am-7pm.

Stupingi
Villa Reale di Stupingi
Open: 10am-12.30pm and 2-5pm, closed Monday and Friday.

Susa
Museo Civico
Castle
Open: summer Tuesday-Saturday 3.30-5.30pm, Sunday 9.30-11.30am and 3.30-5.30pm, winter Thursday and Sunday 2.30-4.30pm.

Torre Pellice
Museum
Open: Monday and Thursday 4-7pm, Sunday 10am-12.30pm and 4-7.30pm.

Tortona
Museo Civico
Palazzo Guidobono
Via Emilia

Varallo
Pinacoteca & Museo di Storia Naturale
Palazzo dei Musei
Open: summer 10am-12noon and 3-6pm, winter on request. Closed Fridays.

Verbania
Museo del Paesaggio & Museo Storico Artistico del Verbano
Via Cavour 40
Open: April-October Tuesday-Sunday 10am-12noon and 3-5pm, November-March Saturday and Sunday 10am-12noon and 3-5pm.

Villa Taranto
Open: April-October 8.30am-7.30pm.

Vercelli
Museo Leone

Via Verdi 7
☎ (0161) 65604
Open: April-November Tuesday and Thursday 3-5pm, winter with prior notice Sunday-Friday 10am-12noon.

Museo Borgogna
Via Borgogna 8
Open: Tuesday and Thursday 3-5pm, Sunday 10am-12.30pm, other days by prior arrangement, write.

Vicoforte
Museo M. Ghislieri
Santuario di Vicoforte
Open: March-October 9am-12noon and 3-6pm.

Voltaggio
Pinacoteca
Convento dei Cappuccini
☎ (0143) 9301237
Open: on request.

Museo della Civiltà Contadina
Palazzo Galliera
☎ (0143) 9301148
Telephone to ensure museum is open.

3 • Lombardia

Bordered by the crest of the central part of the Italian alpine range to the north, Lago Maggiore and the Ticino river to the west, Lago di Garda and the Mincio to the east and the Po to the south, Lombardia (Lombardy) is, at 9,200sq miles, one of the larger Italian regions. The southern half of the region is a thick alluvial plain which slopes almost imperceptibly upwards towards a fairly narrow band of hills and then the pre-Alps and the Alps. These last are composed of three main groups: the Retiche Alps to the east of the Spluga river, the highest of which is Monte Bernina (13,280ft) and where even the lowest of the mountain passes reaches over 7,600ft; the Lepantine Alps, more uniform in height — 10-11,000ft — with passes around 6,500ft; and the Orobie Alps which vary from a minimum of just over 8,000ft to the 12,800ft Ortles. All three alpine groups are crystalline rock while the pre-Alps are mainly calcareous and dolomitic.

Most of the famous Italian lakes are to be found in the Lombardian pre-alpine zone: Maggiore, Lugano, Como, Iseo, Idro, and Garda at the foot of the valleys separating the major Alps. The effect of the lakes on the area immediately surrounding them is to raise the naturally cold winter temperature by several degrees permitting a wide range of plants to grow outside their normal geographical limits. Not only vines and olives can be seen around the larger lakes but even crops of citrus fruits and some palm trees. Other smaller, often picturesque lakes are to be found in the hilly area of Lombardia where scattered homesteads and vineyards are interspersed with occasional infertile ridges which protrude through the alluvial deposits of which the hills are formed.

The plain is almost all either intensively farmed or built on and its main interest lies in the many old towns which, while once strong independent *comunes*, now serve mainly as dormitory towns for Milan. In the third century AD Milan was already an important city, the capital of the Western Roman Empire, although by the end of the seventh century it had been superseded by Pavia as the capital of the

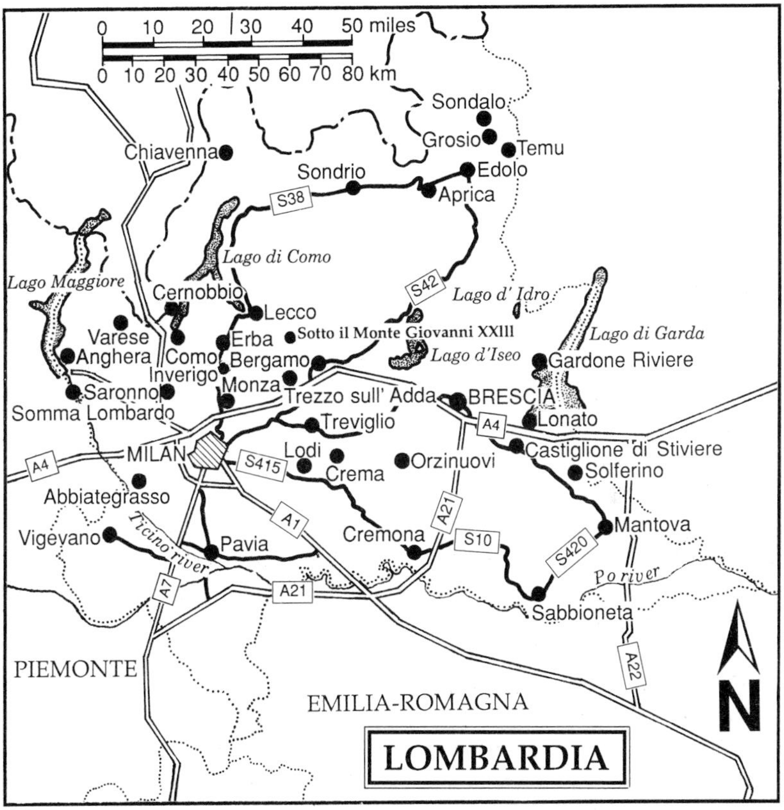

Longobard kingdom from which the present region takes its name. By the end of the millennium the Longobard rule had become decentralised with Milan, Pavia, Bergamo, Brescia, Como, Crema, Cremona, Lodi and Mantova becoming strong independent *comunes* often warring amongst each other for supremacy, a system of government which rapidly spread throughout northern and central Italy. Despite frequent disputes among the cities, most of them thrived in this period, exporting their own style of religious architecture and their banking organization (the Lombard Bank) throughout Europe.

During the medieval period, Milan gradually re-established itself as the most important city in the region, although many of the others continued to be important cultural centres, the testimonies of which can still be admired today. From the sixteenth century, however, the region was governed by Spain and went into decline for 200 years, a process accentuated by the rigorous repression of the Counter Reformation. The Austrians, who took over the region in 1714, were more stimulating and by the time of the 'Unification of Italy' in the 1860s, Milan in particular, and the region in general, was ready to assume the mantle of industrial, commercial and financial leadership.

Lombardia is best visited during spring or autumn, as in summer the plain is very hot, while in winter it tends to be cold, wet and foggy. Weekdays are best for visiting the lakes and mountains as during these periods good weather at weekends provokes a mass exodus from the cities towards the lakes. The mountains are at their best climatically in summer although those prepared to brave the occasional heavy downfall will be quite comfortable in spring and autumn. Like most of Italy's mountains the Lombard mountains are well equipped with winter sports facilities, although again they tend to get very busy at weekends.

Sondrio is best situated for use as a starting point for exploring the mountains while Brescia and Milan are best for visiting the towns on the plain.

Excursions from Milan

The first excursion from Lombardia's capital touches both legs of Lago di Como and visits important cities such as Como, Bergamo and Crema, as well as several smaller, much lesser known towns before returning to Milan. Leave the city on the SS36 to **Monza** 8 miles to the north. The city has long been an important one, at times overshadowing even Milan, particularly in the seventh century under the Longobards. Although it has grown rapidly in the last century there are still many important things to see in the city which, owing to its proximity to Milan, tends to be neglected by tourists.

The most important building in Monza is the royal palace, built in the late eighteenth century, just in time to become the favourite residence of Eugénie de Beauharnais, Napoleon's stepson and viceroy. The gardens are open to the public as is the chapel and one wing of the palace which contains an art gallery. Beyond the ornamental gardens is a vast park which contains a golf course and the Grand-Prix motor racing circuit.

The other monument of great importance in the town is the thirteenth-century Gothic cathedral with its white marble façade. Inside the altar is an iron crown which is said to have been forged from the nails which were used to crucify Christ. The church's treasure is housed in the Museo Serpero below the left-hand nave of the church. Other interesting buildings are to be found around Piazza Roma about 100yd west of the church.

After Monza, head due north for about 12 miles to the attractive town of **Inverigo** on one of the first hills of the pre-Alps. The town has no really important monuments but several fine villas and excellent views of the surrounding countryside.

Shortly after Inverigo, turn left and head for **Como** which stands at the foot of the lake of the same name. Como is a lively city with a pleasant mixture of the old and the new, and has been prevented from becoming too big by the amphitheatre-like hills which provide a magnificent backdrop. Many of the finest exponents of Romanesque architecture and sculpture were from around Como and not surprisingly the city's cathedral dates from that period, although it was not completed until 1770. Adjoining the cathedral is the Broletto, once the centre of the city's government. The building, with its elegant porticoed loggia, was built in the first half of the thirteenth century as was the tower alongside, although it was shortened in the fifteenth century when the façade of the cathedral was built. The tower was completely rebuilt along the original lines in the 1920s. Four hundred yards further down Via Vittorio Emanuele are the civic museums which contain several collections of great interest. Visitors with a scientific bent should visit the Tempio Voltiano, the small mausoleum and museum of Alessandro Volta, the man who gave his name to the volt. The Tempio is situated on the shore of the lake, to the north-west of the centre. Continuing round the shore in the same direction one finds the magnificent neo-classical Villa Olmo which is used for congresses, concerts and exhibitions. Just outside the city to the south-west is the twelfth-century Castel Bardello with a magnificent view over the lake.

The road around the shore of the lake is magnificent but as it is far from off-the-beaten-track it is outside the scope of this book. Should you be willing to make a small exception, however, it is well worth visiting the small town of **Cernobbio** 3 miles to the north. The village is full of characteristic alleyways and interesting old buildings. At the northern end of the town is the magnificent sixteenth-century Villa d'Este, now one of the world's most luxurious hotels.

The excursion continues to the east of Como. Proceed to **Erba** where the fine archaeological museum should not be missed. The magnificent neo-classical Villa Amalia and the Buco del Piombo caves (2 and 3 miles north of the town respectively) may be visited with the permission of the Comune (☎ (031) 641006). A large open-air theatre is being built on one of the hills overlooking the town and will soon be hosting concerts on summer evenings.

After Erba visit **Asso** 6 miles to the north-east, a pleasant town between the two branches of Lago di Como, well placed for walking in the surrounding hills with their fine views of the lake and the Alps beyond. The village is fairly popular in the summer months but the tourist trade there is relaxed and not obtrusive.

Continue to the north-east until the road drops down to the lake again and turn right along the shore to **Lecco**, centre point of the action in Alessandro Manzoni's classic novel *The Betrothed*. The beautiful setting described in the first two pages of Manzoni's book has not changed although the town has grown somewhat. A Manzoni museum has been established in the house where the author stayed in the town, while part of the civic museum is housed in the castle tower which also has Manzonian connections. A funicular railway takes just over 5 minutes to climb up to the Piani d'Erna — 3,500ft above the town — which offers excellent possibilities to skiers in winter as well as fine walking in summer.

From Lecco, take the road towards Bergamo alongside the minor lakes, Garlate and Orlinate, until the right turn for Brivio where the main road swings away from the Adda river. Turn left at Brivio and continue until a sign to the left directs you up to the abbey of Fontanelle Sotto il Monte Giovanni XXIII. Only the church of Santo Egidio remains of the eleventh-century Cistercian abbey but this is one of the finest of its period. Traces of fifteenth-century frescoes can be seen in the naves, each of which has its own apse. The road from Sotto il Monte Giovanni XXIII, the road to Bergamo, is pleasant although not spectacular. It has the advantage however of being reasonably free of traffic.

The city of **Bergamo** was already important in Roman times and for centuries was a keen rival of Milan and Venice before finally succumbing to Venetian rule. There are two distinct parts of the city: a rapidly expanding sector on the plain and the old town 300ft higher up, which is still contained by a circle of defensive walls. Until the nineteenth century the lower part of the city consisted of a few small villages and stately residences which remain as interesting islands among the modern buildings. One of these, the Palazzo dell' Accademia built at the beginning of the last century now houses the Accademia Carrara, one of the most important museums and art galleries in Italy, containing paintings by Tintoretto, Bellini and Mantegna amongst others. The old city on the hill is mainly medieval with narrow winding streets but its centre is the Piazza Vecchia, an attractive Renaissance square created in the late fifteenth century when several older streets were demolished.

Palazzo della Ragione separates Piazza Vecchia from Piazza del

Bergamo cathedral

Duomo, the city's religious centre which predates the rest of the square having been built in the twelfth century. The façade which faces the square, however, was modernised to unify the square during the fifteenth century. The early thirteenth-century *Duomo* has been restored several times since then and contains an important *Martyrdom of St John the Bishop* by Tiepolo. More impressive, however, is the twelfth-century Romanesque basilica of Santa Maria Maggiore which occupies another of the sides of Piazza del Duomo. Outside the church are several important sculptures by Giovanni da Campione, one of the finest sculptors of the fourteenth century, while inside are many important paintings, sculptures and wood-carvings. The Colleoni chapel on the site of the original sacristy was the first truly great piece of Renaissance architecture in Lombardia when it was built in the 1470s. The tomb of Bartolomeo Colleoni, the greatest of the Bergamasque leaders, is in the chapel which is decorated by some of the finest Renaissance paintings including the *Holy Family* by Angelica Kauffman, probably the finest of the female Renaissance painters. The small baptistry on the fourth side of the square was originally situated inside Santa Maria Maggiore until being resited on the edge of the 'Bishop's Garden' in 1898.

The city's castle was begun in 1334 and added to by several later rulers of the city. The outer circle is now a memorial garden while the main building now houses a museum of the Resistance with sections dedicated to the various wars of independence as well as to the partisans of the last war. The city's walls were built in the 1560s by the Venetians as the city had outgrown the previous medieval circle. The complete walk around the walls is over 3 miles and takes just under an hour. Besides the important buildings already mentioned Bergamo has several other important museums and the visitor could quite easily use up 2 or 3 days in the city.

From Bergamo, follow the Milan road until **Trezzo sull' Adda**, where the remains of one of the most formidable castles in Lombardia can be seen. From Trezzo head south alongside the Adda to **Treviglio** where several fine old churches and the civic library, which contains many important manuscripts, deserve a visit. A minor road which forks off to the left at Calvenzano, a mile south of Treviglio, allows you to avoid the bulk of the traffic between Treviglio and Crema, the next city on this itinerary. The old centre of **Crema** is extremely beautiful with several interesting Renaissance *palazzi* and many magnificent churches in widely divergent styles. Of these the most important is the sixteenth-century Venetian-style cathedral with its magnificent plain brick façade. While the cathedral lacks the marble coverings and the external statues of many other Italian cathedrals, the harmonious qualities of the architecture make up for this. The façade is wider and much higher than the rest of the building with every aspect having been designed on classical principles. The interior is lofty and austere, bearing some resemblance to the English cathedrals of the late medieval period.

The church of the Santissima Trinità is a complete contrast to the *Duomo*, being an excellent example of the baroque where almost every detail gives a feeling of space and refinement. The large former monastery of Sant' Agostino, built between the fifteenth and seventeenth centuries and then closed by Napoleon, now houses the civic museum and art gallery where the most important exhibit is Gaetano Previati's *The Hostages of Crema*. A third church of great importance is the late fifteenth century Bramantesque sanctuary of Santa Maria della Croce. Outside, the church is round with four external chapels giving it the shape of a Greek cross, while a fine loggia runs around the top. The interior is octagonal and contains some well executed frescoes.

The second excursion from Milan also leaves the northern side of the city but this time the first port of call is **Saronno**, 20 minutes drive to the north-west. Again, the town's main claim to fame is a church, this time the rectangular sanctuary of the Madonna dei Miracoli, one of the finest Bramantesque churches in the whole region. Saronno also has several hotels and could be used as an alternative base.

After Saronno continue on the same road through countryside, which becomes steadily more attractive, to the pleasant, though modern, city of **Varese**. Built on the side of a hill sloping gently down to the shore of Lago di Varese, the town is much more open than most modern Italian towns, with many of the houses having their own gardens. The city itself is of no great interest but the possibilities for walking and skiing in the nearby mountains, and the ease of access to several lakes make Varese an ideal place to have a meal and use as a temporary base. Within 4 miles of the city centre are places of interest such as Lido di Varese on the shore of Lago di Varese; Bizzozero, where the fine Romanesque church has foundations dating back to the eighth century; Monte Campo dei Fiori, a long mountainous ridge with fine views and an astronomic observatory open to the public at weekends; Prima Cappella with its fourteen chapels and the interesting Villa Lodovico Pogliaghi museum; and the small village of Santa Maria del Monte with its interesting old church and another small museum.

After leaving Varese, follow the road around the shore of Lago di

Varese in an anti-clockwise direction until the small village of Cassinetta Rizzone, pass in between the two small lakes, Comabbio and Monate, run up the western shore of the latter then cut across the SS629 on the shore of Lago Maggiore. One mile to the south a minor road to the right takes you even closer to the lake before finally arriving in **Angera**, a pleasant lakeside town. The thirteenth-century castle still belongs to the Borromeo family whose most famous member was a saint of the Roman Catholic church.

To avoid the traffic south of Angera leave the town to the east on the minor road which passes through the villages of Taino and Oneda. Five miles south of Oneda at **Somma Lombardo** is another fine castle, this time dating from the fifteenth century and containing some archaeological exhibits in the courtyard. Just over a mile outside the town to the east, two Romanesque buildings of great interest can be seen in the village of **Arsago Seprio**. The baptistry dates from the eleventh century while the village church itself predates it by at least two centuries and the foundations are believed to be mainly Roman.

A few miles to the south is the airport of Malpensa, one of the busiest in Italy. Few of the many thousands of tourists who pass through the airport each week know, however, that there is an aviation museum at the airport with a collection of planes dating from as far back as 1908.

Head south-west from the airport and then turn left immediately before the road crosses the Ticino river and continue southwards on the secondary road which roughly follows the course of the river as far as **Abbiategrasso** where the fourteenth-century castle has been undergoing a restoration programme which will eventually lead to the opening of an archaeological museum. The town's thirteenth-century church of Santa Maria Nuova has a magnificent Renaissance portal, the last of Bramante's great works to be built in Lombardia (1497). Just off the road towards Pavia, 4 miles south of Abbiategrasso is the late twelfth-century Cistercian monastery of Morimondo. The monastery was founded earlier in the twelfth century by a group of French Cistercians and traces of their influence can be seen in the building.

Continue towards Pavia until just after Bereguardo then turn left and work eastwards along a succession of minor roads to **Certosa di Pavia**, 5 miles north of the city of Pavia itself. The Certosa di Pavia is a magnificent monastic complex founded in 1396 by Gian Galeazzo Visconti to his wife's memory. The monastery, which has two attractive cloisters, is full of precious works of art produced by many of

Panorama of Angera

Italy's greatest artists over the 300 years which followed the foundation of the church. The façade is divided into five sections by marble pillars and has a richly decorated portal portraying the lives of various saints and relating the story of the foundation of the monastery.

Situated as it is at the confluence of the Po and the Ticino rivers, **Pavia** was already an important town in the Roman period and later, under the Longobards, was the capital of the Regnum Italicum. Even after falling under Milanese rule the city continued to be one of Italy's foremost centres of culture and learning with one of the first Italian universities. The area between the Certosa and the fourteenth-century castle at the northern end of the city was once a hunting park as the castle was one of the Milanese dukes' favourite residences. After the death of the last of the Sforza family in 1535 the palace became a barracks, and only in the last 50 years has it been restored to anything like its original splendour. It now houses the civic museum, where one of the finest exhibits is an exquisite wooden model of Pavia's cathedral, a fine Renaissance building where the influence of Bramante can be seen clearly, particularly in the crypt.

Other important churches in the town are the twelfth-century basilica of San Michele where several kings and emperors were crowned in the medieval period; the large Romanesque church of San Pietro in Ciel d'Oro where the remains of St Augustin are kept under a Gothic arch, and the Gothic Carmine church. The covered bridge over the Ticino was built in 1354, but the present bridge is a reconstruction built after the original was destroyed during the last war.

The rest of this itinerary crosses the flat Lombard plain which is fairly monotonous and uninteresting with the exception of a few old towns. The next of these which should be visited is **Sant' Angelo Lodigiano** with its magnificent medieval tower. The central part of the castle was modernised in the 1370s and despite passing through several sieges is little changed since then. Two museums are housed in the castle, one which recreates the appearance and atmosphere of a late medieval noble residence, and the other, based in the stable block, an agricultural museum.

At first sight, **Lodi** 8 miles to the east, appears to be an uninteresting modern dormitory town, but at the centre, Piazza della Vittoria is very attractive with some important old buildings around and nearby. As usual, the churches in the town are of far greater interest than any of the other buildings. The most important are the twelfth-century *Duomo* with its raised Romanesque presbytery; the Incoronata sanctuary, an attractive Renaissance church with four important paintings by Bergognone; and San Francesco, a fine example of the Lombard Gothic. Besides these the visitor should try to see the town's museum and art gallery in the ex-monastery of San Filippo, and the Broletto, an imposing building next to the *Duomo* which, despite its eighteenth-century baroque façade, was built in the late thirteenth century. If staying in Milan, the best way to return there from Lodi is on the motorway as this allows you to miss out the rather uninteresting outskirts of the city.

Excursions from Brescia

Brescia has expanded rapidly over the last hundred years, but the historic centre still retains the same street plan adopted on the site by the Romans more than 2,000 years ago. The old centre is dominated by the town's castle, mostly dating from the sixteenth century. Besides having a fine view over the city, the castle also has a very pleasant park, part of which has been turned into a zoo. Since the end of the last century, the castle has belonged to the town council and two museums have been set up there: a weaponry museum with

The Certosa at Pavia

over 1,300 exhibits, and a museum dedicated to the period of the Italian Unification. Other museums in the town are the Pinacoteca Civica Tosio Martinengo which contains mainly paintings by local artists, housed in a fine Renaissance *palazzo*; the museum of modern art which unfortunately lacks paintings by the futurists, the most important artistic movement in modern Italian art; the civic Christian museum, in the ex-monastery of San Salvatore, and more importantly the archaeological museum in a restored section of the Roman Tempio Capitolino erected by Vespasian in AD73. A viewing gallery allows the visitor to the museum to see part of the Roman theatre, the bulk of which, however, is covered by Renaissance buildings.

Three hundred yards away is the magnificent Piazza della Loggia which has been the city's historic and civic centre for the last 500 years. The most impressive building, from which the square takes its name, is the Palazzo del Comune commonly known as the Loggia as most of the ground floor is open with four columns giving on to three vaulted naves. The architecture of the building is Venetian Renaissance as is the Monte di Pietà alongside it. The many Roman inscriptions, written in gem-stones, which are embedded in the outer walls were recovered from local excavations in the fifteenth century and by placing them on public display the building can claim to have been Italy's first lapidary museum.

Until the fifteenth century the city was governed from the Broletto, an eleventh-century building in Piazza del Duomo, which contains many fine frescoes. The *Duomo* itself is a seventeenth-century mannerist building in the form of a Greek cross. Far more interesting is the old cathedral which stands alongside it. The main part of the church is round with simple severe decoration while a flight of steps gives onto a regular shaped presbytery with two parallel side chapels which were added to the original eleventh-century structure in the fifteenth.

From Brescia take the SS237 eastwards and then cut across to **Gardone Riviera** on the shore of Lago di Garda. One of the most important and elegant resorts on the lake, a large number of open-air concerts are held on the shore during the summer. Half a mile from the town is the Villa Vittoriale where the revolutionary poet Gabriele d'Annunzio once lived. The villa has magnificent gardens and besides containing the poet's mausoleum also holds a museum dedicated to his life and works. Two miles south of Gardone is **Salò** where Mussolini formed a new capital after the Allies had taken Rome. Now the town is an attractive resort with an archaeological museum and an interesting museum dedicated to the period between Napoleon's occupation of Italy and the partisan resistance to fascism, Museo del Nastro Azzuro.

The coast road below Salò is likely to be busy in good weather so take the secondary road a mile or so inland, through Polpenazze and Padenghe before reaching **Lonato**, a pleasant little town overlooking the southern end of the lake. The area around the town where Napoleon scored a great victory against the Austrians in 1796 is known to have been inhabited since the Bronze Age. If you are lucky enough to be in the area on a weekday outside the main tourist season, one place which should not be missed is **Sirmione** situated on a long thin peninsula into the lake. The most interesting building is the thirteenth-century Rocca Scaligera castle which is entirely surrounded by water. A lapidary museum is situated inside the castle, while the battlements may also be visited. At the extreme northern end of the peninsula are the Grotte di Catullo; the remains

Piazza Castello, Mantova

of an Imperial Roman villa with several underground rooms.

The next port of call is **Castiglione delle Stiviere,** 5 miles south of Lonato, where several fine paintings by Francesco Bassano can be seen in the Museo Storico Aloisiano which is situated in a fine Renaissance building, formerly the Collegio delle Nobili Vergini convent. To the west of Castiglione is **Solferino,** the site of the most famous battle of the Italian wars of independence, where, in 1859, Napoleon III's army, led by MacMahon, crushed a much larger Austrian army. The town's museum contains many relics of the battle while others can be seen in the castle half a mile outside the town which dates from the eleventh century.

South-east of Solferino is one of the finest cities in Lombardia, if not in Europe. Surrounded on three sides by the Mincio river, **Mantova** is full of magnificent buildings, most of which date from the fifteenth and sixteenth centuries when the Gonzaga family made it one of the finest courts in Europe. There are many literary references to Mantova as two of Italy's finest writers, Virgil and Castiglione, were born there. Virgil tells us that the city's origins were Etruscan but the descriptions of the city we see today are to be found in the letters of Castiglione who grew up in the area in the late fifteenth century. The ducal palace was built in various stages between the thirteenth and eighteenth centuries and consists of over 500 different buildings (including a basilica) and fifteen separate gardens or internal squares. One of the greatest artists to work for the Duke of Mantova was Rubens and many of his greatest works can be seen inside the palace. The best way to see the palace is to join one of the tours organized by the local tourist board. Facing the palace is the city's cathedral built in the Middle Ages but almost completely reconstructed in 1545 following a design by Giulio Romano, Raphael's leading assistant.

While designing the cathedral, Romano was following established architectural conventions but the real extent of his brilliance as an architect can be seen in Via Poma 3, the house which he designed for himself. Even more important was Andrea Mantegna, another native of the city who designed his own tomb in the fifteenth-century basilica of Sant' Andrea designed by Leon Battista Alberti, 2 years before his death. Most of Mantegna's best works were painted for the Venetian Doges but the *Holy Family* on one side of the chapel where his tomb is situated is by him, while other paintings in the chapel are by his son.

Follow the SS420 to the west, across the Oglio river to **Sabbioneta**, an almost exemplary Renaissance town. During the Renaissance the town was ruled by a cadet branch of the Gonzaga family and under Vespasiano Gonzaga earned itself the nickname of 'little Athens' by establishing an academy, a museum, a library, a mint and one of the first printing presses in Europe. The town has retained its defensive walls and can be visited fairly comprehensively in 2 or 3 hours.

From Sabbioneta take the main road towards Parma until just before the Po and then turn right to **Cremona**. Piazza del Comune, the centre of the city, is considered by many to be the finest medieval square in Italy. Dominating the square is the 370ft-high Campanaria tower where the reward for climbing the 487 steps is a magnificent view of the city. The ornate surround of the clock on the tower represents the hours, the days, the phases and eclipses of the moon, and the signs of the zodiac, painted in 1671. A loggia at the base of the tower continues along the whole of the façade of the cathedral, unifying the two monuments. The cathedral itself is a vast Romanesque building which picked up Gothic and Renaissance elements as improvements were carried out over the centuries which followed its construction in 1107. In the Palazzo del Comune three violins are on view in the room known as the 'Violin Room', one by Andrea Amati (1566), one by Nicolo Amati (1658) and the third by Antonio Stradivari (1715) the most famous violin-maker of all time, whose violins are now worth almost half a million pounds each. A Stradivari museum has been established in the Palazzo dell' Arte where documents relating to the craftsman's life, designs for his violins, and even the tools he used can be seen. The city's civic museum has a large and varied collection, and is situated in the fine Renaissance Palazzo Affaitati, built in 1561 for a family of bankers.

Take the road northwards to Verola Vecchia until the left turn signposted 'Quinzano d'Oglio' shortly after crossing the river Oglio. Cross the main road and continue to the north-east until **Orzinuovi** where part of the fortifications erected by the Brescians in the medieval period to defend their border against the Cremonese can still be seen. Also of interest is the large elongated central square surrounded by porticoed buildings.

The historic centre of **Soncino**, $2^1/_2$ miles west of Orzinuovi, on the other side of the Oglio, is still surrounded by its medieval walls and defensive towers. The fifteenth-century castle at the centre of the town is surrounded by a moat with two drawbridges, and has not changed much since it was built despite having become a residence rather than a fortress during the seventeenth century.

Follow the road northwards for 8 miles alongside the river until the right turn for **Chiari**, which has an interesting medieval centre despite the modern look of the town. Both the *Duomo* and the church of Santa Maria Maggiore date from the fifteenth century, while in the Pinacoteca Repossi, the town can boast an interesting art gallery with a particularly fine collection of etchings.

Excursions from Sondrio

Situated halfway along the Valtellina valley **Sondrio** is a typical example of a flourishing alpine town ideally placed as a centre from which to visit the smaller walking and skiing centres of the Valtellina, the Valchiavenna and their side valleys. The fourteenth-century castle which overlooks the town is the only remaining castle in the Valtellina, the others having been destroyed by the Grigioni family who ruled the area from Sondrio in the sixteenth and seventeenth centuries. All the town's museums are currently housed in the neo-classical Palazzo Quadrio along with the public library. Most of the province's important pieces of religious art are contained in the diocesan museum, while the Valtellinese museum of history and art which will eventually be moved to the austere Palazzo Sassi dei Lavizzari in the public gardens, contains various articles relating to the valley, including several Roman and North-Etruscan inscriptions found during local archaeological excavations.

Due north of Sondrio is one of the most important of the side valleys, the Valmalenco. Fifteen miles long, the valley offers spectacular scenery from the road and a number of walks of varying degrees of difficulty into the surrounding mountains. **Chiesa in Valmalenco** has established itself as one of Lombardia's finest ski resorts over the last 20 years and a vast array of facilities are available during the winter. One of the most pleasant and easiest ascensions which can be made from Chiesa is to make the 20-minutes' walk up to the village of **Caspoggio** (3,600ft) and from there the chair-lift to Piazzo Cavalli (5,640ft), while a slightly more arduous excursion is that to Lago Palu which entails taking a cablecar to the Alpe Palu and then walking over the mountains for about 2 hours to the lake. A mountain shelter on the north shore of the lake offers refreshment and in peak periods also functions as a hotel. This area of the Alps is particularly well provided with shelters connected by marked footpaths. Before embarking on any of the longer or more difficult walks, however, visitors must provide themselves with a detailed map, proper walking equipment and inform his or her hotel where he or she plans to go that day.

For a mile and a half after Chiesa the valley is very narrow and forbidding before opening out again for the last 5 miles to **Chiareggio** at the head of the valley. The view from Chiareggio is magnificent, overlooking as it does the vast glacier of Monte Disgrazia. The glacier can be reached on foot at several points without too much difficulty, while some of the more difficult paths which continue from the shelters on the edge of the glacier lead over the border into Switzerland.

Follow the SS38 for 10 miles eastwards until the right turn for **Aprica** at Tresenda. Aprica is a small village on the steep Aprica Pass which has developed into a well known skiing centre over the last few years and offers excellent walking possibilities in summer. One of the shorter walks offering excellent views is the climb to the top of Monte Belvedere which can be accomplished in about an hour.

Just after Aprica take the right fork and continue over the moun-

Aprica offers good skiing and excellent walking

tains along the Val di Corteno until the road drops down to meet the SS42 at **Edolo**. A picturesque little town where the church of San Clemente is believed to be on the site of the important Roman temple of Saturn, destroyed by the Longobards in the seventh century, Edolo can be very busy at peak times with people on their way into the Valtellina or up the SS42 towards the Dolomites.

Take the SS42 as far as Ponte di Legno, pausing on the way to look at the sixteenth-century carvings in the parish church at **Temù**, which is also the ideal starting point for walks into the Adamello group of mountains which cover an area of almost 400sq miles and which was an important stronghold during World War I. Situated in a green valley whose grassy slopes slowly give way to spectacular mountain sides, **Ponte di Legno** has been developed into an important centre for summer walking holidays as well as being fairly near to some of the most extensive ski-slopes in the region. Of the many tracks which leave the town the most interesting historically is the one leading to the summit of Monte Tonale which offers the best view of the site of some of the bitterest fighting of World War I in Italy.

A very steep rough minor road leads north from Ponte di Legno, climbing spectacularly over the Gavia Pass (8,600ft) before dropping down, just as steeply towards Bormio. Part way down where the Val di Gavia meets the Val Furva is **Santa Caterina Valfurva** from where it is possible to ski all the year round, as well as to begin many walks and climbs.

Bormio is now one of the busiest of the Italian ski resorts and beyond the scope of this book. Skirt the southern end of the town and take the main road down the Valtellina. After 12 miles, a minor road on the right leads up the side of the valley to the village of **Sóndalo** in the magnificent scenery of the Stelvio National Park with its many footpaths and interesting geological nature. The Val di Rezzalo which faces Sóndalo is also outstandingly beautiful and although the area attracts a fair number of visitors one never has the sensation of being just one of the many while walking or skiing among the rugged mountains.

A little further down the main valley is the summer resort of **Grosio**, overlooked by the imposing ruins of the medieval Visconti Venosta castle. In the town itself the fifteenth-century church of San Giorgio has an interesting marble portal. Grosio is situated at the point where the beautiful Val Grosina joins the Valtellina. The first part of the valley can be seen from a car but the most attractive section leading up to the Malghera sanctuary and mountain shelter can only be ascended on foot and requires about 4 hours.

In **Tirano**, further down the main valley, there are many fine sixteenth- and seventeenth-century buildings, but the finest of all is without doubt the sanctuary of the Madonna built in the first decade of the sixteenth century after an apparition of the Virgin Mary had appeared on the site. The magnificent bell tower with its three lighted mullioned windows and the dome was added towards the end of the same century.

Most of the Valtellina to the west of Sondrio can be reached without using the main road as the villages along the north side of the

Villa Monastero, Lake Como

Winter scene at Sesto-Sexten, north-east of Cortina d'Ampezzo, Dolomites

Piazza Vecchia in Bergamo, Lombardia

The winter resort of Pampeago in Trentino

valley are mostly linked to each other by small twisting mountain roads, which are far more scenic than the more direct route. The Valtellina comes to an end where the Adda flows into Lago Como. Just before that a right turn leads up into the Valchiavenna beyond the small lake of Mezzola. **Chiavenna** itself is situated 10 miles above Lago Mezzola and is a pleasant little town still preserving much of its original medieval aspect. Besides the old buildings, the visitor to Chiavenna should not miss the Crotti, a group of caves which for centuries have been used as wine-cellars and meeting places by the townsfolk; the Paradiso archaeological and botanical park; and the Marmitte dei Giganti park where many pot-holes may be visited. Beyond Chiavenna itself the valley is very rugged and beautiful with many possibilities for walkers and winter sports enthusiasts.

Further Information
— Lombardia —

Airports

Bergamo
'Orio al Serio'
☎ (035) 217315

Milano
'Internazionale Forlanini'
Linate
☎ (02) 74852200

'Intercontinentale della Malpensa', Gallarate ☎ as above.
Buses for both airports from Piazza Luigi di Savoia, next to Central Station.

Tourist Information Offices

Lombardia is divided into eight provinces each of which has its own tourist information board. Local information is also available in many of the more popular towns.

Province of Bergamo
Ente Provinciale per il Turismo
4 Viale Vittorio Emanuele II Bergamo
☎ (035) 242226

Province of Brescia
Ente Provinciale per il Turismo
38 Corso Zanardelli
Brescia
☎ (030) 43418

Province of Como
Ente Provinciale per il Turismo
17 Piazza Cavour
Como
☎ (031) 262091

Province of Cremona
Ente Provinciale per il Turismo
8 Piazza del Comune
Cremona
☎ (0372) 23233

Province of Mantova
Ente Provinciale per il Turismo
6 Piazza Andrea Mantegna
Mantova
☎ (0376) 350681

Province of Milano
Ente Provinciale per il Turismo
1 Via Marconi
Milano
☎ (02) 809662

Province of Pavia
Ente Provinciale per il Turismo
1 Corso Garibaldi
Pavia
☎ (0382) 22156

Province of Sondrio
Ente Provinciale per il Turismo
12 Via Cesare Battisti
Sondrio
☎ (0342) 214463

Province of Varese
Ente Provinciale per il Turismo
5 Piazza Monte Grappa
Varese
☎ (0332) 283604

Museums and Other Places of Interest

This information has been arranged alphabetically by town. Opening times have been given where reliable information was available at the time of going to press. Church opening times are 7am-1pm, 3-6pm as a general rule.

Abbiategrasso
Museo Storico Archeologico
Castle

Asola
Museo Archeologico
8 Via Brescia
Open: Sunday 3-6pm (winter 2-5pm).

Bellagio
Villa Serbelloni
Open: Tuesday-Sunday, 10am-4pm.

Villa Melzi
Open: March-October, 9am-12.30pm and 2.30-6pm (summer 9am-6.30pm).

Bergamo
Cappella Colleoni
Open: 9am-12noon and 3-6pm.

Museo di Scienze Naturali
Cittadella (2nd floor)
Open: Tuesday 9am-12noon, Wednesday-Friday 9am-12noon and 3-5.30pm, weekend 3-6pm.

Pinacoteca dell'Accademia Carrara
Piazza G. Carrara
Open: 9.30am-12.30pm and 2-5.30pm, free entry on Sundays.

Museo del Risorgimento e della Resistenza
Rocca
Open: Tuesday to Saturday am, sometimes at other times.

Museo Diocesano di Arte Sacra
Casa dell'Arciprete
3 Via Donizetti
☎ (035) 211001
Visit by appointment.

Museo Donizettiano
Palazzo della Misericordia
9 Via Arena
Open: Monday-Friday 9am-12noon and 2-6pm (to 5pm October-April).

Botanical Garden
Entrance on Viale Beltrami
Open: Tuesday and Thursday 10am-12noon, Saturday and Sunday 10am-12noon and 3-6pm.
Closed July-March.

Birthplace of G. Donizetti
14 Via Borgo Canale
Open: June-September, Saturday and Sunday, 10am-12noon and 3-6pm.

Bormio
Museo Civico
Palazzo de Simoni
Open: Tuesday-Thursday 9am-12noon and 3-6pm, Friday and Sunday 10am-12noon, Saturday 5-7pm.

Breno
Cividate Camuno
$2^1/_2$ miles SW of new centre
Museo Archeologico della Valcamonica
Open: Tuesday-Saturday 9am-12noon,
Sunday 9am-1pm.

Brescia
Rotonda Church
Piazza del Duomo
If locked see Sacrestan.

Tempio Capitolino
Piazza del Foro
Open: Tuesday-Sunday 9am-12noon and 2-5pm, includes Lapidary Museum.

Museo Romano
Behind Tempio Capitolino
Open: as above.

Basilica of San Salvatore
Via dei Musei
Visitable Monday with permission, apply 1 Via Martinengo da Barco or ☎ (030) 59120.

Museo della Città
Church of Santa Giulia
Above San Salvatore
Planned to incorporate exhibits from former Christian Civilisation Museum.

Pinacoteca Tosio Martinengo
1 Via Martinengo da Barco
Open: Tuesday-Sunday 9am-12noon and 2-5pm.

Museo Diocesano d'Arte Sacra
Church of San Giuseppe
Open: Monday-Saturday 10am-12noon and 3-5pm.

Museo del Risorgimento
Castle
Open: Tuesday-Sunday 9am-12noon and 2-5pm.

Museo delle Armi Marzoli
Castle
Open: as above.

Museo Civico di Scienze Naturali
4 Via Ozanam
Open: Tuesday-Saturday 8.30am-12.30pm.

Cadenabbia
Villa Carlotta
Open: April-September 9am-6pm, March and October 9-11.30am and 2-4.30pm.

Cantù (Galliano)
Basilica and Baptistry of San Vincenzo
Open: 9am-12noon and 2-6pm.

Caravaggio
Sanctuary of the Madonna of Caravaggio

Castiglione delle Stiviere
Museo Storico Aloisiano
Collegio delle Nobili Vergini
Open: 9-11am and 3-6pm.

Museo Internazione della Croce Rossa
Palazzo Trineri-Longhi

Castiglione Olona
Palazzo Branda Castiglioni
Open: Tuesday-Friday 2.30-5pm, Saturday and Sunday also 10am-12.30pm.

Museo della Collegiata
Baptistry
To visit see Custodian of Collegiata Church.

Cavernago
Castle of Malpaga (1 mile from village)
☎ (035) 840003
Open: Sunday 2.30-5.30pm. Other days by appointment.

Cavriana
Museo Archeologico dell'Alto Mantovano
Open: March-November, Thursday, Saturday, Sunday 9am-12noon and 3-6pm.

Certosa di Pavia
Monastic Complex
Guided visits, March, April, September, October, closed on non-holiday Mondays, 9-11.30am and 2.30-6pm.

Chiari
Pinacoteca Repossi
9 Via B.Varisco
Open: Tuesday-Saturday 9am-12.30pm and 2.30-6pm.

Chiavenna
Archaeological and Botanical Gardens and Archaeological Museum
Open: Tuesday-Friday 2-5pm, Saturday and Sunday 2-6pm.

Chiesa in Valmalenco
Museo della Valmalenco
Parrocchiale
Open: July-August 5.30-7.30pm every day, September-June Saturday pm only.

Como
Tempio Voltiano (Physics Museum)
Lungolario
Open: April-September 10am-12noon and 3-6pm Tuesday-Sunday, October-March 2-4pm Tuesday-Sunday.

Civic Museums
Palazzo Giovio
Via Vittorio Emanuele II
Open: Tuesday-Saturday 9.30am-12noon and 2-5pm, Sunday 9.15am-12noon.

Crema
Museo Civico
49 Via Dante
Tuesday-Thursday 3-7pm, Monday, Friday and Saturday 3-6pm, Sunday 10am-12noon.

Cremona
Torrazzo Tower
Piazza del Comune
Open: Sunday 10am-12noon and 3pm-sunset.

Palazzo del Comune
Saletta dei Violini
Open: 9am-12noon and 3-5pm Tuesday-Friday, weekend am only.

Museo Civico di Storia Naturale
Palazzo dell'Arte
Piazza Marconi
Open: Tuesday-Saturday 10am-12.15pm and 3-5.30pm, Sunday 9.30am-12.30pm.

Museo Civico
4 Via Ugolani Dati
Open: Tuesday-Saturday 9.30am-12.30pm and 3-6pm, Sunday am only.

Museo Stradivariano
17 Via Palestro
Open: as above.

Museo della Civiltà Contadina
51 Via Castelleone
Open: Tuesday-Saturday 9am-12.30pm and 3-6pm, Sunday 9.30am-12.30pm.

Dalmine
Museo del Preseppio
Open: December and mid-January, February-November Sunday only.

Desenzano del Garda
Villa Romana
Via degli Scavi
Open: Tuesday-Sunday 9am-1 hour before sunset.

Erba
Civico Museo Archeologico
23 Via Ugo Foscolo
Open: Tuesday-Friday 9.30am-12noon, Saturday 3-7pm.

Esino Lario
Museo Civico delle Grigne
Open: July-August Monday-Friday am only, Saturday and Sunday am and pm, September-June apply to *Municipio*.

Gallarate
Museo
4 Borgo Antico
Open: 2-6pm, Sunday 10am-12noon, or ☎ (0331) 899281.

Civica Galleria d'Arte Moderna
Palazzo della Pretura
Viale Milano
Open: Tuesday-Sunday 10am-12noon and 3-6pm.

Museo della Tecnica e del Lavoro
3 Via Matteotti
Open: Sundays and holidays 9.30am-12.30pm and 3-6.30pm.

Museo Aeronautico Caproni-Taliedo
Malpensa Airport (4 miles)

Gandino
Museo della Basilica
Basilica di Santa Maria Assunta
Ask for Sacrestan in 2 Via Loverini.

Ganna
Museo della Badia
Priorato di San Gemolo
☎ (0332) 719795
Visitable on request.

Gardone Riviera
Hruska Botanical Gardens
Via Roma

Open: March-October 8.30am-sunset.
Vittoriale
Gardone di Sopra
(House of Gabriele d'Annunzio)
Open: 8.30am-12noon and 2-5pm.

Gravedona
Museo delle Barche Lariane
Calozzo ($3^1/_2$ miles)
Open: Saturday and Sunday 10am-12noon and 2-5pm.

Grosio
Castle and Park
☎ (0342) 845047
Closed Sunday.

Laveno
Civica Raccolta di Terraglia (Ceramics)
Palazzo Guilizzoni-Perabò
Cerro (2 miles)
Open: April-October, Friday-Sunday 10am-12noon and 2.30-6pm, Tuesday-Thursday pm only.

Lecco
Museo Civico del Risorgimento e della Resistenza
Torre del Castello
Piazza XX Settembre
Open: Tuesday-Saturday 10am-12.30pm and 2.30-5.30pm, Sunday 10am-1pm.

Museo di Scienze Naturali
Palazzo Belgioioso
Corso Matteotti
Open: as above.

Villa Manzoni and Galleria Comunale d'Arte
Via Amendola
Open: as above.

Legnano
Museo Civico
2 Via Mazzini
Open: Tuesday-Thursday and Saturday 9am-12.30pm and 2.30-5.30pm, Friday am only.

Museo d'Arte Moderna della Fondazione Pagani
Via Gerenzano
Castellanza
Open: 9.30am-12noon and 3-6pm.

Lodi
Museo Civico
63 Corso Umberto I
Open: Sunday 3.30-6.30pm, Tuesday-Saturday on request.

Museo Diocesano d'Arte Sacra
Palazzo del Vescovado
Open: Saturday 10am-12noon and 4-6.30pm, Sunday pm only.

Lonato
Casa del Podestà
Rocca Viscontea
Open: Monday-Friday 2.30-6pm.

Lovere
Galleria dell'Accademia Tadini
14 Piazza Garibaldi
Open: May-September Monday-Saturday 3-6pm, Sunday 10am-12noon and 3-6pm.

Luino
Museo Civico
Via Dante

Mantova
Rotonda di San Lorenzo
Piazza delle Erbe
Open: 9am-12noon and 3-5pm.

Teatro Scientifico
47 Via Accademia
Open: Monday-Saturday 9am-12noon and 3.30-6pm.

Palazzo Ducale
Guided visits
Open: Tuesday-Saturday 9am-2pm, Sunday 9am-1pm.

Museo del Risorgimento
Piazza Sordello 42

Museo Diocesano d'Arte Sacra
55 Piazza Virgiliana
Open: mid-March-June and September-October, Tuesday-Sunday 9am-12noon and 3-6pm. Other months only Saturday pm and Sunday.

Palazzo d'Arco
Open: March-October, Thursday,

Saturday and Sunday 9am-12noon and 3-5pm, Tuesday, Wednesday and Friday 9am-12noon, November-February, Saturday and Sunday 9am-12noon and 2.30-4pm, Thursday 9am-12noon.

House of Andrea Mantegna
47 Via Acerbi
Open: Monday-Saturday 8am-1pm, Monday and Thursday also 3-6pm.

Palazzo Te
Open: Tuesday-Sunday, April-October 9.30am-12.30pm and 2.30-5.30pm, November-March until 5pm.

Merate
Observatory
Open: 1st Friday of month, 2-5pm.

Monza
Museo Serpero
Duomo
Open: Tuesday-Saturday 9am-12noon and 3-5pm, Sunday pm only.

Pinacoteca
Villa Reale
Closed Monday.

Morbegno
Museo Civico di Storia Naturale
1 Via Cortivacci
Open: Tuesday, Thursday, Saturday and Sunday, summer 3-6pm, winter 3.30-5.30pm.

Pavia
Museo Civico
Castello Visconteo
Open: Tuesday-Sunday, April-June and September, 10am-12noon and 2.30-5pm, February, March, October, November 2-4pm, July, August, December and January 9am-1pm.

Piadena
Museo Civico 'Platina'
☎ (0357) 98125
Open: Monday-Friday 9.30am-12.30pm and 3.30-6.30pm, Saturday am only, by appointment except Saturday and Tuesday am.

Pizzighettone
Torrione
Ponte sull'Adda (bridge over Adda)

Museo Civico
12 Via Garibaldi
Open: Tuesday-Saturday 3-7pm, Sunday 10am-12noon.

Rho
Museo Archeologico Rhodense
291 Corso Europa
Open: 9am-12noon and 2.30-6pm, Monday and Thursday pm only, Saturday am only.

Museo Storico Alfa Romeo
(Arese $2^1/_2$ miles)
Open: Monday-Friday 10am-12.30pm and 1.30-5pm.
☎ (02) 93392108 (previous day).

Rovetta
Casa Fantoni
1 Via Fantoni
Open: July-September, Thursday-Tuesday, 3-5pm.

Sabbioneta
Guided visits to monuments of town
Open: March-October 10.30am-12.30pm and 3-6.30pm, November-February 2-4.30pm. Apply to Pro Loco Tourism any day except Monday.

Salò
Museo Civico Archeologico
Palazzo della Magnifica Patria
Open: Tuesday-Sunday April-September.

Museo del Nastro Azzurro
49 Via G. Fantoni
Open: April-October Saturday and Sunday 10am-12noon.

San Benedetto Po
Museo Civico Polironiano
Cloisters of San Simeone
Open: March-May 10am-12noon and 1.30-5pm, June-October 10am-12noon and 4-7pm, closed Mondays and in winter.

San Martino della Battaglia
Museo della Battaglia
Behind tower
Closed Tuesday, hours variable.

Sesto Calende
Museo Archeologico
Municipio
Open: Tuesday-Saturday 8.30am-12.30pm and 2.30-4.30pm, Sunday 10am-12noon and 3-7pm.

Sirmione
Rocca Scaligera
Open: Tuesday-Sunday summer 9am-1pm and 2.30-6.30pm, winter 9am-2pm. When Monday is public holiday closing day changes to Tuesday.

Grotte di Catullo
Open: 9am-2 hours before sunset, closing day as above.

Solferino
Museo Storico
Open: Tuesday-Sunday (November-February see custodian).

Soncino
Rocca
Open: Saturday and Sunday, 10am-12noon and 4-7pm (summer), 10am-12noon and 3-6pm (winter), other days 9am-12noon with permission of local tourist office.

Sondrio
Museo Valtellinese di Storia e Arte
Via IV Novembre
Open: Monday-Friday 9am-12noon and 3-6pm.

Sotto il Monte Giovanni XXIII
(Brusico) Birthplace of John XXIII
Open: 8am-12noon and 2-7pm.

Suzzara
Galleria Civica d'Arte Contemporanea
3 Via Don Bosco
Open: April-September Sunday 10.30am-12.30pm and 4-7pm (other months 3-6pm), Tuesday-Saturday pm only.

Teglio
Palazzo Besta
Open: May-September Tuesday-Saturday 9am-1pm and 2.30-5.30pm, Sunday 9am-1pm, other months Tuesday-Saturday 9am-2pm, Sunday 9am-1pm.

Tirano
Museo del Santuario della Madonna
Open: June-September 10am-12noon and 2.30-6.30pm, other months Saturday 3-6pm, Sunday 10am-12noon.

Treviglio
Museo Civico
14 Via dei Facchetti

Varenna
Museo Ornitologico
Open: summer 10am-12noon and 3.30-6.30pm, Sunday am only, winter Thursday and Saturday 3-5pm.

Varese
Musei Civici
Villa Mirabello
Open: Tuesday-Saturday 9.30am-12.30pm and 2-5.30pm, Sunday am only.

Vigevano
Museo del Tesoro
Duomo
Open: Sunday 3-5pm.

Castle
Open: Saturday and Sunday 10am-12.30pm and 3-6.30pm.

Museo Civico
82 Via Cavour
Open: September-July, Sunday 9.30am-12.30pm.

Voghera
Museo Storico di Voghera
Open: Sunday 10am-12noon.

4 • The Northern Uplands

The Valleys of Piemonte and Lombardia

For the first Piemontese stop, begin at the Gran Paradiso National Park, by taking the Val di Locana which lies north-west of Turin, and following its river, the Orco, back into the park. From almost any point on the road between Rosone and Ceresole Reale, tracks lead off into the park, offering splendid walking among excellent scenery. The narrow road beyond Ceresole can be used to reach the twin lakes of Agnel and Serru, each beautifully set, and from them an excellent, though not always easy, path crosses the Colle di Nivolei to the Valsavarenche, entering Aosta as it does.

On its eastern side, Piemonte reaches as far as Lago Maggiore but to the north-west of the lake there are still mountains that lie within the region, a fine series of valleys radiating out from the Val d'Ossola into which those who cross the Simplon Pass from Switzerland arrive. The **Val Anzasca** is the most southerly of the side valleys of Val d'Ossola, leaving the main valley almost due west towards Monte Rosa. **Macugnaga**, at its head, is rightly famous as a ski resort, but is equally good in summer when there are fine walks with a backdrop of the tent-like mass of Europe's second highest mountain. Macugnaga is a Walser village, and there is a museum to the Walser tradition in **Borca**, a link with the Val di Gressoney in Aosta. The Walser were a German Swiss people who migrated south of the Alps in the Middle Ages. Their language, a German dialect, is still spoken in some villages. For a good walk go to Lago di Fate, south of Borca, and follow the river back towards the pass which, if crossed, leads to Alagna-Valsesia. For a lazier day, go to **Vanzone**, once a gold-mining village, now a most picturesque place, left much as it was when the mines were abandoned.

Val Antrona, which leaves the main valley at Villadossola, is a quieter, more secretive place, than Val Anzasca, with a surprisingly mild climate that makes it ideal for summer exploring. At its head there is a fine collection of excellent mountain villages, and a number

The Val Anzasca

of mountain lakes which are good targets for a day's walking. From **Antronapiana**, go north for Lago Alpe di Cavalli, a tree-shrouded lake with a fine backdrop, or go south for a series of lakes, culminating in Lago del Cingo, set in truly wild and rugged country, but a good day's walking from the village. The main valley leads to **Val Formazza**, where a visit to the Toce waterfall is a must, the water falling down an elegant sweep of clean-swept rock. Not surprisingly the waterfall has been considered the most beautiful in Europe. Further on there is the interesting chance of a walk into Switzerland over the San Giacomo Pass, while just before the waterfall, at **Premia**, there is a fine series of, now-dry, glacial gorges that are both geologically unique and very impressive.

The real gem, however, is found by leaving the main valley at Baceno, and taking the **Val di Devero**. This little valley, barely 6 miles long, is a truly marvellous place, a mixture of lake and river, trees and meadow, and a backdrop of both jagged and snow-capped peaks. No one spot stands out, the whole is delightful.

By way of complete contrast, is the **Val Vegezzo**, which leaves the main valley at Domodossola, and which can be used to reach Switzerland near Locarno. This valley has long been a favourite with artists because of its colours and the purity of its light, and offers fine

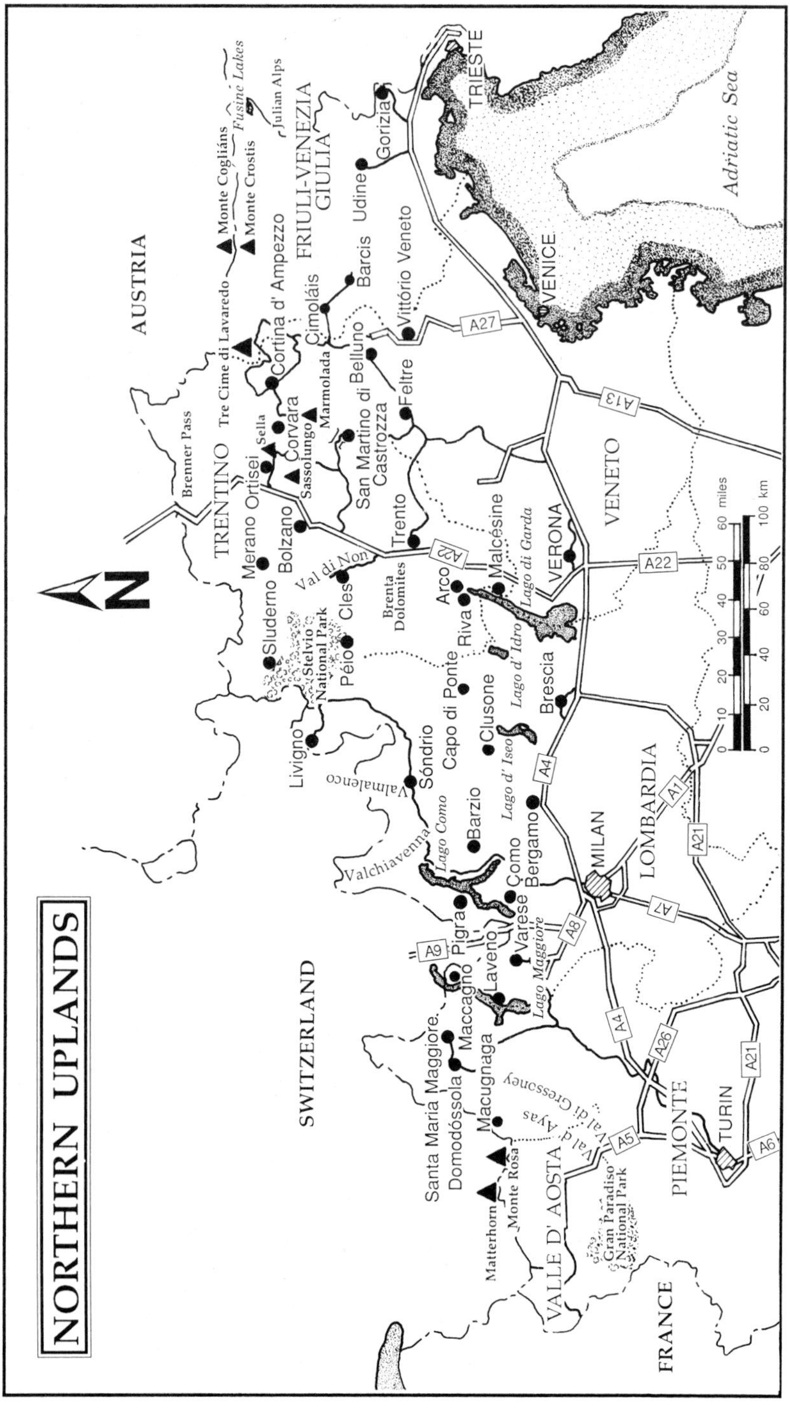
NORTHERN UPLANDS
N
AUSTRIA
SWITZERLAND
FRANCE
TRENTINO
FRIULI-VENEZIA GIULIA
VENETO
LOMBARDIA
PIEMONTE
VALLE D' AOSTA
Adriatic Sea
Brenner Pass
Tre Cime di Lavaredo
Monte Cogliáns
Monte Crostis
Fusine Lakes
Julian Alps
Sella
Sassolungo
Marmolada
Corvara
Ortisei
Merano
Bolzano
Cortina d' Ampezzo
Cimoláis
Barcis
Udine
Gorizia
TRIESTE
VENICE
Vittório Veneto
Belluno
Feltre
San Martino di Castrozza
Trento
Val di Non
Cles
Brenta Dolomites
Sluderno
Stelvio National Park
Pèio
Livigno
Valmalenco
Sóndrio
Capo di Ponte
Arco
Riva
Malcésine
Lago di Garda
VERONA
Lago d' Idro
Clusone
Lago d' Iseo
Brescia
Bergamo
Barzio
Lago Como
Valchiavenna
Como
MILAN
Pigra
Varese
Laveno
Lago Maggiore
Maccagno
Santa Maria Maggiore
Domodóssola
Macugnaga
Val di Gressoney
Val d' Ayas
Monte Rosa
Matterhorn
Gran Paradiso National Park
TURIN
A4
A5
A6
A7
A8
A9
A1
A21
A22
A26
A27
A13
0 10 20 30 40 50 60 miles
0 20 40 60 80 100 km

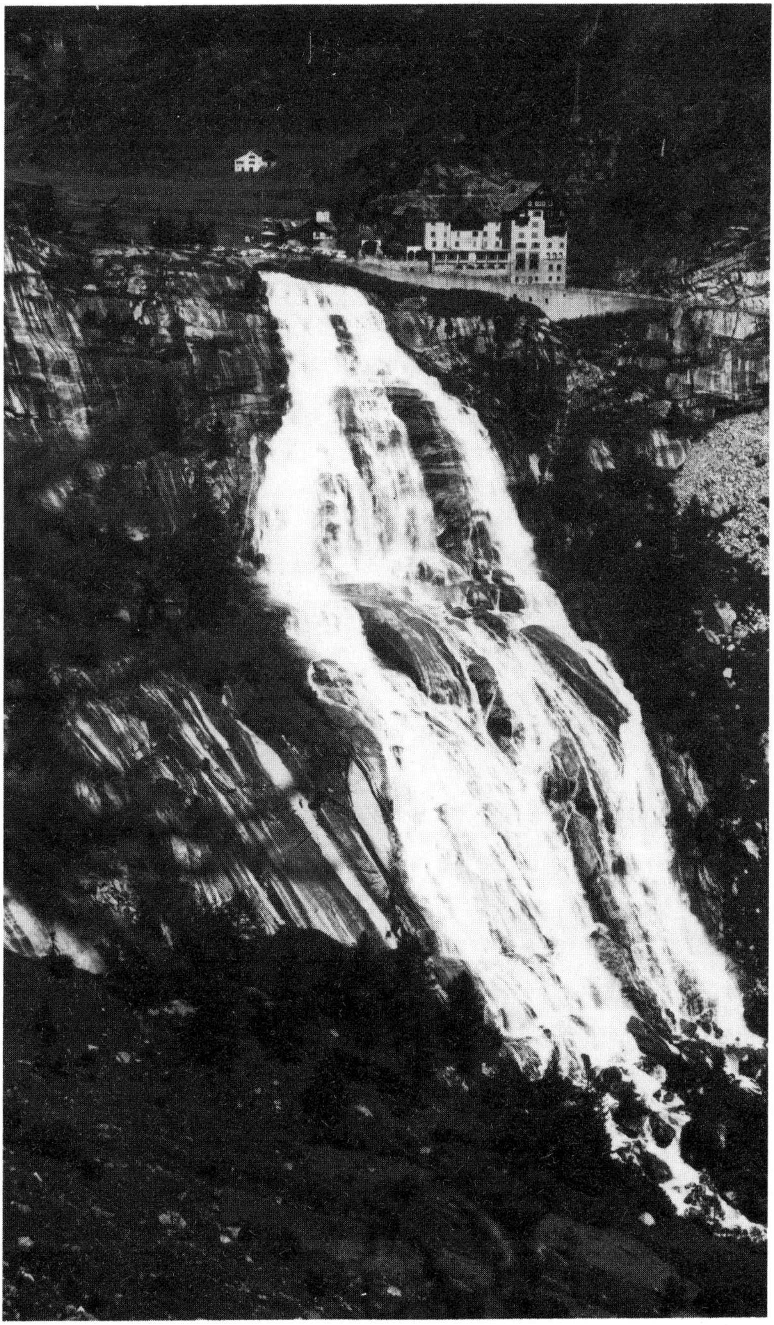

The Toce waterfall, Val Formazza

walking, but especially fine are the church at **Re**, a huge, building, sumptuously furnished; the chimney sweep's museum at **Santa Maria Maggiore**, a collection of old sweep's memorabilia — the local smoked ham is also very good; and the museum of **Gurro** in **Val Cannobina** which leaves Val Vegezzo at Santa Maria Maggiore. In 1537, Scottish mercenaries, fleeing after the defeat of their chosen army at the battle of Pavia, settled in this remote valley, marrying local girls. The museum shows local costumes, and the tartan influence is still apparent. And, for those who have not had enough of odd museums, there is one to the history of umbrellas and parasols at **Gignese** on the side of the Mottarone, the mountain above Stresa, a mountain which offers an excellent view of both Monte Rosa and Val d'Ossola, and Lago Maggiore.

On the opposite side of **Lago Maggiore** from Stresa is Lombardia. Go first to **Arcumeggia**, a tiny village reached by a difficult drive from Val Cuvia, a valley running east from Laveno. Here contemporary artists have painted frescoes on the outside walls of the village houses — to be invited to paint here is an honour — making a walk around the equivalent of a visit to a gallery.

To the north, a road from Maccagno, on Maggiore's shore, leads up **Val Veddasca**. Take this and go left for Lago Delio, and climb Monte Borgna above it — a walk of about an hour — for one of the finest views of Lago Maggiore. A road on the other flank of Val Veddasca can be used to reach Curiglia from where one must walk — there is no road — to **Monteviasco**, one of the most remote and, therefore, unspoilt mountain villages in Italy.

Like Lago Maggiore, **Lago di Como** also has surrounding mountains offering fine views to the Alps and to the lake itself. **Pigra**, above Argegno — and reached from there by a *funivia* (cable railway) — has what many consider the best view of the lake, and an equally fine view towards the **Val d' Intelvi**, a fine valley connecting the lakes of Como and Lugano. The Intelvi has some excellent odd corners and a good museum to valley life at **Scaria**. To the north, the hills above Como, occasionally reached from small valleys which penetrate from the lakeshore road, offer good walking, with excellent views to the lake, or to the High Alps.

On the eastern side of Como, the **Valsassina** is a fine valley, not remote in the sense of being far from civilisation, but empty in comparison with the lakeside sites. **Barzio** is a good, but quiet, winter sports centre, while the best walking is from the Piano del Resinelli, reached by turning off at Ballabio before reaching Barzio. Here the scenery is wild and wierd, the rocky towers and pinnacles of the

Grigna are an excellent small(-ish) scale introduction to the Dolomite peaks to the east.

East again, visit the **Val Seriana** which runs north-east from Bergamo, that most exquisite of northern Italian towns. The whole valley is off-the-beaten-track and worth a slow journey. Look out for the beautiful arcaded church in **Vertova**, and the two fifteenth-century 'skeleton' frescoes in the church at **Clusone**. In the upper reaches, two fine spots stand out. The first is the side valley of Valcanale, set among tremendous scenery, and with an excellent walk — allow a long half-day — to the rock-enclosed Lago Gemelli. The real valley classic, however, is the trip from Valbandione, near the head of the main valley, to the **Cascata del Serio**, Europe's highest — or perhaps second highest — waterfall, at around 1,035ft. Why is all this so vague? You see when you go — there is no waterfall, the water has been diverted down a hydro-electric station pipe line. Only at certain — advertised — times of the year is the water allowed to flow as nature intended.

East again a most interesting and unusual sight awaits the visitor who is brave enough to take a side road from Marone on the eastern shore of **Lago d'Iseo** that goes steeply — and at first, disconcertingly narrowly — up towards Zone. Just below the village of **Cislano**, at an obvious hairpin bend, there is a good view of Europe's finest set of erosion pyramids, glacial oddities, termite-like pillars of an earthy conglomerate, invariably topped by a flat boulder. It is possible to reach the pyramids on foot, but do not attempt to climb on them: they are not wonderfully stable and are a national treasure. Northward beyond Lago d'Iseo, Val Camonica should be followed in order to visit the National Park of Rock Engravings at **Capo di Ponte**. Here there are almost a quarter of a million rock engravings, chiefly hunting scenes and religious themes, dating from 8,000 years ago through to the Roman era. So good is this site that in 1979 it was given international protection as a site of world importance.

East of Lago d'Iseo is **Lago di Garda**, the largest of the northern lakes, with two worthwhile high-level sites, one on each shoreline. On the west are the twin regions of Tremosine and Tignale, regions so beautiful that words seem inadequate to convey their exquisiteness. There are pretty villages perched on rock ledges high above the lake, and excellent scenery, well explored by a series of footpaths.

On Garda's eastern shore, go to **Malcesine** (Veneto) and then visit one or other — or perhaps both — nature parks on the flanks of Monte Baldo, the ridge that separates Garda from the Val Laga. High on the mountain is the Selva Pezzi Park, called the 'Botanical Garden of Italy' for the number and excellence of its plants, which include many rarities. This park is reached from the top station of the cableway from Malcesine, and extended walks onto the long, high ridge are also possible and worthwhile. The second park, the Gardesana Orientale, lies beside the road $2^1/_2$ miles north of Malcesine, and it too is criss-crossed with paths.

To the north of the lake country, the **Valtellina** runs east-west splitting the Orobie Alps — in which sit the Val Seriana and the Val Camonica — from the main alpine chain. The **Valchiavenna** leads off northward to the Splugen Pass and Switzerland, a fine valley with some excellent walking. Arguably the best walking country lies north of Chiavenna itself, closer to Madesimo and the border. Two especially fine walks start from **Isola**. The first goes north towards Stuetta and then runs along the shore of Lago di Montespluga, reaching Montespluga itself. This walk, allow about 3 hours, offers excellent valley walking through fine scenery. A tougher, but not too tough, alternative is to go westward from Isola, up the Val Febbraro to the Passo di Baldescio, beyond which it is downhill all the way, to Switzerland. For this walk it is better to allow a half-day, perhaps using Borghetto as a watering-hole.

Sondrio is a pleasant town, and from it the **Val Malenco** heads north towards the alpine chain which separates Italy from Switzerland. This is an excellent valley, rich in crystals and with cableways that allow easy access to the High Alps so that the interested visitor has a real chance of finding an excellent souvenir. The quarries that supply Malenco marble, a green serpentine, can be seen, and at **Chiesa** there is a fine museum to the history and natural history of the area.

At the far eastern end of the Valtellina is the Stelvio National Park, and, at the extreme tip of Italy, the Val di Dentro and Val Livigno. The former is an exquisite valley lying along the edge of the Stelvio, while the latter is one of the most magnificent areas in the whole of alpine, as opposed to dolomitic, Italy. It is an almost perfect mix of alpine meadow, high, rocky peaks, snow dusted; lakes and pretty villages with exquisite wooden houses. The nearby Stelvio, whose symbol is an eagle, is a sanctuary for wildlife, and the whole area is threaded by footpaths. Do not leave this valley off your itinerary.

The Dolomites, Trentino, Veneto and Friuli-Venezia Giulia

Ironically, the so-obviously Italian Dolomites were named after a

Lago di Caldonazzo

French geologist, Déodat Dolomieu who lived in the last half of the eighteenth century. Strictly, the peaks lie in an area to the east of the A22 *autostrada* which runs up the valley of the Adige from Verona to Trento, and on over the Brenner Pass to Austria. Here we also include the mountains of Trentino for completeness.

In one sense, the Dolomites are the most inaccessible of the alpine peaks, an array of limestone pinnacles and towers which are so steep that only the rock climber can safely negotiate their walls and summits, and yet the peaks are accessible, cableways giving access to cols and plateaus, and high-level walking is everywhere possible because of the lack of glaciated snow-fields. Here we explore ways of getting right up into the peaks without — or with rare — requirement for ropes and other climbing equipment.

Begin though, at **Trento**, a fine city, famous for its council which sat for 18 years, from 1545-63, yet did not really succeed in helping the Roman Catholic Church face up to Lutheranism. The council sat at the cathedral, an eleventh- to twelfth-century building with a fine interior. Look out for the sixteenth-century Flemish tapestries, the much earlier frescoes and the array of bishops' tombs. Also worth visiting is the Buonconsiglio castle, a fine building dating, in part, from the thirteenth century and with a museum to the Risorgimento, the movement for Italian national unity, which was especially, and bloodily, important in this area near the disputed border with the Austrian Empire.

Trentino is, perhaps, the most complete of all Italy's regions, as good as any we have so far encountered. Lago di Caldonazzo, to the east of Trento, is a larger lake, set close to two spa towns below Monte Panarotta, while to the north and south of it the tiny lakes of Lases and Lavarone are equally well set. In the south there is Lago di Garda, with its almost tropical climate, there are the Marmolada and Adamello, peaks well over 10,000ft and snow-capped, and the Brenta Dolomites, one of the most famous of all the Dolomite groups. Trentino boasts 297 lakes, so it would be unseemly not to go to one or two. But do not go to Lago di Garda, journey north instead from **Riva** to the little **Lago di Tenno**, or north through **Arco** to **Lago di Cavedine**. Each of these lakes is superbly set, and in the area of each there is fine walking and fine views. Cavedine is interesting in having been formed comparatively recently — geologically speaking — behind a landslide and is set close to some very diverse landscapes. To the south, the **Marocche** is an almost lunar landscape, though still very picturesque, well seen by a footpath signed from the lake's southern tip, while the western and eastern shores offer open mountain and wooded slope scenery.

Further west, the **Val di Chiese**, following the river from the flanks of the Adamello group to Lago d'Idro, is a fine valley, its sides deeply wooded, its villages and hamlets well set among meadows.

North of here is the **Brenta**, an archetypal Dolomite group, huge towers and pinnacles of limestone, more massive blocks with sheer faces and soaring arrêts, the whole comprised of an orange rock that catches the light, especially fading light, to offer astonishing colour shows. The Brenta can be viewed from the valleys to the east or west — it is a north-south running rock mass — and either of these valleys is worth visiting for its own sake. **Val Rendenna** is a fine pastoral valley with **Madonna di Campiglio**, a well known ski resort, at its head. From the village of Carisolo, go into the Val di Genova for about a mile to visit the **Cascata di Nardis**, the Nardis waterfall, a magnificent bifurcated sheet of water. Or, if the handful of other

Lago di Tovel

visitors who might be at the falls is too many for you, take the footpath — No 210 — which runs up an even smaller side valley just below the falls to visit another, less dramatic but rarely seen falls.

To the east, **Val Molveno** is equally good, the Brenta standing above it like a castle, occasionally reflected in the blue water of Lago di Molveno. This lake has footpaths on both sides: on the shore to the west, the path lying between the Brenta and the lake; above the road to the east which can be used for a quiet day, or for contemplation of an assault on the Brenta itself. From Tuenno further up the valley — actually reached off the N43 road — take a steep, narrow mountain road to **Lago di Tovel**, perhaps the prettiest of all the lakes, once famous for being red at the height of summer, due to a growth of red algae in the hottest surface waters. Of late this strangely beautiful phenomenon has not occurred.

The best routes on the main rock mass are fairly difficult, they consist of Via Ferrata — literally, iron paths — where progress is occasionally aided by ladders or rungs fixed to the rock, and protection is offered by means of a wire cable also fixed to the rock — and mountain paths. The Via Ferrata are sensational in all senses of the word, but they require a head for heights and a sureness of foot. To follow one it is necessary to have a guide to the route, the correct equipment and a sound understanding of belaying techniques. They are no place for complete novices. One of the easiest Via Ferrata is the 'Sentiero Orsi' on the Brenta. To reach it, take the cableway from Madonna di Campiglio to **Passo del Groste** and from there take path 316 to the Tuckett hut (Rifugio del Tuckett). This 2-hour walk is itself a wonderful experience, really close to the rock, but the Via Ferrata beyond is fantastic. The 'Sega Alta' is a broad ledge (protected by a handrail) between a huge overhang and an even bigger drop. Beyond is a great viewpoint, and, on again, the Campanile Basso is reached, an elegant needle of rock towering into the sky. Just to see it makes the route worthwhile. The route finishes at the Pedrotti hut — after about 4 hours — but as descent from there is long and into Val Molveno, it might be better to reach the Campanile Basso and return.

North-west of the Brenta is the **Stelvio National Park**, mentioned briefly in the Lombardian section. The Val di Dentro and Val Livigno have already been mentioned. To see some of the best of the rest, take the path along the Noce Bianco, the stream falling southward from Monte Cevedale to the hamlet of **Cogolo**, near Péio, which stands at the head of the valley of the same name. This path is followed to Rifugio Torbi, from where path 102 and then mountain path 123 lead to the secluded **Lago del Càreser**. The path continues, past several smaller lakes and waterfalls into the very heart of the Stelvio National Park, with its ibex, deer and marmots, eagles and flowers.

For those who wish to go higher, use the cableway from Péio to get high on the flank of Péio mountain. From there, at 9,480ft, the Rifugio Mantova at 9,790ft can be reached by path 138, a hut standing on a summit commanding a great view over Monte Cevedale.

The Stelvio National Park can also be reached via the Val di Solda

Colfosco near Bolzano

which leads off from Stelvio (Stilfs in German) itself. Paths from Solda di Dentro (Innersulden) offer a close view of the Ortles group. The cableway to Schaubach can also be used to gain high ground and some good, but not easy, walking. Nearby, at **Sluderno** (Schluderns) in the region of Alto Adige, the castle (do not miss the arcaded courtyard) holds a very fine collection of weaponry. The knight in armour on the armoured horse is stunning, a real medieval tank.

East from the Stelvio National Park is a trio of very pleasant towns, Merano, Bolzano and Bressanone, enclosing an area of Italy almost as closely allied, culturally, to Austria as when the Austrain Empire ruled here. **Merano** is a delightful spot, now living down the notoriety of having once staged a Karpov-Korchnoi chess match.

The name Tyrol — and not only for this region of Italy, but for the Austrian Tyrol as well — derives from the Tyrol castle at Merano, which must be visited by all interested in the history of the area. The view from it is stunning. **Bolzano**, the capital of Alto Adige — the South Tyrol — is certainly worth a visit. The town's two churches, the

Franciscan church near the centre of the town, and the parish church of Gries, the suburb of the town to the north-west, beyond the Talvera river, each have artwork of interest. The Franciscan church, a fourteenth-century building, has frescoes and a sixteenth-century frieze. There was once a marvellous altar of carved wood, but this has been removed following an attempted theft (?!). There remains a fine carved altar in Gries church, a masterpiece of the late fifteenth century. The Maretsch and Runkelstein castles at Bolzano are also worth visiting, as is the oddly house-like Englar castle at **Eppen**.

From Bolzano, cableways lead to some interesting country. Try the cableway to **Colle** (Kohlarn), the large wedge of rock to the south of the town, from the top of which several very pretty villages set among woods and meadows can be reached. Or, try the cable to **Renon** (Ritten), from where a rack railway continues to **Collalbo**. From here, a 30-minute walk towards Longomoso leads to a fine set of erosion pillars, more abundant, but not quite as dramatic as those above Lago d'Iseo. Beyond (allow a further $3^1/_2$ hours), is the Rifugio Corno di Renon (about 3,600ft above Collalbo) which offers a fine view to the north.

From the Bolzano-Bressanone road, the **Val Gardena** leads off eastward, one of the highlights of any trip to the Dolomites. The valley is one of the last strongholds of a third language in the area, Ladine. Ladine is a Romance language, once spoken over the whole of Central Europe, but has been gradually eliminated by influxes of foreign settlers. Today it exists here, in a small part of Switzerland, and further east in the Friuli region of Italy. At one time the language was under threat, but it has now been afforded official status with Italian and German and is used in the early stages of school. A by-product of this status is that those visitors who have been impressed by the bilingualism of the majority of South Tyroleans have now to come to terms with the trilingual inhabitants of the Val Gardena and Val di Fassa. Those interested in finding out more about the language, should visit the library in **Ortisei** (St Ulrich) where information on the language's origins and evolution is available. One astonishing fact is that it was not until 1864 that the Ladine grammar was written down.

Another wet weather alternative is a visit to the folk museum, also in Ortisei, a fascinating place which exhibits not only the area's woodcarving and history, but the local geology, flora and fauna.

Chiefly though, the best thing to do in Val Gardena is walk, and the first place to visit is the **Seiser Alm**. An *alm* is an alp in Italy, but the Seiser Alm is different, being a high plateau, a huge meadow set on top of a truncated peak, a table mountain, rather than the high, sloping meadows normally associated with alps. Seiser Alm is reached by a cableway from Ortisei, and is an extraordinary place, a vast field, dotted with old chalets, now mostly used as solid tents by lucky visitors, the whole dominated by the spiky peaks of the Sassolungo — or Langkofel as it is known in German. In early July the *alm* is carpeted with flowers, delightful and fragrant mountain orchids, and a host of others in pinks and yellows. There are no fences here, so the visitor is free to wander at will.

The top section of the Sassolungo is, not surprisingly, reserved for the rock-climber. Indeed, the group's only Via Ferrata is not for the inexperienced. However, the gap between the spire of Sassolungo (the Langkofelspitze) and the curiously sloping Sasplat (Plattkofel), is reached by cableway, and this spot is definitely worth reaching, offering a real 'in-the-Dolomites' feel to the visitor and an exciting view. The best way to do the trip is to make half a day of it, using the chair-lift from St Christina to reach Monte Seura at 6,725ft and taking Fr. Stradal Weg and the mountain path beyond to go between the rock masses and up to the cableway top station at 8,790ft. This trip — the valley bus can be used to regain St Christina — is extremely exciting and goes right among the rock towers, and although the latter part of the path is rough, it is easily negotiated with care. It goes without saying that this trip, and the others described in this section, require at least the minimum of walking equipment — boots, spare clothes, wet-weather equipment etc.

From the Sassolungo/Langkofel the view is dominated by the **Sella**, a huge rock mass, castle-like in construction, even to the extent of having a walkway at half-height, above which are embattled towers. There is a route that goes all the way around that half-height walkway, but there is a fine excursion across the top of the Sella plateau, with occasional snow patches even in the height of summer. The best way to make the trip is to leave a car at the Passo Pordoi one evening, using the bus to return to base, although buses can be used to eliminate all use of cars. The route starts at Passo Gardena (Grödner) where Route 666 is used to gain the Sella plateau 1,650ft above. Nowhere is this climb difficult, in the sense of requiring particular skills, though it does require effort. From the top of the climb the walk goes through some excellent country, high rocks, patches of greyish snow, lunar hollows, to reach the top of the cableway at Sass Pordoi, from where the view to the Marmolada is excellent.

Those requiring a more gentle introduction to the area's charm, should go to the other side of the valley from the Sella, again using Passo Gardena as base, following the marked path to the plateau of Tschierspitzen. This path, like that across the Sella, forms part of Alta Via 2, High Path 2, which crosses the Dolomites from Bressanone to Feltre. It is one of a number of such paths, all of which are excellently signed, and go between huts (*rifugi*) offering food and overnight accommodation.

For an alternative gentle walk go to **Corvara** — beyond the Passo di Gardena — and take the cableway to Col Alto, from where a walk rounds the plateau edge, with glorious views to the angular Sassongher and the mighty wall of the Fanis, to the top of the cableway coming up from La Villa Stern. From the village, either take the bus back to Corvara or walk along the river between the villages.

And before leaving Val Gardena, those interested in skiing should seriously consider **Selva** (Wolkenstein) as a base before it becomes too popular.

The **Marmolada**, which dominated the view from Passo Pordoi, is comfortably reached by cableways. One from the Passo di Fedáia, on the border of Trentino and Veneto, beside the reservoir reaches the foot of the Marmolada glacier, but do not venture onto the ice unless you are experienced. It is better just to admire the scenery, or to take one of a number of paths that skirt the base of the glacier, with excellent views back towards the Sella and the Sassolungo. From the eastern side, another cableway reaches close to the top of the highest peak, which is also the highest peak in the Dolomites, but the 'Queen of the Dolomites', should not be attempted by anyone who is not an experienced mountaineer. The casual visitor must content him or herself with a view of the last 330ft pyramid, and a view over the only glacier in the Dolomites.

Before moving east to Cortina d'Ampezzo, the Dolomite's most famous village, go south, back into Trentino to visit a pair of fine and little visited valleys. The first is the **Val di Non**, which goes left (north-west) off the main valley running from Trento to Bolzano. It is entered from Roccheta, and lasts just a few miles to Cles, standing on the edge of the lake of **San Guistina** which provides water for a hydro-electric power station. From its start, the entrance guarded by the very fine castle of Ton, to its end, where there is another castle high above Cles, the valley is superb. Not surprisingly it has often been described as Trentino's most beautiful valley, though its relative remoteness, and the nearness of the rock spires of the Dolomites means that it is little frequented. In **Cles**, be sure to visit the twelfth-century church of San Vigilio which has fine frescoes, and to go up

Val di Non

to the Dos di Pez from where the whole valley can be seen, together with the lake and the castle of the barons of Cles.

The **Val di Cembra** lies to the other side of the Trento-Bolzano road, heading off towards the high Dolomites. It too is tucked away, a pastoral haven among the hills. **Cembra**, the chief town, has a long history, not least because its excellent climate and soil provide good vine growing conditions and the local wines are famous — as is the local *grappa*, which is, apparently, not to be toyed with! The valley is also excellent for the standard of its restaurants, and is *the* place to go for those interested in cuisine and good wines. From the valley the high plateau of Piné can also be reached, good walking country with nicely set villages and lakes.

From the Val di Cembra, the Dolomite groups of Sassolungo, the Sella and Marmolada can be reached along the Val di Fiemme. At Predazzo the beautiful **Val di Fassa**, a German-Ladine valley, leads off to the Ladine Val Gardena, or, the Val Travignolo can be taken, leading to distinctly Italian country. From the Passo Rolle at its head take the path to **Lago del Colbricon**, a final Trentino mountain lake, and one of the finest.

From the Sella region it is only a few minutes' drive along the dolomite highway to **Cortina d'Ampezzo** in Veneto, justly famous and a spot few visitors will wish to miss. For a different view of things, visit the ski-jump, the *trampolino*, now standing unused and forlorn, but offering an interesting insight into what it must be like to be touched by the madness that makes you want to use one.

North of Cortina, go to **Misurina**, a splendid village set on a lake used for skating in winter, and then take the road past the smaller Lago d'Antorno that leads to the Rifugio Laveredo. Now walk, or just stare at, the Tre Cime di Laveredo (the Drei Zinnen in German), the three massive bulks of rotten limestone rising vertically from the scree slopes. These towers have long been famous with climbers — the central tower's north face is one of the six great north-face climbs of the Alps, and is also climbed by a route engineered over one of the Alps' largest overhangs — but is less famous with the non-climbing public. There is a path along the foot of the cliffs, but do be careful, especially if there are climbers on the route, the cliffs are not wonderfully sound, and it is easy to be surprised by, and damaged by, a falling stone. A very good walk goes right around the peaks, but equally good from the hut is to follow route 101, then 104 below the Cime Patterno to Lago di Cengia, going south down to Val di Cengia and returning northward through Val di Lavaredo. This circuit (about 6 miles) takes about $2^1/_2$ hours.

The country around Cortina is magnificent, the peak of the **Cristallo** being especially fine. One of its highest peaks can be reached by a Via Ferrata from the top of the cableway from Cortina, but if you are a newcomer to these iron ways, go to the Rifugio Dibona, reached by a forest track off the road from Cortina to the Passo Falzárego, take path 404 and at the obvious start point, try the short Via Ferrata to the Grotta Tofane, a cave on the side of the rock mass of the Tofane. The sure-footed will not need elaborate protection on this route which involves one long traverse on a reasonable ledge and a short vertical section. The cave is interesting, but not spectacularly so. It does offer an excellent viewpoint, and a strange one at that, of the Dolomites towards Monte Pelmo.

Move south towards Feltre, and if you are driving, there is one more trip in this area that you must make, around the Pale di San Martino. This route, from the Passo di Rolle down to San Martino di

Lago del Colbricon

Castrozza, then up the Val di Cismon towards Fiera di Primiero, not quite reaching the village before turning off along N347 to Agardo, is an exciting drive, with fine views. The N203 is now followed back to the pass. If one or two of the little villages en route are visited, perhaps eating at one of the off-the-beaten-track restaurants, then this fine outing can fill a whole and leisurely day.

Feltre is a fine place, its ancient walls circling a town that was almost entirely rebuilt in the early sixteenth century following a devastating raid, and so offers a glimpse of an almost complete Renaissance town. Go to Piazza Maggiore, where the geometrically tiled square is surrounded by a fine array of buildings, including the castle, the town hall with a Palladian loggia, and the church of San Rocco, in the forecourt of which is a fine Lombardian fountain. Some of the nearby houses have external frescoes including some believed to be by Morto da Feltre, who died here in 1512. His masterpiece, a Transfiguration, can be seen in the sacristy of the church of Ognissanti. In it Christ is painted in white on a white background which is an astonishing show of confidence by the painter. More of Morto's work can be seen in the civic museum, but a better museum is the Rizzarda which has a quite remarkable collection of wrought iron work, and also has a modern art gallery.

East of Cortina the visitor enters Friuli-Venezia Giulia. Go first to an area reached along the N355 which branches off the Tolmezzo to Ampezzo road at Villa Santina. When the N465 crosses this road, go right (east) along it and turn off to the village of Solârs. North of here is **Monte Crostis**, a mountain area that extends all the way to the, now very near, Austrian border. It is an area of outstanding scenic beauty, not high enough to hold much permanent snow, but with handsome rock, part grassed, part tree-covered, rising from flower-carpeted meadows. Monte Crostis itself can be comfortably climbed, for a fine view of Monte Cogliáns, along the summit ridge of which the border with Austria actually runs. This peak too can be climbed, the best way being from the Rifugio Marinelli — reached from Sigilleto — but this climb (about 2,300ft) is not for the very inexperienced.

Now go to **Tarvisio** at the extreme eastern edge of Italy near the border with Yugoslavia. Follow the N54 from the town towards the border, and take the road in the last valley in Italy, to the lakes of **Fusine**, set in a nature park. This is wonderful country, and about as off-the-beaten-track as it is possible to be, as the Dolomites become the **Julian Alps**. It is difficult to tear yourself away from the lakes, but those that do can amble over the lower slopes of Monte Mángart, whose summit ridge divides the two countries.

Equally beautiful is the **Val Bruna** which lies the other side of Tarvisio, a wide valley, its floor a sea of alpine flowers and a fine range of grey mountains at its head.

North of Belluno, Friuli is entered by a road from Langarone, passing the excellent Lago di Váiont for Cimoláis. Here, go north, following a track along the Val Cimoliana for some 10 miles to the Rifugio Pordenone, beside the delightful Lago di Meluzzo Sorg. From the hut take path 353 which heads north towards, and beyond, the Perugini Bivouac. This path reaches the Campanile di Val Montanaia, a huge apparently tottering mass of limestone, similar in appearance to, but half as high again as, the Old Man of Hoy in the Orkneys. The tower is about 2 miles from the hut and it is best to return by the same route. There is a path from the Perugini, No 360,

Further Information

The Valleys of Piemonte and Lombardia

Museums and Other Places of Interest

Capo di Ponte
National Park of Rock Engraving
Open: daily except Monday 9am-1 hour before sunset.

Gignese
Umbrella Museum
Open: daily April-September, 10am-12noon, 3-5pm.

Santa Maria Maggiore
Chimney Sweep's Museum
Under reconstruction (1987). Ask at local tourist office for details of opening hours.

Scaria
Museum
Open: daily, July-mid-September 3-5pm.

The Dolomites and Friuli-Venezia Giulia

Museums and Other Places of Interest

Feltre
Rizzarda Museum
Open: daily except Monday 9am-12noon, 3-6pm.

Ortisei
Folk Museum
Open: daily except Sunday mid-June-mid-July 3-6pm; mid-July-August 10am-12noon, 3-6pm; September-mid-October 3-6pm.

Sluderno
Castle
Open: daily except Monday 9am-12noon, 2-5pm.

Trento
Buonconsiglio Castle and Museum
Open: daily except Monday 9am-12noon, 2-5pm (6pm in summer months).

that goes over the eastern ridge of the valley, returning to the Pordenone along a parallel valley, but it is not for the inexperienced walker.

Beyond Cimolàis, the road goes along the Val Cellina, a fine, little-frequented valley, reaching **Barcis**, a very pretty village set beside a very blue lake.

Finally, east again, to the strange land of the **Carso** lying south of Gorizia and along the tongue of land that separates Yugoslavia from the sea, from Monfalcone to Trieste. It is a gently rolling landscape of very white, sun-bleached rocks and low scrub, with the occasional *dolina*, or swallow-hole, clear proof that this is a cave area. Around Gorizia there are indeed some of the finest showcaves in Europe, the best being over the border in Yugoslavia. At **Duino** near Monfalcone, the rock climber should try the white slabs that rise out of the sea, a nearby headland dominated by a medieval castle. Nearer Trieste is the **Val Rosandra**, a last piece of mountain, a fabulous place in autumn. Within the valley are waterfalls and water scooped gorges and always the multi-hued alpine flowers.

5 • Veneto

The 7,100sq miles of land and water which go to make up the region of Veneto have a mixture of natural-historic boundaries and more recent politically motivated boundaries. The prehistoric Veniti people inhabited the large plateau around Venice and the sub-alpine hills which precede the more mountainous inland areas, while the Venetian Republic, which was one of the richest and most important in Europe until being over-run by Napoleon, controlled not only the mountains behind the hills but also the whole of Friuli to the east and part of Lombardia to the west. The region's natural boundaries are formed by the Adriatic coast and the Po to the south and Lago di Garda to the west. The north of the region comprises part of the Dolomites to the west and part of the Carniche Alps to the east, while below Lago di Garda, an arbitrary border divides the region from Lombardia as the ragged line linking the rivers Tagliamento and Livenza divides it from Friuli to the east.

Of the mountainous areas, the most important is the Dolomite group which, unlike the other alpine ranges, does not form a crest but rises up in several almost vertical groups of white peaks with wide green valleys in between. The pre-Alps are more compact and uniform, being made up of various types of calcareous rock including 'Red Verona' an important type of marble. The sub-alpine band of hills which separate the mountains from the plain are highly seismic and many earthquakes have struck the area over the centuries.

The plain itself was originally formed by the alluvial deposits brought down from the mountains by the glaciers and only very rarely does it exceed 150ft above sea level making the region prone to flooding, both by exceptionally high tides and by the major rivers. Some areas of reclaimed land, particularly in and around the Po delta are below normal sea level, and water is pumped off in raised canals.

In general, the region has a fairly damp subcontinental climate with most rain falling in spring and autumn. The lowland areas have between 80 and 100 days of rain while in the mountains this figure

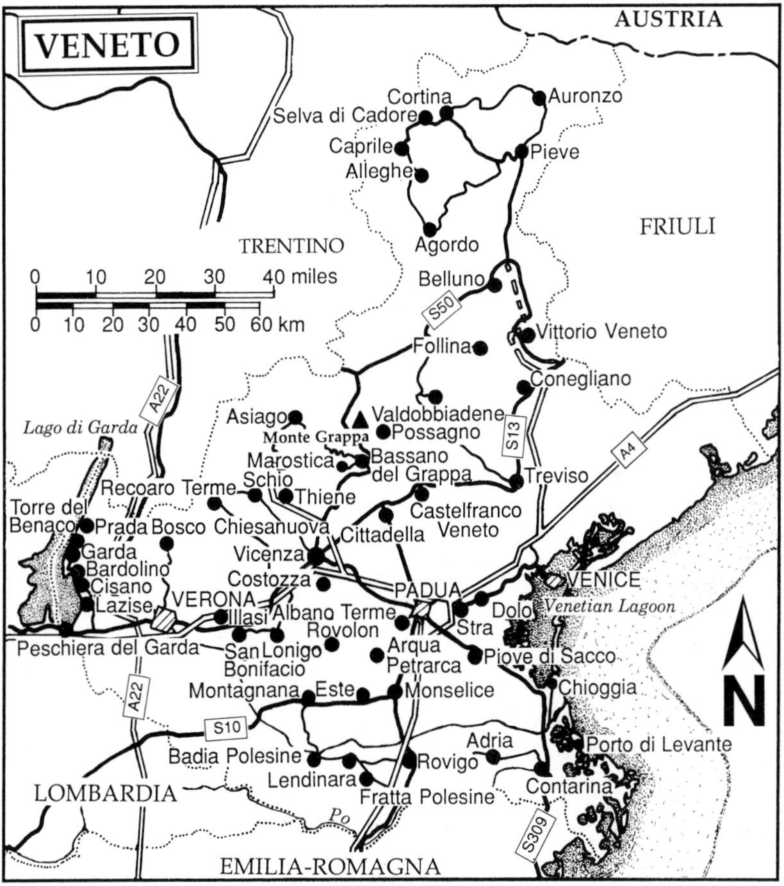

rises to between 120 and 130 days. Winter temperatures in the mountainous areas vary greatly, a factor which depends more on the direction in which each valley faces than on altitude. At Arabba on the border with Trentino, snow is to be found for about 150 days in the year, while at Cortina d'Ampezzo it only lasts for around 100.

Despite the great interest which the area holds for the general tourist; winter sports, walking in summer, art, historic cities and seaside resorts, the extremely varied terrain, the effect of the sea and the differences in climate between one area and another make it highly interesting for the botanist and nature lover. A large variety of species of flowers and trees are to be found in the region, including the Cistus Laurifolius, found in the Eugenean hills, south-west of Padua, which is extremely rare.

Of the major cities and towns in the region, Venice is outside the scope of this book, being one of those cities which attracts millions of visitors every season. Verona and Padua tend to be neglected by international visitors but attract many Italian tourists during the peak summer period, while the other main centres — Vicenza, Rovigo, Treviso and Belluno — tend to be overlooked by almost everyone.

This chapter assumes that the visitor will be based in either Padua, Vicenza, Treviso or Belluno as these are the cities best placed for visiting the region. For the visitor who is more inclined to move from place to place each day, however, the region is well equipped with camp sites and hotel facilities. For those driving to the region, the most practical route to take is the Brenner Pass, as this reduces to a minimum the distance to be travelled on the Italian motorway system witn its expensive tolls. For those who intend to arrive by air, the region is well served by three international airports at Venice, Verona and Treviso.

Excursions from Padua

The city of **Padua** has its origins in the sixth century BC as a humble fishing village, which gradually grew in size and importance until becoming an important Roman *municipium* in the second century AD. One of the most striking aspects of the city is the amount of covered walkway in the centre of the town where almost all the pavements are covered by porticoed loggias. These were first introduced in the medieval period and the tradition has been continued since then giving the city its unique atmosphere. The general aspect alone would make the city well worth visiting, but it can also boast some of Europe's greatest works of art, particularly the contributions of Giotto and Donatello.

Giotto's Scrovegni chapel was built at the end of the thirteenth century by Enrico Scrovegni in the area known as the Arena, which was once the site of the Roman amphitheatre. The outside of the chapel does not immediately attract attention being relatively simple; once inside, however, the spectacle is magnificent as both side walls and the wall behind the altar are covered by Giotto's frescoes. The thirty-eight frescoes which tell of the origins of Mary, the birth, life and death of Christ, ending with the Ascension and Pentecost, belong to Giotto's last period and are considered to be the most important works of art of the medieval period. Beneath the main series of frescoes are a further fourteen (seven on each side) representing the seven virtues and the seven vices, while around the

Traditional methods of ploughing

door on the entrance wall is Giotto's *Last Judgement.*

Outside the Arena is the thirteenth-century church of the Eremitani which, despite serious damage during World War II, has been restored to its original state, although with the sad loss of many of its fine frescoes.

Vying with the Scrovegni chapel as the most important Paduan monument is the basilica of Sant' Antonio, the construction of which began in 1232 to house the tomb of Sant' Antonio of Padua. Built in the form of a Latin cross, the basilica mixes with a surprising degree of harmony Romanesque, Gothic, Islamic and Byzantine elements. Outside the church, possibly the most interesting part is the roof where eight domes coexist with a variety of different styles of bell tower. Inside, the most interesting points are the 'Chapel of the Arch of the Saint' where the silver coffin of Sant' Antonio is embedded in an arch of green marble over the main altar, and the altar of the presbytery designed by Donatello in the fifteenth century, demolished and then recomposed approximately at the end of the last century. The fine bronze statues on the predella of the altar are original works by Donatello.

In front of the basilica is another of the Florentine sculptor's masterpieces — the large equestrian statue of Gattamelata, the greatest of the Venetian condottieres who died in Padua in 1443. The square in front of the basilica is known as Piazza del Santo and around the square the visitor should not miss the school of Santo Antonio which houses important works by Titian, the civic museum and art gallery which, as well as a fine collection of paintings, can also boast a fine archaeological section, and an important numismatic section. Nearby are the botanical gardens (the oldest in Europe).

Other important buildings to visit in Padua are the basilica of Santa Giustina with the adjacent Benedictine monastery, dating from the twelfth century; the twelfth-century baptistry of the *Duomo* with its fine frescoes; Palazzo della Ragione; the early sixteenth-century Loggia della Gran Guardia, built as the council chamber and frescoed by leading artists of the period; and the Arco dell' Orologio, housing the first clock in Italy — designed in 1344, the clock shows the time, the day of the month, the phase of the moon, the signs of the zodiac and the motion of the sun and of the planets.

Leaving Padua on the SS11 towards the coast, 5 miles brings you to the small town of **Stra** situated at a fork in the river Brenta, and notable for its many fine villas. The most famous of these is the Villa Pisani, built in the mid-eighteenth century when Alvise Pisani was elected Doge of Venice, on a scale to rival most European royal palaces. The villa later belonged to Eugène de Beauharnais (Napoleon's stepson), the Austrian imperial family, and the Italian royal family, and in 1934 was the site of the first meeting between Hitler and Mussolini.

From Stra continue along the SS11 to Dolo and then turn south-east to reach the coast road. At this point the coast road goes directly southwards for 10 miles hugging the edge of the Venetian lagoon (Laguna Veneta) offering unusual and interesting views. At the end of the lagoon the road sweeps round to the east until it reaches **Chioggia**, a smaller version of Venice with a much smaller proportion of tourists. The town is divided by three large canals while a long bridge connects it with the suburb of Sottomarina built on a spit of sand facing Chioggia. Sottomarina has excellent beaches but these tend to get crowded in summer. Chioggia is connected by ferry to the Littorale di Pellestrina, one of the long, sandy embankments which divides the Venetian Lagoon from the Adriatic. A road runs along the 7-mile-long embankment which is then connected by another ferry to the Littorale di Lido, where another 5 miles of road leads to Lido from where a network of passenger ferries will take you to the peripheral Venetian islands of Murano (craftsman-run glassworks), Burano, and Torcello (with its famous monastery) not to mention Venice itself.

Val di Cembra, Trentino

Lake Tenno, Trentino

Lake Molveno, Trentino

The other coastal area which deserves to be visited by those based in (Padua) Padova is the National Reserve of the Foci del Po (Mouths of the Po or Po delta), an excursion which permits the visitor to see other places of interest on route. Leave Padua on the SS516 and follow the road as far as **Piove di Sacco**. This former Roman settlement has changed little over the last few centuries and the busy Piazza della Incoronata and Via Garibaldi offer an insight into the many styles of architecture which have influenced the region. **Adria,** 20 miles south of Piove di Sacco was, before the silting up of the Po estuary, one of the most important sea ports in the eastern Mediterranean, and although it is now situated 15 miles from the sea it can still boast of having given its name to the Adriatic. The Museo Archeologico is of considerable interest as are the Byzantine frescoes in the old cathedral (reached by passing through the left nave of the new cathedral).

From Adria it is possible to follow the course of the Po along minor roads until reaching the Strada Romea coast road at **Contarina**. From Contarina the visitor has a number of choices, all of them on fairly minor roads. To the north of the Po delta, Rosapineta and Rosaline Mare have fine beaches set against a background of pine forests, but these can occasionally get very busy in summer. An alternative way of seeing the delta is to take the road from Contarina to **Porto di Levante**, a small fishing village reached via a road which, after passing first through cultivated reclaimed land, then finds itself in the midst of wild misty marshes which are characteristic of the zone. From Porto di Levante a small road leads southwards across a series of sand spits and small islands on the lagoon until finally reaching a larger road on the bank of the main branch of the Po, where, depending on the time available, the visitor can either turn seawards to explore more of the delta or turn inland to rejoin the coast road.

Twenty-five miles south of Padua on the SS16 (and A13 motorway) is the city of **Rovigo**, main town of the Polesine area and therefore of the south of the region. The city became important after the millennium which makes it relatively young by Italian standards and this is reflected in its lack of popularity with the tourists. The oldest building is the sixteenth-century *Municipium* with its graceful open loggia over a three-arched portico. Next to the *Municipium* in the central square is the other main focal point of the city, the Palazzo dell' Accademia dei Concordi (1814) which houses the civic library and art gallery with many important works by, amongst others, Giovanni Bellini and Tiepolo.

The town where the famous socialist M.P. Matteotti was born and lived until his assassination by the fascists in 1924, **Fratta Polesine,** is located 10 miles west-south-west of Rovigo. The town is famous for its many fine villas, the best of which is the Villa Badoer built by Palladio in 1569, now the headquarters of the Board of Venetian Villas. Matteotti's study in Casa Matteotti has been restored to its original state by his family and can be visited. Archaeological excavations in Fratta have revealed traces of ancient pre-Venetian civilisations.

Lendinara, a few miles to the north, is a small, though lively, town with a particularly attractive older quarter. Being away from the normal tourist centres, the town is a useful place to take a break for a meal at a reasonable price.

Badia Polesine, 5 miles to the west, takes its name from the tenth-century abbey of Vangadizza. Substantially modernised in 1233 and again in the fifteenth century, the abbey was finally supressed by Napoleon and is now in ruins. Enough remains, however, to give a good idea of what it was originally like.

Directly north of Badia Polesine is **Montagnana** which is enclosed by one of the finest and best preserved fortified city walls in Europe. Built and strengthened between 1200 and 1400, the four equal sides have a total length of almost $1^1/_4$ miles. Each side is broken by one gateway and surmounted by battlements and seven fortified towers (mainly pentagonal in form). The most impressive of the gateways is the Porta Legnano where the rooms which formerly housed the garrison are now used as a youth hostel. Inside the town the most important building is the cathedral, whose portal takes the form of a triumphal arch.

The ancient capital of the Veneto, **Este,** is situated 12 miles east of Montagnana. At the centre of the city is the fourteenth-century castle built in 1339 on the ruins of an earlier one. The interior of the castle has been turned into a public garden, while for the visitor perhaps the most interesting part is the sixteenth-century Palazzo Mocenigo built over part of the castle wall, which houses the Atestino museum, one of the most important in Italy for the pre-Roman period. Many of the exhibits come from the nearby Eugenian Hills where the prehistoric Veniti had their major settlements.

Behind the castle, a small road leads out of the town up a small twisting road to the attractive village of **Calaone** $3^1/_2$ miles away. This is also a pleasant walk for those with an afternoon to pass in a relaxing way.

Five miles to the east, built on the side and at the foot of a hill is

Mule transport can still be seen in rural parts of Italy

the town of **Monselice**. The visitor should start in Piazza Mazzini in the lower part of the town where the Torre Civica (1244) with its loggia, battlements and fifteenth-century bell, is the most notable of several fine buildings. From the *piazza*, Via del Duomo leads to the picturesque Salita al Colle. Soon after the beginning of the rise is the castle whose fine courtyard is overlooked by a variety of examples of different styles of medieval architecture. Higher up the hill is the Duomo Vecchio, an ogival-Gothic construction which, like the castle, dates from the thirteenth century. Higher still is the fine early seventeenth-century Villa Dudda whose perimeter wall houses the sanctuary of the Seven Churches consisting of six small chapels and the church of San Giorgio where the bodies of twenty-five martyrs from the Roman catacombs are preserved. From the villa, a small winding road leads up to a ruined thirteenth-century fortress with magnificent views over the surrounding countryside.

The main road from Monselice to Padua runs alongside the Eugenian Hills which merit at least a whole day to visit them. The nearest of the Eugenian towns to Padua is **Albano Terme** which, although the site of important settlements since pre-Roman times, is relatively modern-looking. The town is an important centre for thermal cures and is well provided with hotels and other facilities for visitors, although being a spa it is much more peaceful than the nearby seaside resorts.

While several towns have been developed as thermal resorts there are still many parts of the hills which have remained unspoilt. **Torreglia**, 3 miles south-west of Albano is a small quiet town from where it is possible to begin some interesting walks. The Villa dei Vescovi at **Luvigliano** is only 20 minutes' walk away, while an hour's pleasant walk will take you to the hermitage of Rua where the rustic bell tower of the fourteenth-century church was originally a much earlier fortified tower. The hermitage is a monastery and entry is restricted to men. Five miles south of Torreglia is **Valsanzibio** where the gardens of the Villa Barbarigo are among the finest to be found in Veneto.

Dropping out of the hills to the main road in order to reach Arqua Petrarca the road takes you to the small **Lago di Arqua**, very picturesque and popular with fishermen. The remains of a Bronze Age settlement have been found on the south bank, most of which have been taken to the museums of Padua and Este.

Arqua Petrarca, which takes its name from the great poet who spent the last 4 years of his life here, and is buried in a red marble tomb in the central square, is a small medieval village in one of the most attractive parts of the Eugenian Hills. Petrarch's house is open to the public and visitors will be adding their names to those of Byron and Carducci amongst others. Half an hour's walk takes you to the even smaller village of Valle San Giorgio from where the summit of Monte Gemola with its ex-convent can be reached in around an hour.

Teolo, 10 miles to the north, is the starting point for many of the most pleasant walks in the area. A detailed local map is advisable, however. Two of the best walks are those to the sanctuary of the Madonna of the Mount and to the hermitage of Sant' Antonio Abate. The first walk, as well as the sanctuary, can also offer one of the areas most beautiful viewpoints, while the second is situated at a point where several extremely rare species of plants can be found.

Another interesting visit to make either on foot or by car is to the **Madonna of Rovolon**, where the attractive village is surrounded by vines and cherry trees. The best time to visit Rovolon is April-May when the trees are all in blossom.

Monasteries and other religious buildings are almost always found in the most attractive parts of the hills and the Abbazia di Praglia is no exception. The fine monastery, which in part dates from the eleventh century, has a view which often extends as far as the Alps on fine days.

Excursions from Vicenza

The second major centre from which to see Veneto is **Vicenza** which offers access to the west of the region, Lago di Garda and the beginning of the mountains. Situated at the confluence of two rivers and set against a backdrop of mountains, the city is unjustly (although fortunately) ignored by the vast majority of tourists. Three distinct architectural styles are immediately evident: the first being the medieval Gothic, the second being the early Renaissance Florentine style of the fifteenth century, and the third, the neo-classical style which takes its name from the famous sixteenth-century Paduan architect Palladio. Palladio spent most of his life in the city and it is his style which predominates. The finest example is the basilica in Piazza dei Signori, where Palladio built two layers of classical loggias surmounted by a balustrade with statues, around the existing late fifteenth-century Gothic palace. The Loggia del Capitanato in the north-west corner of the *piazza* was also built by Palladio to replace an earlier construction. Of older date is the Torre di Piazza, built in the thirteenth century as a private fortified tower and then acquired by the city for use as a bell tower.

The oldest building in the city is the basilica of San Felice, where parts of the original late third-century church can still be seen incorporated into the present building which was rebuilt after the earthquake of 1117. The other religious building in the city which should not be missed is the Temple of San Lorenzo, begun in 1280, and particularly the fifteenth-century Altare dei Poiani in the north transept.

Palazzo Chiericati, which now houses the important civic museum and art gallery is considered to be one of the finest of Palladio's buildings. A Doric portico stretches across the façade supporting the Ionic upper storey where the central section is flanked by two loggias giving an impression of airiness while still retaining its classic severity. On the ground floor, the museum has sections covering all the different civilisations which have occupied the Veneto, while on the upper floor the gallery, which is set out in chronological order, contains fine works by artists such as Paolo Veronese, Tiepolo and Van Dyck.

On the outskirts of the town is Villa Capra 'La Rotonda' which served as a model for Palladian villas all over Europe. The villa is built round a square central hall where six Ionic columns on each side support a graceful dome.

Back in the town the house known as Palladio's House is not

worth visiting if time is limited, as not only did he not design it but he probably never lived there either. What should be seen is Palladio's last project, the Olimpico theatre. The theatre was designed following the rules prescribed by Vitruvius, the famous Roman architect, in his treatise *De Architectura*, with interesting adaptations to utilise the space available.

Monte Berici to the south of the city offers the visitor a number of small quiet centres from which to begin a large number of walks. From **Lonigo**, 15 miles south of the city, which itself has several buildings of interest such as the sixteenth-century *Pieve* and the Palazzo Comunale, it is possible to walk the mile or so to Villa La Rocca or to the fifteenth-century Gothic sanctuary of the Madonna of Miracles in half an hour, while 45 minutes' walk will take you to **Bagnolo**, an interesting little village dominated by a villa begun by Palladio.

The town of **Costozza** in the north-west of the Berici area had its origins in the period of the Veniti, and has been famous ever since for the quality of its wines which should be sampled by all those who eat in the town's small restaurant. From Costozza the energetic walker can reach the small village of **Villabalzana** with its magnificent views in just over an hour, while the peaceful Lago di Fimon in its green basin is situated at a similar distance.

Moving away from the Berici Hills, 6 miles west of Lonigo is **San Bonifacio** where the ruins of a medieval castle destroyed in 1243 can be seen in the memorial gardens. **Soave**, 2 miles to the north has retained much more of its medieval aspect being completely enclosed by defensive walls built in 1369 and protected by twenty-four towers and the castle which looks out from the town's highest point. Inside the town, the parish church and the palace of justice both date from the fourteenth century, while the frescoed Palazzo Cavalli dates from 1411.

From Soave it is possible to take either the SS11 or the motorway to Verona but it is well worth making a slight deviation to the north in order to visit the town of **Illasi**, where two fine eighteenth-century villas dominate the hillside behind the town, which is capped by a ruined medieval castle.

A small tomb in the group of buildings formed by what was once a Franciscan monastery is generally known as the Tomb of Juliet which is one of **Verona**'s most famous monuments. The ex-monastery has recently been adapted to house a Shakesperian museum, the city museum and a museum of sixteenth-century Verona. Culturally and artistically Verona is one of the richest cities in Italy but apart

Statue of Dante, Verona

from July and August when tourists come from all over the world for the operatic season, the city does not get as many tourists as it deserves. Many of the city's finest buildings and monuments date from the Roman period. The following is a selection of those which the visitor spending a day or two in the city outside the main summer season should try to see. The Arena is the third largest surviving Roman amphitheatre and the site of most of the main operatic productions. The amphitheatre is built of white Veronese stone as is the Roman theatre which also dates from the first century AD. The theatre was completely built over in the Dark Ages and the medieval period but in the last 200 years the area has been progressively cleared until the theatre has once again become the site of important theatrical events, mainly during and immediately after the operatic season. Alongside the theatre, in an ex-monastery, is the archaeological museum containing a wealth of relics from the Roman period.

The most interesting ecclesiastical building in the city is the church of San Zeno Maggiore which, while mainly dating from the thirteenth century, is much older in parts. The other main monument is Castelvecchio, an imposing fourteenth-century fortress which controls the main bridge over the Adige. The bridge (Ponte Scaligero) was built out of terracotta in 1375 and despite being virtually destroyed during the last war, has been restored to its original state, mainly from fragments recovered from the river bed. Inside the castle is the civic art gallery which occupies both floors with a very rich and varied collection. It is possible to follow the old city walls around the city in about $2^1/_2$ hours. The walls, which until World War II were in good condition, show how the fortifications were strengthened in successive periods to cope with attacks by enemies armed with ever more powerful weapons.

The Venetian bank of **Lago di Garda** can be reached easily from Vicenza and Verona, taking the SS11 or the A4 to Peschiera del Garda at the southern end of the lake. During the long Italian summer holidays (the schools are closed from the end of June to mid-September) the lake and the many small towns along its banks are very popular, but in May and late September the visitor will find the area fairly quiet except on Sundays.

Peschiera is worth a quick visit as the older part of the town, which is built around a fifteenth-century fortress, is of great interest to those interested in military history. Two more fortresses were added by Napoleon and later the town became one of the major strongholds which allowed the Austrians to hold onto northern Italy until unification. A mile-and-a-half south of Peschiera on one of the hills, around small Lago di Frassino, is the sanctuary of the Madonna of Frassino built in the sixteenth century.

The next town along the lake is **Lazise**, which is still almost

Street market, Verona

entirely enclosed by its medieval walls. The most interesting building is the fifteenth-century Venetian customs house with its small private port. A pleasant short walk (2 miles) leads the visitor up to the small village of **Calmasino** which has fine views over the lake.

The village of **Cisano** with its church of Santa Maria (founded in the eighth century) holds a famous bird festival on 8 September each year. **Bardolino** is more famous for its wines than for anything else but among the many buildings which bear witness to its long history, one, the tiny ninth-century church of San Zeno, is among the most important relics of the Carolingian period in Italy. Three miles east of Bardolino is the seventeenth-century hermitage of the Camaldolesi, with its separate little monks' houses each one of which has its own herb and vegetable garden. A footpath leads back down to the lake at Garda.

Two miles north of Bardolino, **Garda** has been the site of settlements for over 2,000 years although the oldest parts which can be seen easily date from the medieval period. From Garda the main road follows the beautiful and often busy coastline of the San Vigilio peninsula before finally arriving at **Torri del Benaco**. It is possible however to cut across the base of the peninsula following the wild scenery of the Valle Volpara (Valley of the Foxes) almost to Albisano before dropping down to Torri. Originally a Roman fortress the town is interesting mainly for its fourteenth-century castle as well as for the medieval tower from which it takes its name.

A minor road leads north-east from Torri, through the beautiful village of San Zeno di Montagna, until **Prada**, a small and little known skiing centre. Another skiing centre which also offers many possibilities to walkers is **Malcesine** towards the northern end of the lake. From here, it is possible to reach the Tratto Spino mountain shelter in 25 minutes by cablecar or in 5 hours on foot. From Tratto Spino a number of ski-lifts serve a large number of ski-runs suitable for people of all abilities.

An interesting and little frequented route for the return journey to Vicenza leaves the lake from Castelletto di Brenzone. Twelve miles on a minor road take you to the village of **Spiazzi** on the side of Monte Baldo. From the village it is possible to ascend easily two of the smaller mountains. The summit of Monte Cimo can be reached in 20 minutes while the more dedicated walker may wish to make the longer ascent of Monte Maggiore which requires around 6 hours for the ascent and slightly less for the descent.

After Spiazzi cross the Adige at Rivalta and head south-east to **Sant' Anna d'Alfaedo**, a small town where many of the buildings still have the traditional roofs formed of slabs of stone. A small museum has exhibits which document life in the area as far back as the time of the Veniti. Like most of the places in this itinerary Sant' Anna is the starting point for many interesting walks; visitors intending to undertake anything more than short walks in these mountain areas should purchase a detailed map of the area.

The next place of interest is **Bosco Chiesanuova** 15 miles to the east, which, having several restaurants to cater for skiers and walkers, is a good place to break one's journey. From Bosco follow the road south until the left turn for **Rovere Veronese**, another small town which dates from the medieval period. From Rovere head north-east until reaching Valdango and then north on the main road to **Recoaro Terme**. During the last century Recoaro was one of Italy's leading spa towns and much of its architecture dates from then. Although much less popular now, some thermal cures are still practised while, for winter sports enthusiasts, a cablecar connects the town with **Recoaro Mille**, a small town surrounded by woods of pine, chestnut and beech, which is an ideal starting point for excursions into the Small Dolomites.

The quickest way to return to Vicenza is to take the A31 motorway stopping off for a while in **Schio** if time permits, to visit the fifteenth-century Gothic church of San Francesco.

The last of the major excursions from Vicenza begins by taking the SS349 to **Thiene**. Palazzo Porto Colleoni, built in the fifteenth century to replace the medieval castle, is well worth a visit. The Renaissance-Gothic building which contains some fine frescoes is surrounded by a garden and enclosed by a fortified wall. Five miles north-east is **Lugo di Vicenza** where the first villa to be built by Palladio, the Villa Godi Malmarana, now contains a museum, an art gallery and a library. Two British war cemeteries are situated near **Cesuna** 2 miles to the north.

The town of **Asiago** was for centuries the most important town in the area and as such was periodically razed to the ground during the various wars in which first the Venetian state and then Italy were involved. Most of the town has been rebuilt after the damage suffered during World War I, but the white marble Sacrario Militare should be visited in order to appreciate the destruction caused in such a small area by that war. The Sacrario contains the remains of almost 35,000 soldiers who perished in the war.

Of much more aesthetic interest is the town of **Marostica** 22 miles south-west, inside its fourteenth-century defensive wall. Two castles were built at the same time as the walls; one of these at the centre of the town is now the town hall, while the other, situated at the highest point of the defensive system is in ruins. Every 2 years in the central square thirty-two of the townsfolk dressed in medieval costume act out a historic game of chess. Unlike other similar events this is a re-enactment of a real game which was played out in the fifteenth century with the hand of the lord of the town's daughter as the prize.

In **Bassano del Grappa**, 5 miles to the east, many important old buildings have survived despite the large-scale damage which the town suffered during both World Wars. The most characteristic of these is the Ponte Coperta bridge, a covered wooden bridge which has spanned the Brenta since 1209 having always been reconstructed in exactly the same manner after being damaged several times by floods. At one end of the bridge is a small museum dedicated to its history. The town's civic museum and art gallery is of great importance and should, if possible, be avoided at weekends. The castle, situated at the higher northern end of the town, is one of the oldest in Italy, dating from before the millennium.

Eleven miles along the road which leads east from Bassano, around the base of Monte Grappa, is **Possagno**, birthplace of the greatest neo-classical sculptor, Antonio Canova. The house where he was born has been turned into a museum where it is possible to see the more spontaneous works made for his own satisfaction, as well as a fine portrait of the sculptor by Thomas Lawrence. Above the town is the Tempio di Canova, a mini Pantheon designed by the sculptor.

An unmetalled road leads from Possagno to the summit of **Monte Grappa**, the scene of some of the bloodiest battles seen on the Austro-Italian front in World War I. A mountain shelter serves as a bar and restaurant before the 20-mile descent to Bassano.

Returning to Vicenza, take the SS47 to **Cittadella** where the 40ft-high circular city walls with their four gateways and thirty-two defensive towers date from the 1220s. The full circle is just under a mile and makes a pleasant walk. The SS53 leads back to Vicenza.

Excursions from Treviso

The city of **Treviso** is one of the most interesting Italian cities not attracting a large number of tourists. Situated at the confluence of two rivers, the centre is cut across by several canals which in places give it a resemblance to the quieter parts of Venice. The main streets of the city all converge in Piazza dei Signori, enclosed on three sides by the town hall and other civic offices, the porticoed ground floors of which have been turned into elegant shops and cafés. Palazzo del Trecento, with its fortified parapet, was built in 1217 to house the 'Council of Three Hundred' which governed the city. The council chamber on the first floor is frescoed. Many of Treviso's churches are worth visiting; many of them dating from before 1500, particularly the twelfth-century *Duomo* with its baptistry. Many important works of art can be seen in the *Duomo* including an *Annunciation* by Titian. The civic museum is of great interest but perhaps the more fascinating is the museum of the Trevigian house which documents the development of domestic architecture and artefacts in the area.

Twenty miles to the north of Treviso on the SS13 is the attractive town of **Conegliano** (famous for its white wine), where most of the historic centre passed through the bombardments of the last war unscathed. Dominating the town are the remains of the old medieval castle, where two of the original towers house the civic museum and a restaurant respectively.

An interesting route to follow from Conegliano is the 'White Wine Route' which runs along the base of attractive hills, through interesting villages with simple, reasonably priced eating places, for 20 miles, until **Valdobbiadene**, where every September the Venetian Spumante Fair takes place.

Take the road which runs north-east towards Vittorio Veneto passing through **Follina** where the restored twelfth-century abbey is worth a visit. **Vittorio Veneto** itself was, until 1866, two separate communes, Ceneda and Serravalle, which means it has two distinct historic centres. Of these, the former centre of Serravalle has preserved the greater number of historical buildings. The Loggia Cenedese, formerly the Palazzo Comunale, now contains the Museo della Battaglia, commemorating one of the last great battles of World War I, while the Loggia Serravallese contains the Museo del Cenedese with collections of archaeology, painting and sculpture. The most interesting building in Vittorio Veneto is probably the fourteenth-century civic hospital, the inside of which is almost entirely frescoed. To the north-west of Vittorio Veneto is **Monte Pizzoch**, one of the least known of the Venetian mountain resorts, where even in the high season the ski-runs are less crowded than in the more northerly resorts.

Continue northwards alongside Lago Santa Croce and then up the Piave valley until **Pieve di Cadore** and the beginning of the Dolomites. The area is justly famous for its natural beauty and during July, August and the peak winter sports season some parts of the area tend to get very crowded, particularly in the area immediately around Cortina d'Ampezzo. The route described here takes in some of the lesser known valleys which nevertheless provide access to most of the main mountain groups and guarantee magnificent scenery. The town hall of Pieve contains two interesting museums while nearby is the house where Titian was born which contains relics of his life. The parish church contains a *Virgin and Saints* by Titian, previously housed in an older church on the site.

To the left of the road which leads to the fork for Auronzo are many footpaths leading onto the Antelao and the Marmarole group. The path to the very summit of Antelao is only to be attempted by well equipped, experienced walkers. At the fork take the left turn for **Auronzo**, from where a cablecar takes those who wish to see the Dolomites without too much exertion, from the centre of the town to the top of Monte Agudo (5,200ft). The road continues towards Lago di Misurina passing between the Marmarole and Cadini groups, the latter of which is less frequented than many of the other nearby groups despite offering excellent walking and winter sports opportunities. Just before Misurina is a left turn for Cortina which takes you over the magnificent Tre Croci Pass (5,900ft) between the Crystal mountains to the north and Monte Sorapiss to the south. A series of mountain tracks can be followed onto both mountains, those on the Crystal mountains offering the easier going. A number of ski-runs are also to be found in the vicinity.

After Cortina take the SS48 for $3^1/_2$ miles to Poco and then turn left towards Selva di Cadore, leaving behind the three pyramid-shaped peaks of the Tofane group.

Before reaching **Selva di Cadore**, the road climbs up to the 6,035ft Giau Pass from where most of the most important mountains in the Dolomites can be seen. From Selva take the road westwards through the beautiful mountain village of **Colle Santa Lucia** with its fine church until the left turn for Alleghe. From Caprile, shortly afterwards a right turn leads to the Marmolada group, where the only significant glacier in the Dolomites is to be found. **Alleghe** is a small resort in an excellent position on the shore of a small lake which in winter is often used by ice-skaters. The town is an ideal starting point for excursions into the surrounding mountains.

Continue down the valley until **Agordo**, very popular as a base for rock-climbers especially those intending to climb on the Pale di San Martino slightly to the south-west. Take the SS347 to the north-east until you reach the lower Ampezzo valley at Venas di Cadore, and from there return to Pieve. **Borca** and **Vodo** are two smaller resorts in the lower Ampezzo valley offering a wide range of possibilities to walkers, mountaineers and winter sports lovers, particularly on the Antelao and on the tower-shaped Monte Pelmo. Because of their relative nearness to Cortina these resorts are much less frequented, as many people tend to overlook them in their hurry to reach the larger centre.

An alternative base to Treviso is **Belluno** on the north bank of the Piave, 20 miles to the north of Vittorio Veneto. The oldest part of this attractive town is situated on a spur at the confluence of the Piave and the Ardo, one of its tributaries. A town was well established here in the pre-Roman period, but the influence which can be seen most clearly is that of the Venetians who completely revamped the medieval town in the sixteenth and seventeenth centuries, creating several fine piazzas surrounded by graceful Renaissance houses and churches. An interesting civic museum with a wide variety of exhibits is situated in the old Palazzo dei Guiristi in the city's central square.

Further Information
— Veneto —

Airports

Venice, 'Marco Polo'
☎ (041) 661262

Verona, Villafranca
☎ (045) 513039

Tourist Information Offices

The seven provincial tourist boards in Veneto have recently been replaced by thirty-two local tourist offices. The list below contains the addresses of the offices in the provincial capitals.

Belluno
Azienda Promozione Turistica
Via Psaro 21
Belluno
☎ (0437) 22043

Padova (Padua)
Azienda Promozione Turistica
Stazione Ferrovie Stato (Station)
Padova
☎ (049) 35131

Rovigo
Azienda Promozione Turistica
Corso del Popolo 101
Rovigo
☎ (0425) 361481

Treviso
Azienda Promozione Turistica
Via Toniolo 41
Treviso
☎ (0422) 47632

Venezia (Venice)
Azienda Promozione Turistica
San Marco Ascensione 71/c
Venezia
☎ (041) 26356

Verona
Azienda Promozione Turistica
Via della Valverde
Verona
☎ (045) 595333

Vicenza
Azienda Promozione Turistica
Piazza Duomo 5
Vicenza
☎ (0444) 44805

Museums and Other Places to Visit

This information is arranged alphabetically by town. Opening times tend to change fairly regularly and should only be taken as a rough guide. When times are not given assume that the museum is closed on either Monday or Tuesday.

Adria
Archaeological Museum
Closed Monday and Sunday afternoon.

Affi (Incaffi)
Villa of Girolamo Fracastoro

Altino
Archaeological Museum
Piazzetta della Chiesa
Closed Monday.

Arqua Petrarca
Casa Petrarca
Closed Monday.

Asiago
War Museum and Cemetery
Viale della Vittoria
Open: every day.

Asolo
Museo Civico
Loggia del Capitano
Via Regina Cornaro
Closed Monday.

Bassano del Grappa
Civic Museum
Piazza Garibaldi
Closed Sunday pm and Monday.

Museo del Ponte degli Alpini
Taverna degli Alpini
Open: Tuesday-Sunday 8am-8pm.

Museo Francescano
Convento dei Cappuccini
Borgo Margnari
☎ (0424) 23814
Open: By appointment.

Belluno
Museo Civico
Piazza Duomo 16
Open: summer, closed Saturday pm and Monday; winter, closed Saturday pm, Monday and Sunday.

Bolca
Fossil Museum

Brugine
Villa Bozzolato
Open: Wednesday and Friday.

Caltrano
Museum of Rural Culture
☎ (0445) 891348
Open: By appointment.

Castelfranco Veneto
House of Giorgione
Piazzetta del Duomo
Open: Tuesday, Friday, Saturday and Sunday.

Villa Redevin-Bolasco Park
Borgo Treviso 73
Open: Tuesday-Saturday and first Sunday of month.

Castellavazzo
Civic Museum

Chiampo
Fossil Museum
Via Pieve
Open: Saturday-Thursday 8am-5pm.

Cison di Valmarino
Castle Brandolia
☎ (0438) 85109
Open: By appointment.

Colle Umberto
Casino di Caccia
Open: April-October Monday 10am-12noon and 2-6pm.

Conegliano
Castle Museum
Piazzale Castelvecchio
Closed Monday.

House of Giambattista Cima
Via Cima 24
Open: Saturday and Sunday.

Cortina d'Ampezzo
Museo Ciasa de Regoles
Via Parco
Open: July and September 4-7.30pm, August 10.30am-12.30pm and 4-7.30pm; end December-beginning January 10.30am-12.30pm and 4-7pm; 7 January-Easter 4-7pm.

Crocetta del Montello
Natural History Museum
Villa Ancilotto

Open: afternoons Monday, Wednesday, Thursday and Saturday.

Este
Atestino Museum
Palazzo Mocenigo
Via Negri
Closed on Monday.

Falcade
'August Murer' Studio Museum
Molino
Open: 10am-12.30pm and 4-8.30pm.

Fanzolo
Villa Emo
Open: weekends and holidays (afternoon).

Feltre
Civic Museum
Via Luzzo 23
Closed Monday and weekday afternoons.

Rizzarda Gallery
Via Paradiso 8
Open: June-September, Tuesday-Sunday.

Fratta Polesine
House of Matteotti

Giazza
Ethnographical Museum
Chiesa Parrocchiale
Church opening times.

Legnago
Civic Museum
Via Matteotti 39
Open: first Sunday pm of month, March-November.

Lonedo di Lugo Vicentino
Fossil Museum and Art Gallery
Open: mid-March-end October 2-6pm Tuesday, Saturday and Sunday.

Lugo di Vicenza
Villa Godi Valmarana
Open: all year round.

Luvigliano
Villa Olcese
☎ (049) 5211118
Open: by appointment.

Malcesine
Castle Museum
Open: April-October 9am-6pm.

Malo
Museum of Contemporary Art
☎ (0445) 21549
Open: by appointment, Saturday-Sunday 4-7pm.

Rural Civilisation Museum
Via Pasubio 13
Open: by appointment
Monday-Saturday 8am-12noon and Monday-Friday 2-6pm.

Marocco
Sculpture Exhibition
Via Marignana 112
☎ (041) 942111
Open: on request.

Mas
Museo Civico
Municipio

Maser
Carriage Museum
Villa Barbarò
Open: Tuesday, Saturday, Sunday pm.

Monselice
Ca' Marcello (Castle)
Open: April-mid-November am Tuesday, Thursday, Saturday and Sunday.

Montebelluna
Belluna History and Natural Science Museum
Villa Biagi
Closed Tuesday.

Montecchio Maggiore
Juliet's Castle
(now a restaurant)
Closing day Friday.

Museo dello Scarpone
Villa Binetti Zuccareda
Open: Sunday, Tuesday and Saturday pm.

Nervesa della Battaglia
Natural History Museum
Open: Sunday and holidays 9.30am-12.30pm.

Nove
Museo d'Arte Ceramica
Via Giove
☎ (0424) 82022
Open: 8am-12noon by appointment.

Noventa Padovana
Villa Giovanelli
☎ (049) 525066
Open: by appointment.

Villa Grimani Valmerana
☎ (049) 625299
Open: by appointment.

Orderzo
Civic Museum
Via Garibaldi
Closed Monday and Saturday pm.

Alberto Martini Art Gallery
Via Garibaldi 80
Open: Monday-Friday pm.

Onè
Crafts Museum
Via Lastego 52

Padua (Padova)
Cappella degli Scrovegni
Arena
Piazza Eremitani
Closed Sunday pm.

Museo Antoniano
Piazza del Santo

Museo Civico
Piazza del Santo
Closed Monday and pm Saturday and Sunday.

Orto Botanico
Via Orto Botanico
Open: every day am and pm.

Palazzo della Ragione
Piazza delle Frutta
Closed Sunday pm.

Scuola del Santo e San Giorgio
Piazza del Santo
Closed Sunday pm.

Peschiera del Garda
Gardaland Amusement Park
Open: March-September, weekends and holidays.

Piazzola
Villa Contarini
Closed Monday.

Pieve di Cadore
Magnifica Comunità di Cadore Museum
Municipio
Piazza Tiziano
Open: mid-June-mid-September, closed Monday.

Tiziano (Titian) Museum
Via Arsenale
Open: as above.

Piombino Dese
Villa Cornaro
Open: May-mid September, Saturday 3.30-6pm.

Pontecasale
Villa Garzoni
☎ (049) 5349602
Open: by appointment.

Portogruaro
Museo Nazionale Concordiese
Corso Martiri della Libertà 22
Closed on Mondays.

Possagno
Canova's Birthplace Museum
Closed on Mondays.

Riese Pio X
Pius X Museum and Birthplace
Closed Monday.

Roana
War Museum
Via Roma
☎ (0424) 82022

Open: June-September 9am-12noon and 3-5.30pm; May and October by appointment.

Rovigo
Palazzo dell'Accademia dei Concordi (Art Gallery and Library)
Piazza Vittoria Emanuele II
Open: 10am-12noon.

Sant' Andrea Oltre il Musone
Villa Corner and Agricultural Museum
Via Lama 2

Sant' Anna d'Alfaedo
Museum
Municipio

Sappada
Ethnographical Museum
Municipio
Open: mid-June-mid-September, pm Tuesday-Sunday, other periods on request.

Selva di Cadore
Civic Museum
Open: July-August and mid-December-mid January pm.

Solighetto
Museo Toti dal Monte
Via Roma

Stra
Villa Pisani
Closed afternoons, gardens open 9am-6pm.

Susegana
Wine and Agriculture Museum
Open: Tuesday-Sunday 9am-4pm.

Tambre-Pian de' Cansiglio
War Museum
Open: mid-May-end October and mid-December-mid-January and March-Easter.

Open-air Museum
Open: July-October.

Thiene
Castello Parco Colleoni di Thiene
Open: 9-11am and 3-5pm, weekdays pm only.

Treviso
'Luigi Bailo' Civic Museum
Borgo Cavour 22
Closed Sunday pm and Monday.

Museo della Casa Trevigiana
Via Canova 38

Chiesa di Santa Caterina
Via Santa Caterina
Open: end March to end December 9-11.45am.

Palazzo dei '300
Piazza Indipendenza
Open: Monday-Saturday, 8.30am-1pm.

Ethnographical and Archaeological Museum
Seminario Vescovile
Via San Nicolò
Open: October-May, Sunday 9am-12noon and 3-5pm.

Saletta dei Reggitori al Monte di Pietà
Piazzetta del Monte 2
Open: Monday-Friday 8.30am-12noon.

Palazzo Scotti
Via Toniolo 41
Open: Monday-Friday 9am-12noon and 3-6pm.

Museum of Popular Arts and Traditions
Villa Zen
Viale Felissent 2
☎ (0422) 665618
Open: on request.

Vallada Agordina
Valle del Biois Museum
Municipio
Sacchet
Open: July-August, 3-5pm, Monday, Wednesday, Friday and Saturday.

Church of San Simone
Open: July-August, Tuesday-Wednesday 10am-12noon, Thursday-Saturday 2.30-5.30pm.

Valstagna
Grotte di Oliero (Caves)
☎ (0424) 29622

Vas
War Museum
Parrocchia di Vas
Open: summer, on request.

Verona
Arena Amphitheatre
Piazza Bra
Open: May-September 7am-7pm.
Winter 9am-12.30pm and 2.30-6pm.

Capitolare Museum & Library
Piazza Duomo
Open: 10am-12noon, closed Sunday, Thursday and August-September.

Castelvecchio Museum
Open: as above.

Juliet's Tomb
Via del Pontiere
Open: summer 7am-7pm; winter 9am-12.30pm and 2.30-6pm.

Maffeiano Lapidary Museum
Portoni della Bra
Open: every day.

Natural History Museum
Palazzo Pompei
Lungadige Porta Vittoria 9
Open: summer 9am-12noon and 4-7pm; winter 9am-12noon and 3-7pm, Saturday 9-11pm, closed Friday.

Risorgimento Museum and Modern Art Gallery
Palazzo Forti
Via Emilei

Roman Theatre and Archaeological Museum
Rigaste del Redentore

Scagliere Arches
Via delle Arche Scagliere
Open: summer 9am-12.30pm and 3-6.30pm; winter 9am-12.30pm and 2.30-6pm.

Vicenza
Civic Museum and Olympic Theatre
Open: Tuesday-Saturday 9.30am-12.30pm and 2.30-5pm, Sunday 10am-12noon.

Risorgimento Museum
Villa Guiccioli
☎ (0444) 32199
Open: by appointment.

Villa La Rotonda
Open: Tuesday-Saturday 10am-12noon and 3-6pm.

Villa Valmarana
'Ai Nani'
Open: pm, March-November, Monday-Saturday; am March-November Thursday, Saturday and Sunday.

Vittorio Veneto
Museo della Battaglia (war)
Ceneda
Closed Monday.

Cenedese Museum
Serravalle
Closed Tuesday.

Palazzo Minucci
Via Martiri della Libertà
Open: Sunday 10am-12noon and 3-6pm.

6 • Liguria

The peculiar long, thin banana-shaped region between the sea and the mountains is one of the most famous of the Italian regions, continuing as it does the magnificent coastline of the French Riviera. Until the building of the Via Aurelia in the 1830s, all important communications were by sea and the importance of the region's towns was directly proportional to their accessibility from the sea. At that time the well-being of the countryside was assured by the richness of the olive crops which were the only things that could survive on the rugged terrain. The unification of Italy led to fierce competition from the south and the agricultural crisis was made worse by the effects of World War I.

The result of this was the migration of the agricultural workers to the small coastal strip where flower cultivation presented an alternative to a dependence on olives, and the development of the Via Aurelia and then the railway had led to the growth of an embryonic tourist industry. Not all the people from the country found work on the coast and, towards the end of the last century, Liguria had one of the highest levels of emigration in Italy. The development of Genoa as a great industrial centre at the beginning of this century led to a slight reversal of this trend with some immigration from the south of Italy.

Until World War II tourism in Liguria was mainly for a limited elite, but rapid improvements in mobility and a great increase in the average Italian standard of living have since turned it into a mass phenomenon and much of the coastline into a concrete jungle where the occasional old fishing villages are now defined as historical centres. The hills and mountains which rise steeply almost immediately behind the coast host an almost unique cohabitation of mountain species such as fir and chestnut with typical Mediterranean shrubs and olives. Despite the natural beauty of the countryside the most part is virtually abandoned and only a very small number of tourists ever get any more than brief glimpses from the viaducts which link the many tunnels on the motorway.

For the more adventurous visitor, however, there is a great deal to see and do in the interior. The best bases to see the different parts of the region are, from west to east: Taggia (three hotels), Cairo-Montenotte (four hotels), Torriglia (five hotels) and Sarzana (seventeen hotels and two camp-sites). A car is absolutely essential for visiting Liguria as rural depopulation has reached such a level that bus services have been cut to a minimum, while only the main Genoa-Turin railway line goes into the interior.

Excursions from Taggia

Situated 2 miles from the coast, **Taggia** is just far enough inland to have avoided the ribbon of concrete which has covered most of the inhabitable areas of coastline in the last few years. Built around a medieval castle — parts of which still exist — the town is one of the most interesting on the western riviera. The most important monument is the 285yd, sixteen-arched medieval bridge over the Argentina river. Fourteen of the arches were built in 1450 while the other two are Romanesque. The main street through the town is the porticoed Via Soleri where an antiques market is held on the last weekend of each month. The most important churches are situated at either end of the town: the fifteenth-century San Domenico with its adjacent monastery was, for a long time, a great centre for learning. Now a small but impressive museum has been set up in one of the rooms. The Romanesque Madonna del Canneto with its twelfth-century bell tower is situated just outside the town's sixteenth-century northern gate.

To the north, the road is at first flanked by a mixture of olive groves and flower nurseries until just beyond the confluence of the Argentina and the Oxentina, where the small attractive village of **Badalucco**, with its old bridge, is dominated by the church of San Nicolo which is built over the ruins of the castle of the Counts of Ventimiglia. Interesting walks can be enjoyed in the hills around Badalucco, in particular, to the large cave on Monte Faudo which was used as a cemetery during the Stone Age.

At the head of the valley, cross over to **Borgomaro** in the Impero valley. This town, which was once a thriving commercial centre, has lost more than half its population in the last 30 years and is a good example of the gradual depopulation of the inland areas. Further north, **Pieve di Teco**, which grew up during the medieval period where several important roads met, has retained much of its original

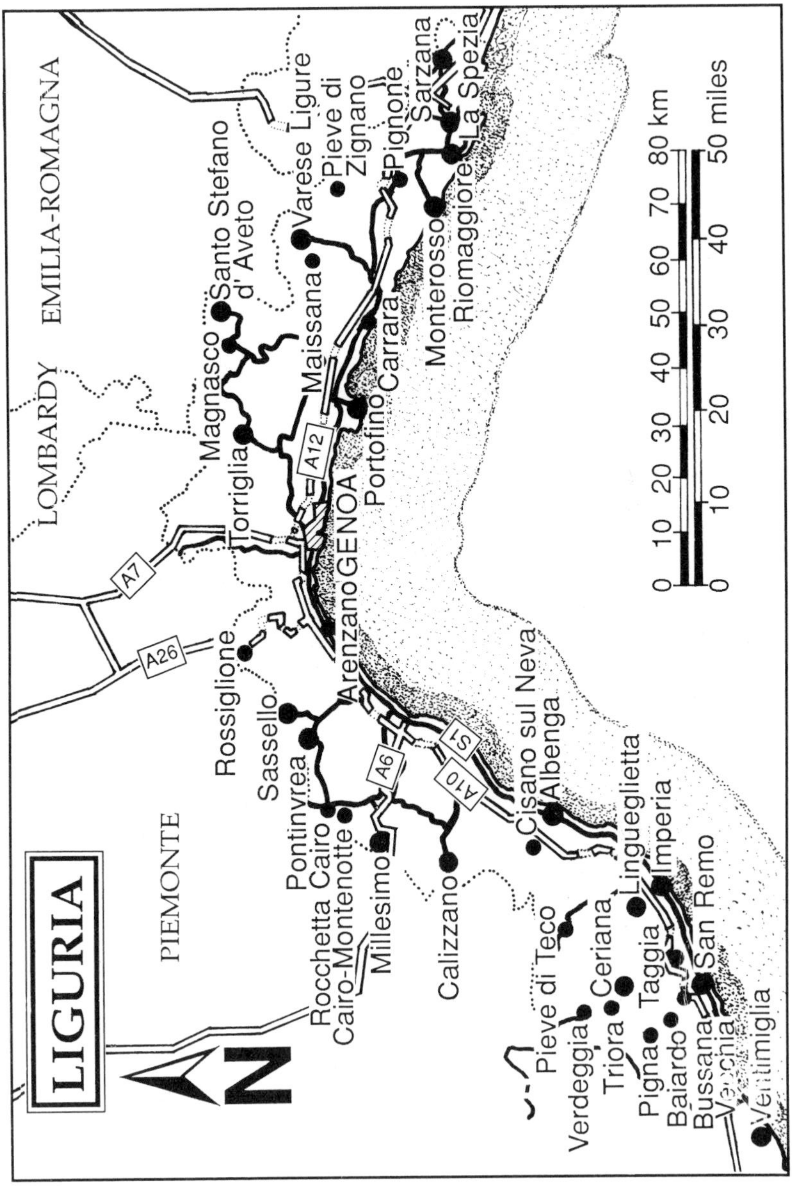

medieval appearance. A pleasant hour can be spent here wandering down the old streets and small arcades which run off the central road.

Head north-east from Pieve, past the ruined castle of Pornassio which, owing to its dominating position over the road linking Liguria with Piemonte, was long disputed by Genoa and the Savoy region, to Ponte di Nava on the region's border. From there, the road twists eastwards spectacularly, along the side of the mountains, for 15 miles until Vignolo and then follows the course of the river Fennavaira until **Cisano sul Neva**. This small medieval village still has considerable remains of its defensive walls, one of the towers of which has been adapted to become the bell tower of the attractive parish church.

The road continues down the valley to reach the coast at **Albenga**. Originally a Roman city, Albenga still has a considerable historic centre grouped mainly around Piazza San Michele where the axis of the Roman city once met. Palazzo Vecchio del Comune and the adjoining Torre Comunale both date from the beginning of the fourteenth century and house the civic museum which is devoted to the history of the town from the pre-Roman to the medieval period. Included in the entrance fee is a visit to the late Roman baptistry situated immediately behind the museum. The floor of the baptistry is much lower than that of the museum, as in the fifth century, Albenga's street level was only 3ft above sea level.

The nearby cathedral dates mainly from the twelfth and thirteenth centuries although it exactly reproduces the form of the original fifth-century church, being built on the same foundations. Stratographic excavations carried out when the building was restored in the 1960s revealed the various decorated pavements laid one on top of the other in the six centuries before the present church was built — the excavations may be visited beneath the presbytery. Other buildings of interest around the central square are the Palazzo Costa del Carretto di Balestrino, once the medieval shoe market which now houses a collection of Roman epigraphs; the Palazzo Vescovile, containing the diocesan museum; and the two fine medieval houses facing the Palazzo Comunale. A third museum in the town, Museo Navale Romano, contains the remains of a Roman ship and its contents which have recently been recovered from a point 2 miles out to sea where it sank in the first century BC.

Head inland again to avoid the traffic on the coast road, turn left near the airport and take the small road through Villalunga and Testico before reaching the SS28 and dropping down steeply towards **Imperia**. The provincial capital was formed in the 1920s by the fusion of two small towns and a number of villages giving a large modern city interspersed with older nuclei. Of these, the most interesting is **Porto Maurizio**, on a headland west of the mouth of the Impero. The large neo-classical building facing the cathedral houses

Folk festivals are frequent events in Italy

the city's art gallery containing works of varying merit. A number of small valleys behind Porto Maurizio offer interesting short walks or quick car trips.

Halfway between Imperia and Taggia, a side road leads off to the right to **Lingueglietta**, a small medieval hill village of great charm and character. Leave Taggia again, this time southwards to Bussana and from there up a narrow twisting road to **Bussana Vecchia**.

Everything in the village except the bell tower was badly damaged by an earthquake in 1887 and lay abandoned until the 1960s when a few artists made the least damaged buildings habitable again and set up a small colony of artists.

The next road inland, up the Armea valley soon brings you to the interesting unspoilt medieval town of **Ceriana** with its mass of apparently interwoven alleyways which are fascinating to explore. At the head of the valley, reached after a considerable climb, is the small town of **Baiardo** with magnificent views in all directions from its 3,000ft vantage point. The atmosphere of the town is rural and friendly. Should you decide to take a break there, be sure to visit the small gallery of contemporary local artists housed in the kindergarten.

The road drops 2,000ft in the next $4^1/_2$ miles, passing through the medieval village of Apricale before turning northwards to the even more impressive medieval village of **Pigna**. The village developed concentrically around a central high point on which a strong fortress stood. The castle has long since been totally destroyed but is still remembered by the open area known as Piazza Castello where it once stood.

Seventeen miles north-east along steep, twisting mountain roads is **Triora** which, although now having a population of just over 500, was once of great strategic importance. A sign of this is that along its interesting old streets there are ten churches, four fountains, the remains of five castles, and considerable remains of the defensive wall which surrounded the town in the medieval period. The most interesting single building is the late thirteenth-century Collegiata dell' Assunta church containing amongst other fine works of art, Taddeo di Bartolo's *Baptism of Jesus.*

Six miles north of Triora at the head of the interesting upper Argentina valley is **Verdeggia**, a small shepherds' village at the start of several pleasant walks on Monte Saccarello, on the northern side of which is the ski-resort of Monesi. The area around Verdeggia and Triora was designated a national park in 1982 and there are plans to set up an ethnographical museum in the area.

Excursions from Cairo-Montenotte

The old section of Cairo on the left bank of the Bormida river has a regular rectangular shape and the many archaeological finds in the surrounding area make it almost certain that a Roman town once stood on the same site. An archaeological cultural centre has been established in one of the old gates in the medieval defensive wall at the end of the central Via Roma. Nearby works of art by local nineteenth- and twentieth-century artists are displayed in a small art gallery in the town hall.

Eight miles to the south-west is another town with Roman origins, **Millesimo**. The town displays an interesting mixture of architectural styles, with the original late medieval nucleus being added to steadily over the following centuries. The most impressive building in the town is the Romanesque church of Santa Maria Extra Muros where fragments of the original frescoes can still be seen in the presbytery and in the left hand nave. The town is dominated by the ruins of its castle built by Enrico II del Carretto at the beginning of the thirteenth century.

From Millesimo, climb up the Bormida di Millesimo valley to the south, running parallel to the French-Italian border until reaching the small town of **Calizzano**. The church of San Lorenzo, originally Romanesque but considerably rebuilt during the early seventeenth century, contains some fine works of art while the bell tower was originally one of the defensive towers incorporated in the town's walls. Leave the town to the east, climbing through the wooded Frassino valley to the top of the Melogno Pass. From there head northwards back towards Cairo through one of the most scenic stretches of the Bormida valley.

Five miles north of Cairo in the woods above the village of **Rocchetta Cairo** are the ruins of an older village of the same name. Walking from the village to the ruins is a pleasant way of passing an hour or so. From Rocchetta continue northwards to Dego and then take the SS542 to Pontinvrea. This road climbs steeply out of Dego and then drops down, crosses the Valla and climbs out of the valley again before descending steeply through the oaks and chestnuts to **Pontinvrea**.

From Pontinvrea head north-east over the Colle del Giovo Pass with its large nineteenth-century fortress and drop down to **Sassello**, one of the most important inland towns in western Liguria. Most of the architecture in the town dates from the seventeenth century although there are still some medieval buildings to be seen. One building which should not be missed is 33 Via del Perrando which, besides housing the town's library, is also the home of the Sassello cultural centre and the Museo Perrando which is devoted to the archaeology of Sassello and the surrounding area.

Continue eastwards to Martina Olba and from there northwards towards Rossiglione. At the top of a steep hill halfway between

Martina and Rossiglione is the Badia di Tiglieto, believed to have been the first Cistercian monastery in Italy. The buildings may only be seen from the outside but they will certainly be of great interest to those interested in architecture for the basic Romanesque structure with French Gothic embellishments. **Rossiglione** is really two villages very close together: Rossiglione Superiore, at 975ft, dates from the fourteenth century while Rossiglione Inferiore, slightly lower at 947ft, predates it by almost 2 years. Both parts of the town are pleasant and although there are no truly outstanding buildings it is interesting to see the difference in styles of the two villages.

Take the main road from Rossiglione down to the coast, over the Turchino Pass (1,750ft) and then bear right along the coast road for 4 miles to **Arenzano**. This is an extremely beautiful stretch of coastline and should you happen to be there outside the summer months it is an extremely rewarding drive. The coast road moves inland slightly after Arenzano then cuts back again to the sea. At this point take the small road on the right signposted 'Arma' and work across the hills to San Martino avoiding the heavy coastal traffic yet passing through attractive little villages, and seeing old churches and monasteries perched on the hillsides. After San Martino it is possible to return to Cairo directly along very minor roads, or alternatively to take the longer but quicker route back via Pontinvrea.

Excursions from Torriglia

Torriglia, situated 22 miles north-east of Genoa, is basically semicircular in form, being backed by a range of mountains, the most impressive of which is Monte Prela (4,610ft). Around the old centre there are a large number of villas where, for over a century, many of the wealthier Genoans have passed their summers. An interesting excursion a few miles north of Torriglia is a visit to Lago di Brugneto, a reservoir popular with trout fishermen and surrounded by spectacular scenery.

Fontanigorda 15 miles to the east is an attractive village which has recently been turned into a fairly quiet holiday centre. It has also developed in recent years as one of the most important animal research centres in Liguria. Originally, the villagers' principal means of support was gathering mushrooms in the surrounding woods. The felling of large areas of woodland in the last century put an end to this traditional way of life and caused widescale emigration.

Leave Fontanigorda in a south-easterly direction until arriving at Cabanne and the SS586. Turn left and head up the valley through the small semi-deserted villages. Two of these, **Magnasco** and **Cerro**, are interesting in that the few remaining inhabitants have preserved, to a large extent, the centuries' old traditional life-style, farming their land on a system of crop rotation already used in the feudal period. Three miles after Magnasco the road crosses the Gramizza river and climbs past the attractive medieval hamlet of Allegrezze to **Santo Stefano d'Aveto**. The old village with the ruins of its old church and the Malaspina castle is worth looking at but the town is more important as the starting place for many fine mountain walks during the summer which in winter become ideal sites for alpine skiing and other winter sports.

Continue through the town and head south-westwards to rejoin the main road through Cabanne. Shortly after Cabanne the road bears left and one of the most scenic stretches of road in Liguria begins. To the right of the road are Monte Cavallo, Monte Ramaceto and Monte Cucco, while on the left, Monte Fascia, Monte d'Abeti and Monte Bregaceto dominate the skyline. At **Borzonasca** turn left and head up the terraced hillside to the abbey of Borzone. The present church was built in 1244 and contains some interesting architectural elements, such as the double series of terracotta blind archways against the stone walls. There is also an interesting fifteenth-century late Gothic polyptych in the presbytery, painted by an unknown artist.

Drop back into Borzonasca and head south to join the main road at Borgonovo. Follow the narrow valley southwards for just over 2 miles and then leave the main road and climb up the Cicana valley into the hills on the right. The highest point of this road is marked by the small village of Chichero which is just below the summit of Monte Mignano, then the road descends again to join the SS225 in the Fontanabuona valley.

When the road reaches Gattorina the visitor can either head straight back to Torriglia or turn left and head for Uscio and the Portofino peninsula. **Uscio** boasts a fine eleventh-century church which has recently been restored to its former splendour. The **Portofino peninsula** is extremely beautiful and attracts a large number of tourists throughout the year. Most of them, however, arrive by car from Rapallo and as there is only a limited amount of parking, most of their time is spent in a long hot traffic-jam between Rapallo and Portofino. It is possible however to park at Recco on the other side of the peninsula and make the final part of the journey on foot.

It is possible to arrive near the highest central point of the peninsula by car but it is much better to walk as much as possible as the

San Fruttuoso

scenery is magnificent and if time allows there can be few pleasanter ways of spending half a day or even a full day. At the central point of the southern face of the peninsula, reachable only on foot or by sea, is the little fishing village of **San Fruttuoso** grouped around the abbey of San Fruttuoso di Capodimonte. The church was built in the thirteenth century when the Doria family obtained sovereignty over San Fruttuoso although the cloister alongside the church predates it, having formerly been part of an eleventh-century Benedictine abbey. For 30 years at the end of the thirteenth century, the abbey was the burial place of the Doria family as their church in Genoa was being rebuilt.

Portofino itself, at the south-eastern tip of the peninsula, was once a small fishing village in a beautiful natural harbour. Nowadays the fishing boats have been replaced by luxury yachts and as already mentioned there is a fairly constant flow of visitors. Should you decide to walk over the peninsula to Portofino excellent fish based meals are to be had in the restaurants around the harbour.

Excursions from Sarzana

Sarzana is situated on the alluvial plain formed by the river Magra and dividing Liguria from Tuscany. It was this important border position which led to the establishment of a castle on the site in the tenth century, which by the thirteenth had developed into a flourishing fortified town. Only a short length of the city wall remains to divide the old centre off from the newer mainly post-war buildings which surround it. Still standing, however, is the Cittadella fortress built by the Florentines in the late fifteenth century after they had seized the town from the Genoans. For many years the Cittadella served as a prison but it has now been abandoned for several years while projects for restoration and a new use are discussed. The historic centre has two distinct focal points, one civil and one religious. Piazza Matteotti is surrounded by fine fifteenth- and sixteenth-century *palazzi* built to house the town's administration and civic dignitaries. Under the double loggia of the Palazzo Municipale, several fragments of Roman masonry recovered from the nearby city of Luni can be seen. Number 28 Via dei Fondachi incorporates the fourteenth-century tower-house which was the home of the Bonaparte family before their emigration to Corsica in 1529.

The cathedral was built in the early thirteenth century on the site of an earlier basilica when the bishopric was transferred to Sarzana from the derelict Luni. It has been added to many times over the centuries, particularly in the fifteenth when a native of Sarzana sat on the papal throne as Nicholas V. The rose window on the façade is a particularly fine example of Gothic sculpture.

A road with fine views leads out of the city to the north-west and up to the fort of Sarzanello, said to have been begun by Castruccio Castracani, the great Luccan war lord, but which was really begun by the Genoans and completed by the Florentines at the same time as they were building the Cittadella.

During the Roman period, **Luni**, 4 miles south-east of Sarzana and now over a mile from the sea, was an important port and defensive bulwark against the Ligurians. The progressive silting up of the port and the formation of bogs around the town led to its gradual decline however, and by the thirteenth century it was little more than a name. The first organized excavations took place in 1837 and a systematic, scientific series of excavations have been taking place during the last 20 years. In previous years many of the finds on the site found their way to the archaeological museums of Florence, La Spezia and Carrara but more recent finds are kept in a new museum which has been built on the site of the excavations.

From Sarzana follow the main road towards La Spezia until it turns at a right angle to run alongside the A15 motorway. Instead of turning left take the minor road under the motorway and climb up to the attractive town of **Vezzano Ligure**. Until the last century the town consisted of two villages: Vezzano Alto and Vezzano Basso, which gradually fused together. Traces of medieval defensive walls can be seen incorporated into the walls of buildings in the lower town where the five-sided tower was originally part of a tenth-century castle. The upper section of the town which has a fine view of the Apuan Alps and the Gulf of Spezia is built around two squares. The smaller, a fine-paved square with a well in the middle, is surrounded by elegant baroque buildings, while in the larger square, trees mingle with the ruins of a medieval castle.

Continue to Buonviaggio and then to avoid La Spezia take the unmetalled track to the west and drop down into Foce. Take the road towards Riomaggiore which climbs to over 2,200ft and offers spectacular views before dropping down to the coast at **Riomaggiore**. The stretch of coast between Riomaggiore and Monterosso is one of the finest stretches of coastline in Italy and would attract many more visitors than it does had not plans to build a large elevated coast road been blocked by the locals who feared that a massive influx of tourists would destroy the character of the area.

Leave the car at Riomaggiore and take the train from there to **Monterosso**. Most of this line is in tunnels so there is little to see on the way there but once there, there is no finer way of passing a day than walking back leisurely along the coastal footpath. The walk can obviously be terminated at any of the villages along the Cinque Terre and the return journey completed by train. The two extreme points of the Cinque Terre — Monterosso and Riomaggiore — have lost a little of their original character as a number of hotels have been built but the other villages have retained their traditional fishing village looks although the functions of some of the buildings have obviously changed to cater for the walkers and those arriving directly by train.

A number of side paths lead off the main footpath, several to sanctuaries which were often built above the fishing villages to protect them, and others further into the interior. Detailed maps of the area are available locally showing all these footpaths. The most important of the sanctuaries is the Madonna di Soviore which can be reached from Monterosso in about an hour and a half. The sanctuary was built in the ninth century and then modified in the thirteenth, eighteenth and nineteenth centuries. Particularly important is the magnificent ogival portal of the façade.

The most difficult section of the coastal footpath is the first, which climbs high above the sea through the vines and crosses narrow valleys on old foot-bridges before descending to the beautiful village of **Vernazza**, which as an important port of the Genoan Republic in

Trento, Dolomite town

Spectacular scenery, Veneto

The summer and winter centre of Malcésine, on Garda's eastern shore

the thirteenth century, presents a more refined appearance than the other villages.

It takes about 2 hours to reach Vernazza and the following stretch of footpath is only slightly shorter, taking over $1^1/_2$ hours before reaching **Corniglia**. Built on a promontory high above the sea the village's origins lie in farming rather than fishing and it bears more resemblance to the old inland villages than to the others on the coast. Where it differs from the inland villages is that, whereas they have undergone radical changes over the centuries, the original structure of Corniglia has survived unchanged.

Another hour brings you to the village of Manarola perched on the top and side of a spur of rock. A secondary footpath climbs to the village of Volastra (1,000ft above sea level) in about an hour, while the main one, known at this point as the Via dell' Amore (Lover's Walk), reaches Riomaggiore after another 30 minutes' walk.

To see the rest of the area return to Foce and follow the Via Aurelia northwards and then turn left at Pian di Barca towards **Pignone**. Like many medieval towns Pignone has two distinct focal points, one civil where a splendid loggia overlooks the square, and the other religious. The present church was restructured in the eighteenth century although many architectural elements of the original fourteenth-century building can still be seen. The village's origins date back to the pre-Roman period and it is known that a Christian church has stood on the site since the late Roman period.

Head north to join the Via Aurelia just west of Borghetto di Vara and then follow the main road for 8 miles to Mattarana. The Via Aurelia at this point is very hilly and fairly slow (which encourages those travelling longer distances to pay to use the motorway) but an extremely pleasant drive for the sightseer. At Mattarana a minor road leads over the hills to the right, over the Mola Pass and then joins the spectacularly beautiful Col di Velva Pass just below the sanctuary of the Madonna della Guardia. Towards the top of the pass those with labouring engines may choose to take the new tunnel through the upper part of the Velva but the old road which continues up through the chestnuts is far more interesting.

Turn left again at Torza and climb up round the many hairpin bends to the village of Tavarone then follow the road down the other side of the hill alongside the first part of the river Vara before climbing to the hamlet of **Maissana**. The parish church which dominates the hamlet is seventeenth century but most of the other buildings below it are recognisably fifteenth. The many old mills which stand alongside the road as it runs parallel to the Borsa towards Varese Ligure give an idea of what the countryside must have been like before emigration and the drift towards the coast began to take their toll.

From a population of almost 6,000, 30 years ago, **Varese Ligure** has declined to around half that number now, which is typical of many of the inland towns in Liguria. The original purpose of the town was to act as a defensive and commercial station on the route between Genoa and Parma but this function decreased during the nineteenth century when the development of the railway system greatly reduced the traffic through the town. At the centre of the town is the fourteenth-century castle formed on a high inner tower inside a round keep. Behind the castle the old centre — the Borgo Rotondo — is almost perfectly circular having a fine porticoed street running right through its centre.

Leave Varese on the road on which you entered and continue south for 4 miles before turning left at San Pietro Vara and following the road eastwards as far as Sesta Godano. Turn left at Sesta and then right along the quiet minor road which eventually drops down to **Pieve di Zignano**, seat of the *comune* of Zignano which is divided into several small hamlets. The area has been inhabited since prehistoric times and an interesting permanent historical-archaeological exhibition has been established in the local school.

After Pieve, the road descends gently through small vineyards, olive groves and chestnut woods for 4½ miles to Rocchetta di Vara. It is possible to return directly to Sarzana at this point by joining the Via Aurelia or the motorway 3 miles south of Rocchetta. A much more pleasant route, however, is to take a left turn in the town, head north-east to Suvero and Casoni and then follow the minor road round just inside the border with Tuscany, then, after passing under the motorway, run alongside the west bank of the river Magra along the same minor road before joining the Via Aurelia for the last 5 miles into Sarzana.

Further Information

— Liguria —

Airport

Genoa, 'Cristoforo Colombo'
☎ (010) 566532

Tourist Information Offices

Liguria is divided into four provinces each of which has its own provincial tourist board.

Province of Genoa
Ente Provinciale per il Turismo
Via Roma 11, Genoa
☎ (010) 581407

Province of Imperia
Ente Provinciale per il Turismo

Viale Matteotti 54 bis
Imperia ☎ (0183) 24947

Province of La Spezia
Ente Provinciale per il Turismo
Viale Mazzini 47
La Spezia ☎ (0187) 36000

Province of Savona
Ente Provinciale per il Turismo
Via Paleocapa 9
Savona ☎ (019) 20522

Museums and Other Places of Interest

This information is arranged alphabetically by town. Opening times have been given where possible.

Albenga
Museo Civico Ingauno
Palazzo Comunale
Open: 9am-12noon (winter 10am-12noon) and 3-6pm, closed Monday.

Museo Diocesano
Palazzo Vescovile
Church opening times: every day for most of the day.

Museo Navale Romano
Palazzo Peloso Cepolla
Via Cavour
Open: as above.

Albisola
Museo Archeologico
Closed Tuesday.

Centro Ligure per la Storia della Ceramica (pottery museum)
Open: 2-6pm, closed Tuesday.

Villa Faraggiana
Open: Wednesday-Monday 2-6pm.

Bordighera
Museo Bicknell
3 Via Bicknell
Open: Tuesday-Saturday 10am-12noon and 3.30-5.30pm.

Cairo-Montenotte
Centro Archeologico Culturale Valle Bormida
Porta Soprana
Closed Tuesday, opening hours variable.

Pinacoteca
Municipio
Closed Tuesday, opening hours variable.

Camogli
Acquario Tirrenico
Castel Dragone
Open: 10am-12noon and 3-7pm (winter 2-6pm).

Civico Museo Navale
Facing station
Open: Wednesday, Saturday and holidays 9am-12noon and 4-7pm (winter 3-6pm).

Campo Ligure
Museo Filigree
Textile Museum

Finale Ligure
Museo Civico
Santa Caterina Monastery
Via Nicotera
Open: Monday-Saturday 9am-12noon and 2.30-4.30pm, Sunday 9am-12noon.

Imperia
Pinacoteca
Facing the cathedral
Open: Tuesday and Thursday 3.30-6pm.

La Spezia
Arsenale
Via Domenico Chiodo
Open to public on Sunday nearest to 19 March.

Museo Tecnico Navale
Via Domenico Chiodo
Open: Tuesday, Thursday and Saturday 9am-12noon and 3-6pm.

Museo Civico Ubaldo Formentini
Via Curatone 9
Open: Tuesday-Saturday 9am-1pm and 3-7pm, Sunday 9am-1pm.

Luni
Museo Nazionale (and Excavations)
Open: Tuesday-Sunday 9am-12noon and 4-7pm (winter 2-5pm).

Ospedaletti
Pinacoteca Rambaldi
Next to church of San Sebastiano Coldirodi, $3^1/_2$ miles from centre.

Pieve di Zignano
Mostra Storico Archeologico del Zignone, Scuola Comunale
Ask for permission to visit in communal offices.

Santa Margherita
Parco Comunale di Villa Durazzo
Open: 8.30am-6.30pm.

Sassello
Museo Perranda
33 Via del Perranda
Open: Monday 9am-12noon and 2-7pm, Wednesday and Thursday pm only.

Savona
Museo Archeologico
Piazzale della Cittadella
Open: Tuesday-Sunday 10am-12noon and 3.30-6.30pm.

Taggia
Museo d'Arte
Convento di San Domenico

Toirano
Museo Preistorico del Val Varatella

Ventimiglia
Museo Archeologico
Palazzo Municipale
Closed Tuesday.

7 • Emilia-Romagna

Many of the tourists who go to Italy every year pass through Emilia-Romagna, but apart from those whose destination is Rimini only a very small percentage of them do other than just pass through. The reason for this is that the whole region is split into two by the railway and motorway which connect southern and central Italy to the north and the rest of Europe. Either side of these two routes the land is flat and monotonous, offering no incentive to the tourist to break his journey. This is a pity because the region has a great deal to offer anyone who does stop to see it.

Much of the region's coastline has been heavily commercialised in recent years and should be avoided at all costs especially in summer, but the northern section near the Valli di Comacchio and the Po delta are much less frequented, being of particular interest to the naturalist. The rest of the region to the north-east of the motorway and for 5 or 6 miles to the south-west of it, is interesting for the historic towns which are situated there, and which, apart from Bologna with its international airport, can all be visited without meeting hordes of other tourists at any time of the year.

While the northern border of the region is formed by the Po and the eastern by the Adriatic, the south and west are limited by the crest of the Apennines which, with their foothills, constitute over a third of the region's 8,550sq miles. Most of the crest is around 3,500ft high but a few of the peaks are as high as 6,000ft. Over the centuries the oak, beech and fir trees which once covered all the Apennine slopes have been partially cleared for cultivation and from a distance this gives the mountainsides the appearance of a large, uneven chess board. Wolves and golden eagles are occasionally seen in some parts of the mountains but these are becoming rarer with every year that passes.

Despite its fairly extensive coastline, Emilia-Romagna has a predominantly continental climate with extremes of cold and heat in summer and winter. This means that the best time to visit the cities on the plain is in late spring and early autumn while the higher altitude and the north-eastern aspect of many of the mountains reduces the temperature enough to make them pleasant even in summer. In winter the plain is often covered for days on end by thick fog while in the mountains snowfalls are often heavy and long-lasting, which has led to the development of many fine ski-resorts. The Appennino Bolognese is also the site of several spa resorts of various sizes.

The region is rich in artistic treasures; Rimini has important Roman monuments; Ravenna is without doubt the most important testimony to Byzantine civilisation in Europe, and Bologna, after the classical Florentine influences of the Renaissance, became the most important artistic centre in Italy in the late sixteenth and early seventeenth centuries with the school of the Carracci and Guido Reno.

Last but not least, the region is famous for its food and wine. Spaghetti Bolognese is famous throughout the world but the visitor should be sure to sample the tortellini and the ravioli which are the true specialities of the region. The most important local wine is Lambrusco which at its best is excellent, but steer clear of the cheaper mass-produced brands which are of very poor quality.

Excursions from Bologna

Situated as it is at the centre of Italy's communications network, **Bologna** is an ideal base for the visitor wishing to see the south of the region and the coast. Modena, Reggio, Parma and Piacenza can also be easily reached either by car or train but these will be dealt with later as the starting points for trips into the Apennines.

Bologna itself is often quite busy as many tourists decide to spend a day or half a day there between trains or between plane and train. The larger museums however, tend to be much less crowded than similar museums in Florence and Rome, while the churches and monuments outside the centre are usually neglected despite being marked on the free map of the city available at tourist information centres.

A visit to the coast should begin with a visit to the city of **Ferrara** or Ravenna, to the north and south of the Valli di Comacchio respectively.

The focal point in Ferrara is its magnificent castle. The oldest part of the castle is a defensive tower which was built in 1385 after a popular uprising and later connected to the nearby ducal palace by a covered walkway (no longer in existence). The original battlements

Walking in the Modenese Alps

were replaced in the 1570s by the white marble balustrades which give the castle the appearance of a villa.

Near to the castle is the fine medieval cathedral with a particularly noteworthy façade with its twelfth-century sculptures depicting scenes from the life of Christ. Many of the finer sculptures and paintings which formerly embellished the interior of the cathedral have been moved to the ex-church of San Romano, dating from the tenth century and restored to house the Museo dell' Opera del Duomo.

The civic museum is housed in the first great Renaissance building to be erected in Ferrara, Palazzo Schifanoia. The palace was used by the various dukes to hold receptions and banquets and was decorated accordingly. More important than any of the many fine exhibits are the frescoes decorating the Salone dei Mesi where three tiers of frescoes are based on the theme of the months of the year. The lowest series illustrates events at the ducal court, the middle series shows the influence of the signs of the zodiac on the months, while the upper series represents the triumphs of the pagan gods who presided over each of the months.

Other Ferrarese *palazzi* which may be visited are the fifteenth-century Casa Romei, a composition of medieval and Renaissance styles; Palazzo di Ludovico il Moro with its majestic courtyard, the site of the archaeological museum; and Palazzo dei Diamanti which takes its name from the 12,000 diamond-shaped blocks of marble which decorate the façade and one of the sides, the site of the art gallery, the Boldini museum (dedicated to the Ferrarese painter Giovanni Boldini) and the civic gallery of modern art.

The house of Ferrara's most famous writer, Ludovico Ariosto has been restored to its early sixteenth-century state and serves both as a museum and a library.

The city was once enclosed by one of the most impressive city walls in Europe, and although a long stretch of the southern section was demolished in the 1930s there are still over 5 miles of wall still in existence. Walking round the walls allows the visitor to see the various stages in the development of the town's defences, from simple medieval earthworks to the mainly decorative seventeenth-century additions when Ferrara belonged to the papal states.

The **Valli di Comacchio** have only been in existence since the late medieval period when the area around the Po delta (now further north) subsided, creating a series of marshy valleys. The area was then used as a vast hunting and fishing area by the Dukes of Ferrara and their successors until parts of the area were drained in the 1950s to allow agricultural expansion. Much of the area has been made into a national park where a vast number of birds can be seen in their natural habitats. Since the area was drained several roads have been built across the area, opening it up to a wider public, but the best way of seeing the area is by boat. Boat trips begin from several of the towns in the Valli — in general the smaller the boat the closer to nature the trip will be.

At the seaward end of the Valli is the town of **Comacchio** which, for centuries, was isolated from other towns in the area by lagoons and marshland. The town is built on thirteen separate islands divided by canals and connected by a series of bridges, the most important of which, Trepponti, consists of five arches surmounted by two towers and connects several islands. Near Comacchio are the remains of the Etrusco-Roman town of Spina which was found during the drainage programmes of the 1950s. The small towns on the coast around Comacchio were once pleasant fishing villages, but with the improved access of recent years they tend to be filled with bathers in good weather. A little further to the north however, is the magnificent abbey of **Pomposa**. The abbey consists of three important nuclei: the Byzantine-Romanesque church constructed between the eighth and the eleventh centuries with its 156ft bell tower; the monastery, rebuilt in the fourteenth century, which contains impor-

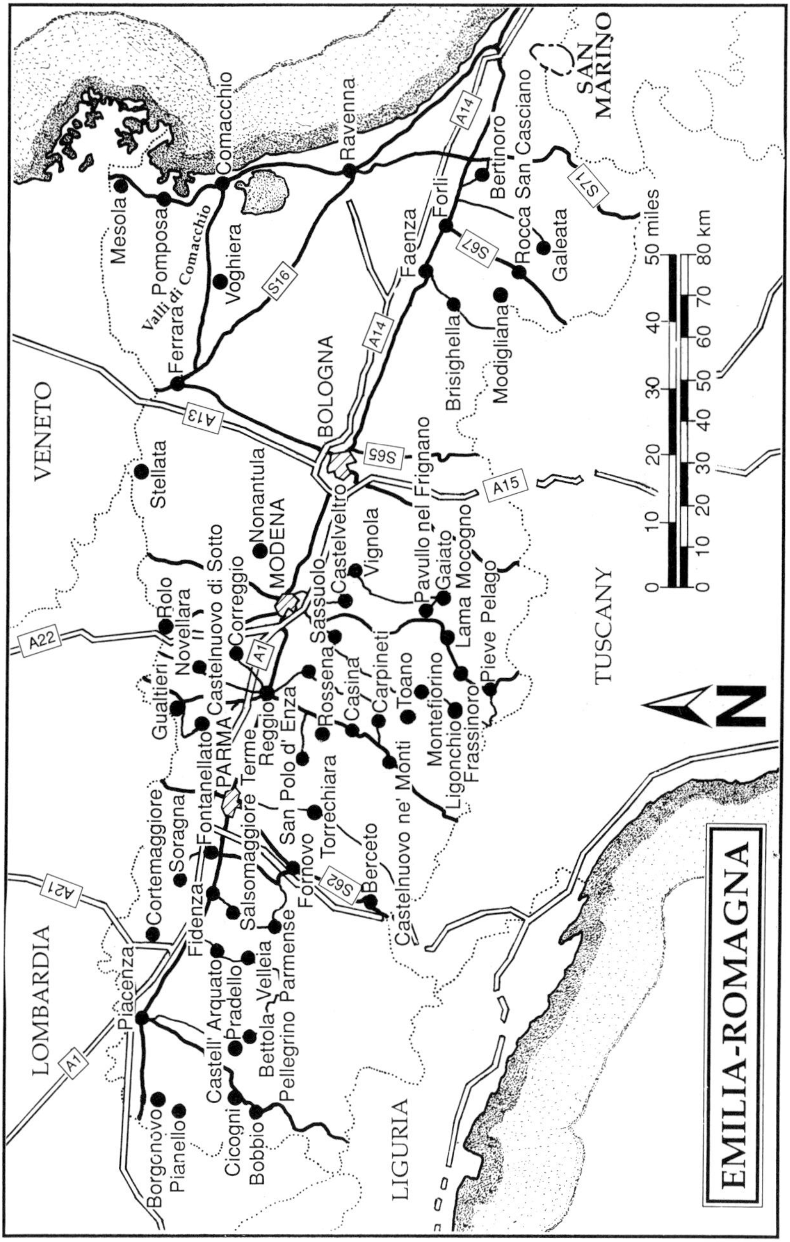

tant frescoes; and the eleventh-century Palace of Reason where the abbot who controlled most of the surrounding area meted out justice to wrongdoers.

Seven miles north of Pomposa, on the same road, is the late sixteenth-century Castello di Mesola built by the Dukes of Ferrara as a hunting and fishing lodge. From a distance the castle seems an impregnable fortress, but near to, the size of the windows reveals that its original function was pacific.

Another Ferrarese castle on the Po is to be found at **Stellata**, 17 miles north-west of Ferrara, built in the form of a star. The castle is not always visitable as its ground floor is often flooded by the Po.

Ten miles south-east of Ferrara are the remains of Belriguardo, the ducal residence at **Voghiera**, begun in 1435 and added to by each successive duke, which was once known as the Versailles of the Estensi. During the first 700 years AD Voghiera was the most important town in the area and the remains of the Roman town are being progressively excavated.

A visit to **Ravenna** is a must while based in Bologna, if only to see the magnificent Byzantine mosaics which decorate most of its churches. The finest examples are to be found in the sixth-century basilica of San Vitale, where the mosaics relate the whole story of the Bible, and in the basilica of **Sant' Apollinare in Classe** 3 miles south of the city which is much less frequented by tourists.

From Ravenna take the SS67 to **Forli** where the most important monuments are all to be found around Piazza Saffi. The cathedral with its twelfth-century bell tower, the fourteenth-century Palazzo del Municipio with its interesting frescoes, and the fifteenth-century Palazzo del Podesta, the façade of which bears the coats of arms of the successive governors, all deserve a visit.

Leave Forli on the SS9 before turning right after 5 miles in Forimpopolo. The next town of interest is **Bertinoro**, a walled medieval town on the side of a steep hill with views of the sea and of San Marino. The defensive walls, restored by Alessandro Borgia, are still standing. A $2^1/_2$-mile walk into the hills brings you to the Chiesa di Polenta and the ruins of the tenth-century castle.

The fine views enjoyed from Bertinoro continue along the following stretch of road until reaching the SS71 where the signs for Florence should be followed. The road rises up into the Apennines at first gently, passing through Sarsina with its Romanesque cathedral and small archaeological museum. After Sarsina the road passes alongside Lago di Quarto before reaching San Piero in Bagno where the visitor should turn right to go over the steep Carnaio Pass to reach **Galeata**, an interesting old town overlooked by the church of Sant' Ellero, built in the fifth century and restored in the seventeenth.

After Galeata the road continues with steep rises and descents to

Rocca San Casciano where footpaths lead to the tops of the Montebello ($2^1/_2$ hours) and Marzanella (2 hours) mountains. Follow the main road for $4^1/_2$ miles towards Forli, then turn left for **Modigliana** from where the hardier visitors may wish to make the 4-hour ascent of Monte Sacco with its ruined fortress. A small road leads from Modigliana to **Brisighella** where the fortress overlooking the town houses a rustic museum. Seven miles north-west the road rejoins the main road for Bologna at **Faenza**, where as well as the main medieval monuments in Piazza del Popolo, the ceramics museum is of great importance housing collections from all over the world.

Excursions from Modena

The city of **Modena** became the seat of the Dukes of Este after they were forced out of Ferrara by the pope at the end of the sixteenth century and many of the city's monuments are worthy of its former status as a capital. A tour of the city should begin in the magnificent eleventh-century cathedral where all the majestic severity of the Romanesque at its best is in evidence. Of particular note is the crypt where the group of five, near life-size terracotta sculptures dates from 1480. The three naves of the crypt are supported by sixty marble columns.

In the outer wall of the apse which backs onto Piazza Grande, the old Modenese measures are still fixed where they were placed centuries ago to ensure the honesty of the market traders who plied their wares there. Not far from Piazza Grande is the massive ducal palace (1634) which, as it houses a military academy, is only visible from the outside and from the courtyard.

A large building built in the first half of the eighteenth century to house the city's poor was adapted a century later to become the 'Palace of the Museums', where most of the city's historic and artistic treasures are housed. Of particular interest is the permanent bibliographical exhibition in one of the rooms of the library (opened on request, free of charge).

The Romanesque church most closely comparable to Modena cathedral is the abbey of **Nonantula** 6 miles east of the city. Most of the present building dates from the twelfth century when the bulk of the original eighth-century abbey was destroyed by an earthquake. The crypt however, was originally part of the older construction and its sixty-four marble pillars were probably the inspiration for the crypt of the cathedral.

From Modena take the SS623 along the Panaro valley as far as

Vignola where the well preserved early fifteenth-century castle may be visited free of charge. All parts of the castle are visitable, including the four towers and the dungeon where the poet Ugo Foscolo was kept prisoner.

The remains of the castle at nearby **Castelveltro** deserve a quick look before joining the SS12 at Maranello and beginning the long southwards ascent of the Apennines towards the mountain resorts of the Appennino Modenese. The first reasonably sized town is **Pavullo nel Frignano** from where a number of shorter excursions can be made. The medieval village of **Montecuccolo**, grouped around an impressive castle, is almost 3,000ft above sea level, 3 miles south-west of the town, while the ruins of the castle of **Gaiato** to the south-east is 100ft higher. To reach the castle, pass through the village of Gaiato then when the road begins to descend take the first (unmarked) track to the right for 200yd then make the rest of the ascent on foot. A magnificent view of the confluence of the Dardagnola, Leo and Scoltenna rivers can be seen to the south-east (the sun is only in the right position for photography from mid-afternoon onwards). Ten miles to the west of Pavullo along a narrow road are the remains of the medieval village of Brandola and nearby the 'Bridge of Hercules', a natural rock formation 100ft long and 10ft wide which spans a tributary of the river Rossenna.

Eleven miles beyond Pavullo, dominated by Monte Cimone (7,102ft) is **Lama Mocogno**, the starting point for excursions to several of the ski-slopes in the area. While the slopes are usually very crowded at weekends, during the week they are usually almost deserted even though all the facilities are open. Fifteen miles later the road reaches **Pieve Pelago**, a pleasant town which is the starting point for several interesting excursions. To the east, a footpath leads through the woods up to the top of Monte Cimone (5 hours), while a minor road climbs the 2,350ft to Lago Santo (7 miles) from where footpaths lead to the tops of Monte Giovo, Monte Rondinaio, the Alpe delle Tre Potenze and the Foce a Giovo.

Four miles beyond Pieve Pelago on the way up to Abetone (the mountain resort on the border of Emilia-Romagna and Tuscany) is the hotel-restaurant La Dogana where simple but excellent meals can be enjoyed at very reasonable prices.

Those wishing to return to Modena by an alternative route should take the road for Foce delle Radici until the junction with the SS486. Of interest along this route are **Frassinoro** with its fifteenth-century parish church built over the ruins of a tenth-century Benedictine monastery, **Montefiorino**, with its restored thirteenth-century castle and its magnificent viewpoints, and finally after passing through much fine scenery, **Sassuolo**, an important ceramics centre where all the products of the Italian ceramics industry are displayed in a permanent exhibition.

Excursions from Reggio

A visit to **Reggio nell' Emilia** can be confined to the area immediately surrounding Piazza San Prospero at the centre of the city, as much of the rest of the city was rebuilt after damage suffered in the war. The *Duomo* is basically of thirteenth-century Romanesque construction which has undergone several radical changes through the course of the centuries. The white marble which adorns the façade was added in the early sixteenth century as was the tripartite apse.

Despite its eighteenth-century neo-classical façade, Palazzo del Municipio is an early fifteenth-century building. It was here in 1797 that the representatives of the Emilian cities which formed the Cispadana Republic adopted the red, white and green flag which eventually became the flag of Italy. On the other side of the *Duomo*, the Palazzo del Capitano del Popolo was restored in the 1920s to its original thirteenth-century form. The building now houses the tourist information centre for the province of Reggio.

The church of San Prospero is one of the finest in Reggio. Originally built in the eleventh century, the façade was added in the eighteenth century, while the unfinished octagonal bell tower dates from the first half of the sixteenth century. Of particular interest are the magnificent wooden choir stalls and the six white marble lions in front of the church.

Yet another eighteenth-century façade on an older building around the central square is that of the church of San Domenico. The interior of this twelfth-century church is formed of a single nave surmounted by two domes and contains some interesting medieval carvings. Of the museums in Reggio, perhaps the most interesting is the Museo del Tricolore, which contains exhibits showing the important part the city played in the Risorgimento movement for the liberation of the Italian states and for a unified Italy in the eighteenth and nineteenth centuries.

To visit some of the towns around Reggio on the plain, leave the city on the SS468 to **Correggio** where the fine early sixteenth-century Palazzo dei Principi is well worth a visit. Part of the *palazzo*, which has wooden ceilings throughout, has been turned into a museum exhibiting a series of Flemish tapestries and Mantegna's *Head of Christ*. Ten miles north of Correggio is **Rolo** where many old craft skills, especially woodcarving, are kept alive today by initiatives promoted by the Institute of Peasant Civilisation. From Rolo go south-east to **Novellara** where the sixteenth-century castle contains two museums — one dedicated to local traditions and artefacts while the other, the Gonzaga museum, contains more usual museum pieces.

Gualtiera, 8 miles to the north-west on the banks of the Po, has a fine central square, dominated by the Comunale Tower. Three sides of the square are occupied by porticoed buildings while the fourth is occupied by the remaining wing of the sixteenth-century terracotta Palazzo Bentivoglio. Several of the rooms of the *palazzo* contain important frescoes. Ten miles to the south is **Castelnuovo di Sotto** with its tenth-century castle which was adapted in the seventeenth century to become an elegant country residence. Campeggine, 3 miles from Castelnuovo, was one of the first centres of organised resistance to fascism in the region and the house of the seven Cervi brothers, executed by the Germans in 1943, has been turned into a small museum of the Resistance.

In the foothills of the Apennines to the south of Reggio, many medieval castles in various states of conservation dominate the hilltops. To visit a representative selection of these, take the road from Reggio to Montecchio where much of the medieval castle remains, although parts of it are hidden by later buildings at its base. The castle of **San Polo d'Enza** is again virtually intact although it was demilitarised in the eighteenth century to house the offices of the civic administration. The nearby gate in the town wall was originally the site of the drawbridge.

From San Polo take the road to **Ciano d'Enza** and there begin the winding ascent to the castles of **Rossena** and **Canossa**. The nucleus of the castle of Rossena was built in the tenth century by the Counts of Canossa to defend the western approach to Canossa itself and the castle was gradually amplified to deal with improved weaponry. The northern side of the castle is protected naturally by an almost sheer cliff-face while a series of concentric defensive walls defend the more accessible southern side. The castle is now privately owned and is open to visitors. Not much remains of the nearby castle of Canossa as the outcrop on which it was built proved to be prone to landslides which eventually carried away most of the outer defensive walls. What remains of the castle has been turned into a museum where material relating to its history is on display.

From the road which descends from Canossa to the town of **Quattro Castella**, four conical hills can clearly be seen to the left. On the tops of these hills the Canossa family erected four forts to defend the northern approaches. Three of these were destroyed during the medieval period and only a few suggestive ruins remain, while the fourth, Bianello, was converted to an elegant country residence. Although the main body of the castle has been greatly changed, the system of defensive walls which surround it are virtually intact, allowing the visitor to study the principles of medieval military science which governed their construction.

Other castles in the territory of Reggio can best be visited while on the road leading up to the Appennino Reggiano. Leave Reggio on the SS467 to **Scandiano** where the fine castle dates from 1262, although some alterations were carried out in the sixteenth century. The part of the town around the castle also dates from the late medieval period. From Scandiano head for the village of **Viano** where the ruins of the old castle can be seen half an hour's walk to the west near the medieval hamlet of Castello Querciola. After passing through Baiso, where the bulk of the castle is the result of an imaginative early twentieth-century restoration, the road reaches **Carpineti**, the starting point for several interesting walks. One of the shortest of these brings you in 40 minutes to the ruins of the castle where in 1092, Countess Matilda of Canossa instigated the war against the emperor. The path to the summit of Monte Valestra (80 minutes) passes near to the entrances of two large grottos with stalactites and stalagmites.

The church of **Toano**, 12 miles to the south, is one of the most interesting in the area. The twelfth-century pillars are decorated with carvings of stories from the Old Testament while the lower part of the bell tower was once part of a tenth-century castle. Take the road which passes through Villa Minozzo (handily placed for the ski-runs of Civago and Febbio) until reaching **Ligonchio**, the highest *comune* in the Apennines at over 3,100ft. In summer it is possible to begin many long walks here, while in winter it is ideally placed for the ski-slopes of Ospitaletto.

Returning towards Reggio on the SS63, one of the first villages to be encountered is Ceravezza where in summer a large camp-site is open. **Castelnuovo ne' Monti** is situated at the foot of three hills, on top of one of which are the ruins of the castle which gives the town its name. The oldest part of the town is at the foot of this hill. Three miles south-east of the town is the Pietra di Bismantova, a flat-topped hill with mainly vertical sides. The hill is much frequented by rock-climbers now, while archaeological excavations have shown that from prehistoric to early medieval times the hill was prized for its defensive possibilities.

Going towards Reggio the road passes the remaining cylindrical tower of the castle of Felina before reaching **Casina**, another starting point for walkers. The remains of the castle of Sarzana lie 2 miles north-west, the castle of Leguigno 4 miles to the west, while the tenth-century Romanesque church of Beleo and the medieval hamlet of Vercalli are also easily reached on foot. The main road continues back to Reggio.

Excursions from Parma

The city of **Parma** has two distinct medieval centres. The older of the two is the area around the cathedral which was developed in the tenth and eleventh centuries, outside the original city walls when the feudal bishops were at the height of their influence. The cathedral was built to resemble the smaller churches to be found alongside routes used by pilgrims, and the influence of Norman church architecture can also be clearly seen. Inside, the most famous of the many works of art is Correggio's *Assunzione della Vergine* under the dome. The irregular octagonal red marble baptistry is notable for the many fine bas-reliefs and frescoes with which it is decorated. More important frescoes by Correggio can be seen in the church of San Giovanni Evangelista, immediately behind the cathedral. The church was originally part of the adjacent Benedictine monastery where the historic pharmacy (*farmacia*) dating from the ninth century is open to the public.

The second important medieval centre is Piazza Garibaldi, the centre of lay power in the city which is built over the old Roman forum. Like *Piazza Duomo* most of the buildings here were fortified during the medieval period. Now only the rebuilt Palazzo del Municipio in the south-eastern corner of the square, and the adjacent thirteenth-century Palazzo del Capitano del Popolo still sport their original battlements. Palazzo del Governatore which dominates the square was given a face-lift in the eighteenth century which changed its medieval aspect into a neo-classical one.

Just to the north of Piazza Garibaldi is the massive Palazzo del Pilotta begun in the sixteenth century by the Farnese family as a demonstration of their influence in the duchy of Parma. The palace, which was never completed and which was damaged during World War II, is probably the ugliest monumental building ever built in Europe, although its great size makes it an ideal home for most of

Parma's museums.

At the southern end of the city, the large sixteenth-century fortress, of which the outer defensive structures are still intact, now contains a camp-site and Parma's public gardens.

Parma's Palazzo Ducale cannot be visited as it belongs to the armed forces, but two other fine ducal residences can be seen at **Fontanellato** and **Soragna** (12 and 16 miles north of the city). Both of the palaces were medieval castles before being transformed in the sixteenth century.

From Parma take the main road north-east to **Fidenza**, passing by the well preserved Castelguelfo with its frescoed interiors. Fidenza is worth visiting for its fine cathedral, begun in the Romanesque style in the twelfth century and completed in the Gothic in the thirteenth. Among the sculptures on the façade is a statue of St Simon pointing out the road to Rome. Five miles south of Fidenza on the SS359 is the spa town of **Salsomaggiore Terme**, 4 miles to the east of which is the twelfth-century castle of Bargone surrounded by its park. To the south of Salsomaggiore the road passes by the remains of the castles of Contignaco and Gallinella before reaching **Pellegrino Parmense**, where a walk up the wooded hillside to the ruins of the twelfth-century castle is only one of several interesting walks which can begin there.

An even better starting point for walkers (equipped with a detailed local map) is **Bardi**, 21 miles south-east of Pellegrino along a road which gradually rises through magnificent scenery. In the parish church, the first known painting by Parmigianino can be seen. Dominating the town is one of the best preserved eleventh-century castles in the region. From Bardi, take the road to the east which follows the river Ceno down the mountains until it runs into the river Taro at **Fornovo**. To the left of the road can be seen the two rustic towers which are all that remain of the once imposing castle of Varsi, and the well preserved privately owned eleventh-century castle of Varano de' Melegari.

From Fornovo take the SS62 south to **Berceto**, a quiet town just before the border with Tuscany. The town has an attractive cathedral and in summer is an ideal starting point for ascents of the Marino, Cervellino, Montagnara, Cavalcalupo, Borgognone, Polo, Binaghe and Cavallo mountains. A small unmetalled road leads eastwards from the town between the peaks of Monte Borgognone and Monte Polo before reaching a main road which leads back to Parma. The road follows the course of the river Parma down a pleasant valley, eventually passing by the magnificent fifteenth-century castle and village of **Torrechiara**. Of particular interest are the frescoes in the 'Golden Bedroom' which relate the story of Bianca Pellegrini d'Arluno who visited all the castles in the area trying to find her missing lover.

Excursions from Piacenza

The monumental centre of **Piacenza**, northernmost of the Emilia-Romagnan cities, is the beautiful Piazza Cavalli, which takes its name from the early seventeenth-century equestrian statues of Alessandro and Ranuccio Farnese (*cavallo* meaning horse). Dominating the square is one of the most important examples of civic medieval architecture, the late thirteenth-century Gothic palace. The lower part of the building consists of a long porch onto which five arches open out. The upper section has six evenly spaced windows on the façade, surmounted by battlements and three small towers.

On the façade of the eighteenth-century Palazzo del Governatore, facing the Gothic palace, is a solar calendar where the shadow made by the sun at mid-day indicates the day and month of the year. The other main building in the square, the church of San Francesco, dates from the end of the thirteenth century.

Three hundred yards north-east of Piazza Cavalli, the civic museum is housed in the magnificent Palazzo Farnese. The palace, begun in the sixteenth century, was never completed and on one side links up with the remains of a fortress which was to have been demolished to make space for the palace. Piacenza's cathedral, which dates from the twelfth century, contains some fine works of art and is unusual in having the form of an irregular cross. In the rear wall of the bell tower is an iron cage, placed there by Ludovico il Moro in the fifteenth century as a prison for blasphemers. Other churches worth a visit are Sant' Antonino, Santa Brigida and the Madonna di Campagna, one of the finest examples of Italian Renaissance.

Most of the province of Piacenza is occupied by the Apennines and their foothills to the south of the city. To gain a fairly comprehensive understanding of the area, leave the city to the west on the SS10 and take the first turning to **Borgonovo**, a busy small town with a fine fifteenth-century Gothic church. The hexagonal castle in the nearby village of **Montalbo** is also worth visiting. From **Pianello**, 6 miles to the south, an interesting 2-hour walk through interesting scenery leads to the isolated tenth-century castle of Olgisio, the oldest in the area. Halfway down the 150ft-deep well in the courtyard is a secret chamber, once used as a hiding place in times of danger. The first part

Torrechiara castle

of the route to the castle is just suitable for motor vehicles and the scenery around the track make it an interesting alternative to the normal road for the next stage of the excursion as far as Pecorara.

Continuing southwards the road passes through the village of **Cicogni** from where it is possible to climb the slopes of Monte Pietra di Corvo to an alpine garden. **Bobbio** is another 12 miles to the south-west along the Trebbia valley. The town, which is dominated by a fine fifteenth-century castle, grew up around a seventh-century monastery founded by the Irish monk St Columbus. The remains of the abbey now house the St Columbus museum while the church, which was rebuilt in the Renaissance period, contains fragments of the original seventh-century mosaic pavement in the crypt. Bobbio is also a small spa centre and the centre for many walks into the surrounding hills and mountains. Nearby Monte Penice is well equipped with skiing facilities and is not very busy on weekdays.

From Bobbio return up the valley as far as Perino and then take the right turn for Bettola, and from there to nearby **Pradello** and the small museum in the birthplace of Christopher Columbus. From Bettola take the road signposted 'Morfasso' for 7 miles until a left turn takes you northwards along the eastern side of Mont' Obolo. The road climbs steeply until Groppo-Visdomo then drops down through Croviano to ***Velleia***. The Roman city of *Velleia* was lost until 1747 when the first excavations to be carried out in the area brought to light the forum, the basilica and several other buildings. More excavations have been carried on regularly ever since revealing most of the town and its necropolis. An on-site museum houses the works of art which have been found in the town. Only *Pompei* and *Herculaneum* can offer a more comprehensive view of what a Roman town was really like than *Velleia* which seems to have been abandoned at the beginning of the fourth century BC.

Twelve miles to the north-east is another of the most typical towns in the province of Piacenza, **Castell' Arquato**. The lower part of the town is modern, but the hillside site of the original settlement is still typically medieval in appearance. The most evocative sight is of the central square dominated by the apse of the magnificently austere Romanesque basilica, the thirteenth-century fortified Palazzo del Podestà with its pentagonal tower rising above the battlements, and the outer walls and fortifications of the fourteenth-century castle which was the base for a succession of great Renaissance *condottieri*.

Fourteen miles to the north is **Cortemaggiore**, where the churches of Santa Maria delle Grazie and the Franciscan church in the old fifteenth-century centre, both deserve to be visited before returning to Piacenza.

Further Information

— Emilia-Romagna —

Airports

Bologna, 'G. Marconi'
☎ (051) 311578

Rimini
☎ (0541) 33132

Tourist Information Offices

Emilia-Romagna is divided into eight provinces, each of which has its own tourist board.

Province of Bologna
Azienda di Promozione Turistica
Via Leopardi 1E
Bologna
☎ (051) 236602

Province of Ferrara
Azienda di Promozione Turistica
28 Largo Castello
Ferrara
☎ (0532) 35017

Province of Forli
Azienda di Promozione Turistica
Corso della Repubblica 23
Forli
☎ (0543) 25545

Province of Modena
Azienda di Promozione Turistica
Corso Canalgrande 1A
Modena
☎ (059) 222482

Province of Parma
Azienda di Promozione Turistica
5 Piazza Duomo
Parma
☎ (0521) 34735

Province of Piacenza
Azienda di Promozione Turistica
Piazzetta dei Mercanti 10
☎ (0523) 29324

Province of Ravenna
Azienda di Promozione Turistica
Piazza San Francesco 7
Ravenna
☎ (0544) 36129

Province of Reggio-Emilia
Azienda di Promozione Turistica
1 Piazza Battisti
Reggio-Emilia
☎ (0522) 35744

Museums and Other Places of Interest

This information is arranged alphabetically by town. Where museum opening times are not given, assume that they are open mornings from Monday to Saturday.

Albinea
Birthplace of the poet Vicenzo Monti — small museum.

Argenta
Civic Gallery
Church of San Domenico
Via G.B. Aleotti

Bazzano
Civic Museum in the castle.

Bedonia
Art Gallery & Archaeological Museum
Seminary
Colle San Marco

Bobbio
St Columbus Museum
Piazza Santa Fara

Brescello
Archaeological Museum
Municipio
Via Cavallotti
☎ (0522) 687562
Open: Monday-Saturday by appointment.

Brisighella
Museo Civico della Val Lamone
Municipio
Piazza Marconi

Busseto
Civic Museum
Villa Pallavicino
Corso Pallavicino

Verdi's Birthplace
Same entrance ticket as for museum.

Villa Verdi di Sant' Agata
$2^1/_2$ miles from town
Verdi's country villa
Open: May-October 9am-12noon and 3-7pm.

Canossa
Castle
Open: Tuesday-Sunday am and pm.

Carpi
Civic Museum
Castello dei Pio

Monument Museum to those deported for political or racial reasons
Piazza dei Martiri

Castell' Arquato
Geological Museum
Torrione Farnesiano
Open: Tuesday-Saturday 9am-12noon and 2-6pm.

Museo della Collegiata
In front of the basilica

Cento
G. Borgatti Operatic Museum
Teatro Comunale
Corso del Guercino

Civic Art Gallery
16-18 Corso Matteotti
Open: Sunday 10am-1pm (on weekdays ask for permission in Municipio).

Cesena
Biblioteca Malatestiana
Open: mornings Tuesday-Saturday.

Museo Storico dell' Antichità

Colorno
Ducal Palace
☎ (0521) 815418
Arrange visit.

Correggio
Palazzo dei Principi
Corso Cavour 7

Faenza
Museo delle Ceramiche
Via Campidori 2
Open: Monday-Sunday 9am-1pm and Monday-Saturday 3-5.30pm.

Civic Museum and Art Gallery
Via Santa Maria dell' Angelo 1
Open: Monday-Sunday 9.30am-12.30pm and Monday-Friday 2.30-4.30pm.

Modern Art Gallery
Corso Matteotti
Open: Tuesday-Sunday 9.30am-12.30pm.

Ferrara
Casa dell' Ariosto
Via Ariosto
Closed Monday and Sunday pm.

Casa Romei
Via Savonarola 30
Closed Sunday pm.

Castello Estense
Open: June-September 8.30am-12noon and 2-5pm; October-May 8.30am-12.30pm and 2-5pm; Sunday 9am-1pm; closed Mondays.

Civica Galleria d'Arte Moderna
Corso Ercole I d'Este 21
Open: 10am-1pm and 3-7pm.

Museo di Storia Naturale
Via Filippo de Pisis 24
Open: 10am-1pm first and third Sundays of month. Closed in summer.

Museo Archeologico di Spina
Via XX Settembre 124
Open: May-September 9.30am-1pm and 3-6pm; October-April 9.30am-4pm; Sundays 9.30am-1.30pm; Tuesday closed.

Museo Boldini
Corso Ercole I d'Este 21
Open: 9.30am-12.30pm and 2-5pm; Sundays 9.30am-1pm; Monday closed.

Museo del Duomo
Open: 10am-12noon and 3-5pm; Sundays 10am-12noon.

Museo del Risorgimento e della Resistenza
Corso Ercole I d'Este 19
Open: Tuesday-Saturday 8.30am-12.30pm and 3-5pm; Sunday 8.30am-12.30pm; Monday closed.

Palazzina di Marfisa
Corso della Giovecca 174
Closed Sunday afternoon and Monday.

Pinacoteca Nazionale
Corso Ercole I d'Este 21
Closed Sunday afternoon and Monday.

Fidenza
Museo del Risorgimento
Piazza Garibaldi 25

Fontanellato
Castle
Closed on Mondays.

Forlí
Museo Archeologico
Corso della Republica 72
Open: October-July; closed Saturday and Sunday afternoons; August-September closed every afternoon.

Museo Etnografico Romagnolo
Corso Garibaldi 96 & Corso della Repubblica 72
Open: as above.

Museo del Risorgimento
Corso Garibaldi 96
Open: as above.

Pinacoteca Comunale
Corso della Repubblica 72
Open: as above.

Forlimpopoli
Civic Museum
Castle
Piazza Garibaldi

Gattatico
Cervi Museum
Via Fratelli Cervi 11
Closed Monday.

Gualtieri
Palazzo Bentivoglio
Open: all afternoons and Wednesday, Saturday and Sunday mornings.

Guastalla
Library Museum
Via Garibaldi 54
☎ (0522) 826294
Open: by appointment.

Imola
Museo Comunale
Via Emilia 80
Gallery, archives and library.
Opened on request.

Armaments Museum
Castle
Piazzale Giovanni delle Bande Nere

Museo Diocesano
Palazzo Vescovile
Piazza del Duomo

Langhirano
Museo Risorgimentale
Palazzo Municipale
Open: Monday 8.30am-12.30pm and 2.30-6.30pm; Tuesday-Friday afternoons only.

Lido di Spina
Museo Alternativo Remo Brindisi

Lugo
Small museum in Municipio

Mesola
Castle

Modena
Civic Museum
Galleria Camporia, Galleria Estense, Museo Lapidario, Biblioteca Estense
Palazzo dei Musei, Largo Porta Sant' Agostino
Closed Saturday pm, Sunday and Tuesday.

Museo del Risorgimento
Palazzo dei Musei
Open: as above except closed in summer Wednesday, Thursday and Saturday pm.

Museo Lapidario del Duomo
Via Lanfranco 6
Open: every day.

Museo Muratoriano
Via Pomposa 1
Open: 9am-12noon (ask caretaker of Santa Maria Pomposa church).

Montecchio
Villa Aiola
Strada Monte Grappa
☎ (0522) 871132
Open: by appointment.

Montechiarugolo
Castle
☎ (0521) 659343
Open: by appointment.

Novellara
Museo Gonzaga
Piazza Marconi 1
Open: first and last Sunday of month. Closed August, November and December.

Museo della Civiltà Contadina
Piazza Marconi
Open: as above.

Parma
Baptistry
Piazza Duomo
Closed on Mondays.

Historic Pharmacy of San Giovanni
Borgo Pipa

Stuard Art Gallery
Via Cavestro 14
Open: Monday-Friday 8.30am-12noon; Monday and Thursday 3-5pm.

Museum of Natural History
Via Università 12
Open: Tuesday, Wednesday, Thursday and Saturday 3-5pm.

Glauco Lombardi Museum
Via Garibaldi 15
Open: Tuesday-Sunday; Sunday am only.

Museo Archeologico
Palazzo Pilotta
Open: mornings Tuesday-Sunday.

Museo Bodoniano and Biblioteca Palatina
Palazzo Pilotta
Open: as above.

Art Gallery
Palazzo Pilotta
Open: as above except Sunday 9am-7.30pm.

Camera di San Paolo
Via M. Melloni

Chinese Art Museum
Via San Martino 8
Open: Wednesday-Sunday 3-6pm.

Ethnographical Museum
Via San Martino 8
Open: as above.

Botanical Gardens
Via Farini 70
Open: April-October Monday-Friday 9am-12noon and 4-6pm.

Piacenza
Galleria Alberoni
Via Emilia Parmense 77
Apply to custodian for entry.

Galleria d'Arte Moderna Ricci-Oddi
Via San Siro 13

Museo Civico
Palazzo Farnese
Piazza Cittadella

Museo del Teatro Municipale
Via G. Verdi 41
Apply to custodian.

Museo del Risorgimento
Via Sopramuro 60
Apply to custodian.

Pieve di Cento
Civic Art Gallery
Palazzo Comunale
Piazza Costa
Apply to custodian.

Ravenna
Museo Nazionale di Ravenna
Via San Vitale 17

Open: summer Tuesday-Saturday 9am-12noon and 2-5pm, winter 9am-2pm; Sunday 9am-12noon (all year).

Galleria dell' Accademia
Via di Roma
Closed Sunday pm.

Mausoleo di Gallia Placidia
Via San Vitale 17
Open: summer 8.30am-8pm; winter 8.30am-5pm.

Mausoleo di Teodorico
Via delle Industrie
Open: 8am-dusk.

Museo Arcivescovile
Piazza Arcivescovado 1
Closed Sunday afternoon and Tuesday.

Sant' Apollinare in Classe
Open: 8am-dusk.

San Vitale
Via San Vitale 17
Open: 8.30am-dusk.

Dante Museum and Tomb
Via Dante Alighieri
Open: 9am-12noon and 2-5pm.

Reggio-Emilia
Galleria Parmeggiani
Corso Cairoli 2

Civic Museums
Via Spallanzani 7
(natural history, gypsotec, paletnological, Risorgimento, art gallery)
Open: every day.

Rossena
Castle
Open: Sunday afternoons.

Sala Baganza
Casino dei Boschi di Carrega
☎ (0521) 833440 to arrange visit.

San Martino in Rio
Agricultural Museum
Corso Umberto 1

San Secondo
Castle
Open: Monday-Saturday 8.30am-12.30pm.

Sant' Agata di Villanova
Villa Verdi
Open: April-October, Tuesday-Sunday 9am-12noon and 3-7pm.

Santarcangelo di Romagna
Castle
Open: June-mid-September, Tuesday, Thursday, Saturday, 10am-12noon and 4-7pm.

Soragna
Castle
Open: March-November, 9am-12noon and 3-7pm.

Torrechiara
Castle
Open: Tuesday-Sunday 9am-3pm.

Velleia
Archaeological site and Antiquarium
Open 9am-dusk.

Vignola
Castle
Open: every day.

8 • Tuscany

Of all the Italian regions, Tuscany is probably the best known, and it may seem surprising to find a chapter dedicated to the region in a guide to off-the-beaten-track places. When, however, one tries to think of places in Tuscany, there are usually only three cities and one wine-producing area which come to mind. Florence, Pisa and Siena, with the Chianti hills, account for only a small part of the almost 9,000sq miles of the region. Many other places, some of them well known to Italians and others almost completely unknown even to those who live relatively nearby are well worthy of a visit.

The region is roughly bounded by three natural features: the Apuan Alps to the north, the Apennines running from north to south down the east side, and the Tyrrhenian Sea which forms the third side of the triangle. Political events over the last thousand years have influenced the boundaries to a certain extent, particularly the division of central Italy between the Longobards and the Byzantines, but on the whole it is these three natural features which delineate the area.

Within the region there is very little level ground, 20 per cent being true mountain country, with between 60 and 70 per cent being hilly. The bulk of the region is criss-crossed by a series of valleys with the dominant axis being that from east to west. Many of these valleys have rivers flowing through them but the only one of any importance is the Arno, 150 miles long, which runs out of the mountains in the east, through Florence into the sea beyond Pisa.

With its many south-facing hillsides, much of the region's economy is based on the wine and olive oil-producing industry, and it is the sight of the many vineyards and olive groves that dominates the countryside. Other lesser known areas of the region are, however, very different from this, with heavy afforestation or pastureland providing an almost complete change of scenery, and a different lifestyle.

The region is divided into nine provinces, centred on Florence,

Siena, Pisa, Arezzo, Pistoia, Livorno, Grosseto, Lucca and Massa-Carrara, and while each of them has much to offer in the way of off-the-beaten-track attractions, the tripartite division of this chapter assumes that the visitor will be initially based in Pisa and Florence because they are the easiest to reach, and Siena because, apart from being world-famous, it dominates the southern half of the province.

Surprisingly, for a region which attracts visitors from all over the world, Tuscany is very poorly connected with other major centres. There is only one international airport (at Pisa) and that is served mainly by charter flights from other European cities. Florence has a small airport at Peretola which is connected periodically with the major Italian airports at Milan and Rome. By road the region is reasonably accessible, it being possible to drive from Dover to

Florence in less than 24 hours even without using the costly French motorway system. Trains arrive in Florence from London two or three times a day depending on the time of year, this journey also taking about 24 hours. Once in Tuscany, however, a car is almost indispensable, for although many of the places described here are accessible by bus or train, the local services tend to be slow and, above all, irregular.

Excursions from Florence

Chianti

Although a very popular area with tourists and natives alike, particularly in summer, there are many smaller roads in the Chianti area which are virtually free of traffic while still passing through countryside and small villages of exceptional charm and beauty. Take the main road out of Florence signposted 'Siena' as far as the entrance to the motorway, at that point follow the SS2 Via Cassia for 2 miles towards Siena before turning right up a small road marked **Sant' Andrea in Percussina**. This is the village where the famous sixteenth-century writer, Niccolo Machiavelli, had his home, which is marked by a plaque. Across the road is the inn where he is said to have spent his afternoons playing cards, which now enjoys the reputation of a good reasonably priced restaurant.

Beyond Sant' Andrea, turn right and follow the road until it ends at Chiesanuova, then turn left and continue amongst fine scenery to **Montespertoli**. This small hill town was a free city until being overrun by the Florentines in the sixteenth century. The church of Sant' Andrea contains, amongst other works of art, a mid-fourteenth century triptych and a thirteenth-century marble font.

Just over a mile south-east of Montespertoli along an unmetalled road is the fine eleventh-century *Pieve* of San Pietro in Mercato which contains more fine Renaissance works of art. Although the *Pieve* has been altered over the centuries it is still recognisably Romanesque, the style of church architecture to be seen most often in the region.

Leaving Montespertoli, follow the signposts for **Certaldo**. Leave the car in the new town and walk up the winding hill to the old medieval centre. The town is best visited during the week as many weekend trippers come here to see the house of Boccaccio with its original medieval tower, now the town library. Next to the house on the main street is the thirteenth-century church of San Michele and San Jacopo with its attractive fourteenth-century cloister, and the funeral monument to Boccaccio. At the top of the street is the fif-

Volpaia (10 miles south-east of Greve)

teenth-century Palazzo Pretorio containing a small museum (open most mornings).

From Certaldo follow the road to the north-east towards San Casciano until reaching a right turn for Marcialla and Tavarnelle after 6 miles. Just north of Tavarnelle turn right for San Donato in Poggio. Two miles along this road is the small village of **Morrocco**, where the fifteenth-century *Pieve* contains a terracotta *Annunciation* by Andrea della Robbia and several important paintings. **San Donato in Poggio**, reached in another 3 miles, has changed little since the Middle Ages when it was a Florentine border fortress town during the wars against the Sienese. There are several *trattorias* in and around the village but the most characteristic of these is La Toppa, near the ancient Palazzo Pretorio and the Palazzo Malaspina. On the outskirts of the village are two important churches — the Romanesque Pieve di San Donato, with some fine della Robbian terracotta, and the late Renaissance sanctuary of the Madonna di Pietracupa containing an interesting altarpiece by Paolo Schiavo.

The small unmetalled road signposted 'Sicelle' which descends by the side of the sanctuary offers some of the finest views in the whole of the Chianti area, and yet is used only by the handful of people who live in Sicelle and La Piazza. At the other end of the road is the main Greve to Castellina road. Turning towards Greve the road twists upwards until Panzano and then descends in large sweeps to **Greve**, the capital of Chianti Classico. One mile to the east of Greve along a minor road is the early medieval castle of Montefioralle with the nearby church of Santo Stefano containing an important Madonna and Child painting.

Continue westwards along the minor road for 15 minutes to the Badia di Passignano, a tenth-century abbey which was richly redecorated in the sixteenth century. Facing the entrance to the church is the former monastery, now an exlusive hotel, the refectory of which is decorated with a *Last Supper* by the Ghirlandaio brothers (1496). From Passignano take the track towards Rignana and at a fork after $1^1/_4$ miles, leave the car and continue on foot to the abandoned village of **Poggio al Vento** on the hill up to the left. Excellent views of the surrounding countryside are to be had from here.

To return to Florence pass through Passignano and drop down into the Elsa valley where the Florence-Siena *superstrada* will take you back to Florence in 20 minutes.

The Mugello

Leave Florence by the Via delle Gore (alongside Careggi Hospital). The road passes through Serpiolle before climbing up a picturesque hillside to Cercina. Eventually you reach the main Florence-Bologna road where after 3 miles is the village of Pratolino. Take the right fork signposted 'Bivigliano' then follow signs for the Convento di Monte Senario (4 miles). This thirteenth-century monastery, which contains some fine paintings, has excellent views over both the Arno and the Mugello valleys. Drop down to Vaglia and follow the main road to **San Piero a Sieve**. One mile to the north of the town (best reached on foot) is the Medicean border fortress of San Martino (1569). Two miles north of San Piero is the monastery of **Bosco ai Frati**, with a Donatello crucifix and an interesting terracotta *Last Supper*. Following the Sieve river until it meets the Arno is a fairly picturesque route for returning to Florence, or take the SS302 from Borgo San Lorenzo over the Olmo Pass.

Excursion to the Casentino

The first part of the Arno valley from the headwaters to just north of Arezzo is known as the Casentino, and is one of the most attractive areas in the whole of Tuscany. Reached by taking the motorway to Arezzo, the valley is flanked on one side by the Pratomagno range of mountains, and on the other by the Alpe di Catenaia. The main town in the area is **Bibbiena**, once an Etruscan stronghold and for centuries an important frontier town. The early sixteenth-century Palazzo Dovizi is one of the finest examples of rustic Renaissance architecture in Tuscany, once the home of the humanist playwright Bernardo Dovizi, later a cardinal and secretary to Pope Leo X.

Other places to see in the area are **Chiusi della Verna**, dominated by a ruined tenth-century castle and near to the thirteenth-century Franciscan sanctuary where San Francesco (St Francis) received the stigmata in 1224; **Badia Prataglia**, a good starting point for many walks; **Camaldoli**, built round an early eleventh-century monastery, which, despite a rule of complete silence, became a Renaissance cultural centre; **Castel Castagnaio**, a ruined medieval castle near the remains of a Roman temple; **Montemignaio** (the fine church contains Ghirlandaio's *Virgin and Child with Four Church Elders*); **Poppi**, an attractive hill town with many medieval streets lined with covered walkways; **Talla**, where the church of San Niccolò contains a finely decorated sixteenth-century organ; **Caprese Michelangelo** (the restored thirteenth-century castle contains modern works of art and casts by Michelangelo, while Palazzo del Podestà where the artist was born contains the Museo Michelangiolesco).

Many of the small towns are connected by small mountain tracks offering pleasant walks. Inexpensive large-scale maps of the province are produced by the Ente Provinciale per il Turismo.

The SS71 leads to two interesting and attractive towns a few miles to the south of the Casentino. **Castiglion Fiorentina** is situated on the side of a hill on a bend in the Chiana valley and from Roman times was important for controlling important communication routes. Of the several interesting churches perhaps the finest is the Collegiata di San Giuliano containing Signorelli's *Deposition of Christ*. An important art gallery is situated in the rebuilt Palazzo Comunale. The eleventh-century castle of Montecchio was given to the English mercenary, Sir John Hawkwood, in the fourteenth century for services to the Florentine Republic.

Cortona was originally established by the Etruscans about 2,500 years ago, passing through many hands until being taken by the Florentines in 1411. Owing to its distance from Florence the people were treated well to ensure their loyalty, and the town developed as a 'middle class' Renaissance town. The result is one of the most attractive towns in the whole of Italy. There are several interesting museums and fine churches, particularly the former church of Gesú built on two levels because of the steep slope. The diocesan museum is now housed here. Two Etruscan tombs can be visited on the hillside below the town.

Excursions from Pisa

Pistoia and the Pistoiese

Take the motorway from Pisa to **Pistoia**. The provincial capital is a lively bustling town with several points of interest, and tends to attract very few tourists. Of particular interest is the Romanesque cathedral with its fine octagonal baptistry. The capitoline museum is housed within the cathedral while many other noteworthy buildings flank the square, including the Palazzo del Comune which houses the civic museum.

From Pistoia the SS66 leads up into the mountains, passing through several attractive villages. One of these, up a small side-road, **Gavinana**, was the site of the decisive battle between the supporters of the Florentine Republic and the supporters of the Medici in 1530. The battle is commemorated in the Ferrucciano museum. After Gavinana, almost all the towns to Abetone are winter skiing resorts. These towns are only really busy during peak holiday periods and at weekends. At other times they offer excellent opportunities for peaceful skiing (or walking in summer).

Return by the SS66 and then the SS633 until the right turn sign-posted 'Pescia' at Chiesa Nuova. On a bend in this road is the small unspoilt medieval village of **Vellano**, where the fine church contains important works of art. **Pescia** itself is famous for its flowers which are heavily cultivated. The town is built on both sides of the river Pescia, giving two distinct urban centres, one civil and one religious. The civic museum contains important Etruscan pieces and etchings by Dürer and Callot, while the church of San Francesco contains the first frescoes on the life of the saint to be painted after his death.

The Garfagnana and the Orrido di Botri

One of the wildest parts of Tuscany bisected by the Serchio river is the Garfagnana. Take the SS12 past Lucca and Borgo a Mozzano until the SS445, stopping off at the Magdalen or Devil's Bridge (apparently built in a single night by the devil in return for the first soul to cross it — the people cheated him by sending a pig across. Two miles along the SS445, a road to the right leads up into the mountains to the Casentini mountain shelter, passing the medieval castle of **Tereglio** with its interesting church. Three miles after Tereglio a track marked 'Montefegatesi' leads to a car park serving the impressive Orrido di Botri. This natural gorge passes between two almost sheer rock faces, at times only about 8ft wide. Properly equipped walkers can pass through the gorge to the other side of the mountains.

The town of Lucca, Tuscany

Fishermen repairing their nets on the island of Elba

Orvieto cathedral, Umbria

Vellano

Six miles further along the SS445, a left turn leads up into the Apuan Alps on the other side of the Garfagnana area to the Grotta del Vento, almost $^{3}/_{4}$ mile of caves containing stalactites and stalagmites.

Barga, on the other side of the Serchio, is notable not only for its excellent views but also for the eleventh-century cathedral containing one of Tuscany's best preserved medieval altars.

Castelnuovo di Garfagnana, the area's main town, is famous mainly for its association with Ariosto, whose dark dangerous woods in the *Orlando Furioso* are drawn from his memories of the Garfagnana where he was governor for several years. The old fortress (*Rocca*) still dominates the centre of the town.

After Castelnuovo the road continues to Aulla through magnificent scenery for 45 miles. Many footpaths of varying degrees of difficulty are to be found in the mountains on both sides of the

Garfagnana. Detailed maps and advice are available locally.

Volterra and San Miniato

Take the main Florence road until the turning for **San Miniato**. Built around the eighth-century church of San Francesco (restored in the fifteenth), the town has several interesting churches, particularly the church and cloisters of San Domenico. A rich art collection is possessed by the Museo Diocesano, and there are extensive views from the rebuilt medieval tower on the hill above the town.

Follow the SS429 until **Volterra** appears on the signposts to the right. High on a spur above the Era and Cecina rivers, Volterra was one of the most important cities in Italy from about 900BC until the fourteenth century, when the hilltop position which had formerly been its strength meant that it was unable to expand at the same rate as Florence. The town's importance in this era is reflected by the importance of the Museo Etrusco Guarnacci. The early thirteenth-century Palazzo dei Priori, the oldest seat of government in Tuscany, has an unusual pentagonal tower and since 1905 has housed an important art gallery. The south-facing Porta all' Arco is an exceptionally well preserved Etruscan gateway, and another area of archaeological interest are the Roman excavations and Etruscan necropolis to the north of the town. A fairly direct road links the town with Pisa.

Excursions from Siena

The coastal plain in the southern part of the region was avoided for centuries by travellers as it was rife with malaria. In the last 200 years, however, the area has opened up new areas of interest to the visitor. The name given to this coastal plain is the Maremma, the most attractive part of which has been designated a national park. The park is entered on a small road from **Alberese**, where permission should be obtained in Via Bersagliere 5. The small road leads to one of three towers which originally protected the coast against Saracen raiders. The second tower stands on the highest point in the park and nearby are the ruins of the abbey of San Rabbano which previously belonged to the Knights of St John of Jerusalem. Beyond the park is one of the most unspoilt and little used beaches in Tuscany. Be careful inside the park as it is easy to get lost in the thick woods.

A few miles to the south of the park is the Monte Argentario peninsula, very crowded in summer but relatively tourist-free outside the main holiday period and weekends. **Port' Ercole**, the

Ruins at Volterra

peninsula's second largest centre is dominated by Spanish fortresses and the parish church where Caravaggio is buried.

From Porto Santo Stefano on the other side of the island, ferries leave for the islands of Giglio and Giannutri. **Giglio** is now becoming more known to summertime holidaymakers but the old town of Giglio Castello, high up on the hill is a typical medieval hill town clustered around its castle. The few tourists who reach **Giannutri** come not for the two shingle beaches but for the excellent underwater fishing in the area.

Elba, the main island in the Tuscan Archipelago is reached by ferry from Piombino. Although a popular holiday venue the island is only ever really busy during the peak summer period, and can be said to be off-the-beaten-track even during the fairly hot months of May, June and September.

Capraia can be reached either from Elba or from Livorno: part of the island is farmed by a prison colony, while the other two-thirds, composed mainly of volcanic rock, has very few facilities for receiving visitors. A boat trip around the island is to be recommended. The other Tuscan islands are not normally open to the public.

Between Elba and Siena lies the former Etruscan settlement of **Massa Marittima**. The city consists of the old (pre-1225) town where most of the important buildings are to be found grouped around the central square. The *Duomo*, the Palazzo Pretorio and the Palazzo Comunale all contain important works of art. A fourteenth-century Sienese fort separates the old town from the new (post 1225); this is now used as a hospital while another building with military associations, the old armoury, just inside the new town, now houses an archaeological museum. The 'new' town was originally developed as a residential area so the only monumental building to be found in this sector is the fourteenth-century church of Sant' Agostino.

Midway between Massa and Grosseto is the small town of **Vetulonia** which at first sight seems a typical medieval hill town like many others. It is, however, built over one of the twelve great cities of the Etruscan Confederation. Many of the large blocks of stones which the Etruscans used can still be seen, while a more detailed view of Etruscan civilisation can be obtained through a visit to the town's antiquarium. Grosseto itself is of no great interest being a relatively modern city, having been developed after the previously important city of **Roselle**, 4 miles to the north, had been abandoned because of frequent Saracen raids. The medieval buildings of Roselle were gradually dismantled and the stones used elsewhere leaving only the skeleton of the previous Roman and Etruscan centres. The foundations of the square perimeter walls with their six gates can still be seen as can the remains of the amphitheatre and the forum, while traces of necropoli with small chamber tombs can be seen along the roads leading to the city gates.

Another ruined town well worth visiting can be seen 25 miles to the south on the small promontory just to the south of Orbetello. The town of **Cosa** was an important Roman *municipium* until it was destroyed by the Visigoths in the fourth century. The town was then abandoned and its streets may still be walked among the ruins of the forum, the basilica, the senate house, the acropolis and the capitol.

Returning inland again, head for the medieval hill town of **Magliano in Toscana**, built around a tenth-century fortress over the ruins of previous Etruscan and Roman strongholds. The town walls date from the Renaissance period and are exceptionally well preserved. Inside the town, the church of San Giovanni Battista reveals a fine Romanesque church with the later addition of Gothic windows on the left side.

Further inland the small town of **Montemerano** is another interesting halting place. The town which rests on top of an olive-covered hillside is surrounded by the remains of a medieval city wall, and has as its centre a fourteenth-century tower which emerges from a group of characteristic dwellings.

Pitigliano

In a small valley not far from Montemerano is the **Terme di Saturnia**, a well known spa centre where various types of cure can be taken all the year round. The town from which the spa takes its name, *Saturnia*, lies slightly to the north inside the remains of a pre-Etruscan city wall. Many claim that the city of *Saturnia* was the birthplace of the Italic civilisation, and as such the first town on the Italian peninsula. Today little remains as the town was finally destroyed by the Sienese in the fourteenth century, after it had become a refuge for outlaws.

Twenty miles to the east is the town of **Sovana** which became an important town in the eleventh century when Gregory VII, who was born there, became pope. In the fourteenth century, malaria and frequent attacks by the Sienese led to the virtual abandonment of the town which is almost tourist-free and yet has remained virtually unchanged for over 500 years. Several important Etruscan tombs including the Tomba Ildebranda can be seen in the necropolis about a mile to the north of the town.

When the people fled from Sovana, most of them went to **Pitigliano** 5 miles to the south, which, being built on a spur, was much easier to defend. Pitigliano also housed a flourishing Jewish community from the fifteenth century onwards and ruins of the synagogue and the Jewish bakery can be seen behind the cathedral.

There are many interesting buildings to see in the town, the finest of which is undoubtedly the Palazzo degli Orsini with its octagonal tower, in Piazza della Repubblica.

Nearby **Sorano** is another former Etruscan town which has suffered from neglect in much the same way as Sovana, although in a later period. Built on an irregular mound of volcanic tufa, there is hardly a level piece of ground to be seen inside the city, giving an overall impression of unusual beauty when seen from a distance. Of major monumental importance in the town are the two fortresses which protect the south-east and north-west extremities. To the south-east is the Fortezza Ursinea erected by Niccolò IV Orsini in 1552, the entrance to which is surmounted by an impressive sculpted coat of arms, while the north-west is protected by the eighteenth-century Sasso Leopoldino.

Moving northwards, **Castell' Azzara** is to be found 2,000ft above sea level in a magnificent position on the side of Monte Civitella. The surrounding area is good walking country and the town only ever gets busy during the main summer holiday period. Another mountain which is much favoured by Italians looking for peace and quiet is Monte Amiata, used for skiing during the winter and walking during the summer. Around the foot of the mountain there are several interesting towns well worth taking the trouble to see. **Arcidosso** is one of these with its characteristic twisting medieval alleyways in the old centre. One interesting walk lies to the north-west where the Pieve ad Lamulas $1^1/_2$ miles away is an interesting church founded before the millennium, while another $^3/_4$ mile brings you to the ruins of the medieval castle of Montelaterone, destroyed by the Sienese in 1260. Another slightly longer walk (6 miles each way) leads to the summit of Monte Labbro where the ruins of the church of the Giurisdavidici can be seen. This was the church of a religious sect led by the Arcidossan Davide Lazzaretti between 1868-78. Lazzaretti, who believed he was the second coming of Christ, was shot along with many of his followers by the Italian police in 1878.

Another interesting centre is **Piancastagnaio** with its battlemented gateway. Part of the old fortress has been restored and now houses a small private museum. Other noteworthy buildings are the Palazzo Pretorio in the central square and the early seventeenth-century manneristic Palazzo Bourbon del Monte with an important internal stairway.

Abbadia San Salvadore tends to get busy on Sundays during the summer but at other times is fairly peaceful. The town grew up around an eighth-century monastery. Little remains of the original monastery, but the church, which was rebuilt in the eleventh century, is well worth a visit. It contains several important works of art but the most important thing to see is the original eighth-century crypt, built in the form of a Greek cross and supported by thirty-six decorated columns. The medieval centre of the town is exceptionally large and almost unscathed by progress, being filled with Gothic and Renaissance houses which have become black or dark-grey over the centuries. To the west of Abbadia San Salvatore is Monte Amiata (5,706ft), the lower slopes of which are covered by chestnut woods. It is possible to arrive within 600ft of the summit by car, but those with a detailed map of the mountain will find many other pathways.

Thirty miles to the east at the southern end of the Val di Chiana is the historic town of **Chiusi**, another of the twelve cities which once made up the Etruscan Confederation. Most of the old medieval town was renovated at the end of the nineteenth century, losing much of its original character, but the remains of the old fortress at the western end of the town may still be visited. The National Etruscan Museum, opposite the *Duomo*, contains one of the finest collections of Etruscan relics in existence, while among the many important Etruscan tombs, three may be visited: the third-century BC Tomba della Pellegrina, where all the articles which were in the tomb when it was discovered in 1928 have been restored and replaced; the Tomba della Scimmia, containing fine fifth-century BC wall paintings which reveal what life was like in that period; and the third-century BC Tomba del Granduca containing eight urns decorated with bas-reliefs of mythological scenes.

Nearby **Chianciano** has been developed as an important spa town, but the old medieval hill town has remained virtually unchanged as most of the new developments have taken place on the plain below. The small Museo d'Arte Sacra is to be found here.

Another 5 miles to the west is the town of **Montepulciano**, situated on the spur dividing the Val di Chiana from the Val d'Orcia. This important strategic position meant that possession of the city was for centuries disputed by the Florentines and the Sienese. When the former finally gained possession of the town they went to a great deal of trouble to consolidate their rule, sending their best architects to redevelop the town. A new *Duomo* was built and in it a fine funeral monument by Michelozzo Michelozzi can be seen. Michelozzi was also responsible for the construction of the Palazzo Comunale which bears a strong resemblance to Florence's Palazzo Vecchio. Facing the Palazzo Comunale is the Palazzo Cotucci del Monte, designed by Antonio Sangallo the Elder who was also responsible for the fortress to the south of the centre. At the foot of the hill to the west of the town is the church which many consider to be Sangallo's masterpiece, the church of San Biagio. This design, with a central dome surmounting a Greek cross was to become the dominant style in church architecture in the century which followed Sangallo's work.

Pienza, 8 miles to the west, was known as Corsignano until 1458 when Enea Silvio Piccolomini, who was born there, became Pope Pius II. During his reign the town was redeveloped to become almost a second papal court. Not only was his own family house rebuilt as a papal palace, and a new Renaissance cathedral (with Gothic interior) erected, but many of his cardinals also built palaces in the town, including Rodrigo Borgia, later one of the most corrupt and unscrupulous popes ever known (Alexander VI). Before the redevelopment the most important church was the *Pieve* which can still be visited in the fields to the west. The primitive font is that in which Pius II and Pius III (Francesco Tedeschi Piccolomini) were baptised.

Near Pienza, other places to be visited include Monticchiello, a small medieval hill town 3 miles south-east, where every July the people of the town act out moments from the town's history in the central square; the monastery of Sant' Anna in Camprena 4 miles to the north, where the refectory is decorated with frescoes by Sodoma (1502-3); Spedaletto, a large medieval castle in the Val d'Orcia with turrets and battlements, which once served as a subsidiary to the hospital of Santa Maria della Scala in Siena; and Palazzo Massaini, an old manor house which has been preserved in its original state 3 miles to the north.

Returning towards Siena on the Via Cassia, the next interesting town is **Buonconvento**, 16 miles to the north-west. The town was built in the thirteenth century over the ruins of an old fort. A museum of sacred art has recently been opened there, collecting together works of art from many of the smaller churches in the Arbia valley. Six miles north-east of Buonconvento is the headquarters of the Benedictine order of monks. Despite being highly recommended by almost all the better guidebooks the monastery has surprisingly few visitors, except for the occasional coach trip during the summer. Monte Oliveto Maggiore was founded in 1313 and during the Renaissance was one of the major centres of Italian culture. The loggia of the magnificent Great Cloister is decorated with frescoes by Sodoma and Signorelli which recount the story of the life of St Benedict. The monastery's library contains more than 40,000 volumes, many of them original manuscripts, while the 'pharmacy' contains an interesting collection of seventeenth-century jars, formerly used for storing exotic herbs. The village of **Chiusure**, just over half a mile from the monastery is worth taking a walk to, as there are excellent views of the monastery emerging from the trees, and of the typical 'burnt' hillsides characteristic of the area.

Further Information

— Tuscany —

Airports

Pisa, 'Galileo Galilei'
☎ (050) 28088

Florence, 'Peretola'
☎ (0103955) 370123

Tourist Information Offices

Tuscany is divided into nine provinces, each of which has its own tourist board.

Province of Arezzo
Ente Provinciale per il Turismo
Piazza Risorgimento 116
Arezzo
☎ (0575) 20839

Province of Florence
Ente Provinciale per il Turismo
Via Manzoni 16
Firenze
☎ (055) 2478141

Province of Grosseto
Ente Provinciale per il Turismo
Via Monterosa 206
Grosseto
☎ (0564) 22534

Province of Livorno
Ente Provinciale per il Turismo
Piazza Cavour 6
Livorno
☎ (0586) 33111

Province of Lucca
Ente Provinciale per il Turismo
Piazza Guidiccioni 2
Lucca
☎ (0583) 41205

Province of Massa
Ente Provinciale per il Turismo
Piazza 2 Giugno 14
Carrara
☎ (0585) 70668

Province of Pisa
Ente Provinciale per il Turismo
Lungarno Mediceo 42
Pisa
☎ (050) 47290

Province of Pistoia
Ente Provinciale per il Turismo
Corso Gramsci 110
Pistoia
☎ (0573) 34326

Province of Siena
Ente Provinciale per il Turismo
Via di Città 5
Siena
☎ (0577) 47051

Museums and Other Places of Interest

This information is arranged alphabetically by town. Opening times tend to change fairly regularly and those given should only be regarded as rough guides. When times are not given, assume that the museums are open in the mornings from Monday to Saturday.

Abbazia di Farneta
A small museum is housed in the abbey.

Anchiano
Leonardo's birthplace.

Arezzo
Museo Archeologico Mecenate
Via Margaritone 10
Open: Monday-Saturday (except Wednesday), 10.30am-3pm, Sunday, 9am-12noon.

Galleria e Museo Medioevale e Moderno
Via San Lorentino 8
Open: Tuesday-Saturday, 9.30am-3.30pm, Sunday, 9am-1pm.

Museo di Casa Vasari
Via Settembre 55
Open: Monday-Saturday, no fixed time, knock at the door.

Museo Diocesano di Arte Sacra
Piazza del Duomo
Open: Monday-Saturday 10am-12noon and 1-5pm

Asciano
Museum of Sacred Art
Via Bartolenga
Open: summer 9am-12noon and 4-6pm, winter 10am-1pm and 3-5pm.

Etruscan Museum
Corso Matteotti

Buonconvento
Val d'Arbia Museum of Sacred Art
Via Soccini 13

Burano
World Wildlife Fund Oasis
Open: September-May, Thursday and Sunday, 10am-1pm.

Calci
Museo di Storia Naturale
Via Roma 1

Caprese Michelangelo
Museo Michelangiolesco
Palazzo del Podestà

Art Gallery
Castello

Carrara
Art Gallery of the Accademia di Belle Arti
Via Roma 1

Castelfiorentino
Galleria d'Arte
Santa Verdiana church

Castello
Villa Medicea di Castello (Gardens)
Via del Castello
Sesto-Fiorentino
Open: summer 9.30am-6.30pm, winter 9.30am-4.30pm.

Villa Medicea di Petraia (Gardens)
Open: as above.

Castiglioncello
Museum, for admission apply to Tourist Information Office
Via della Pineta 6

Cecina
Museo Civico 'Antiquarium'
Piazza Carducci

Certaldo
Boccaccio's House
Via di Boccaccio

Civic Museum
Palazzo del Pretore

Certosa di Pisa
Certosa
Open: May-October, Tuesday-Saturday, 3-6pm, Sunday, 2-6.45pm; November-April, Tuesday-Saturday, 2-5pm, Sunday, 1.30-4.15pm.

Cetona
Villa Terrosi Vagnoli Gardens

Chianciano
Museum of Sacred Art
Palazzo dell' Arcipretura
Via Solferino 38

Information on Thermal Cures
Direzione Generale delle Terme
Via Roma

Chiusi
Etruscan National Museum
Via Porsenna

Open: Tuesday-Saturday, 8.30am-12.30pm, Sunday, 9am-1pm.

Collodi
Villa Garzoni Gardens
Open: daily, 8am-8pm.

Pinocchio's Park and the Kingdom of the Toys

Cortona
Museo dell' Accademia Etrusca
Palazzo Pretorio
Open: 9am-12noon and 3-6pm.

Museo Diocesano
Chiesa del Gesú
Piazza del Duomo
Open: 9am-1pm and 3-7pm.

Cutigliano
Information Office
Azienda Autonoma di Soggiorno e Turismo
Via Tigri

Elba
Museum 'Antiquario Comunale'
Marciana

Casa di Napoleone
Portoferraio
Open: summer, Wednesday-Monday, 9am-1pm and 3-6pm, winter, 9am-2pm.

Antiquarium
Procchio

Museo Minerario Elbano (minerals)
Near Palazzo Comunale
Rio Marina

Empoli
Museo della Collegiata
Piazza San Giovanni

Fiesole
Archaeological Museum & Archaeological Area
Via Partigiani 1

Museo Bandini
Via Dupre 1

Missionary Ethnographic Museum
Church of San Francesco
Via San Francesco

Fucecchio
Museo di Fucecchio
Church of San Salvatore

Gavinana
Museo Ferrucciano
Open: daily, 9am-12noon and 4-7pm.

Grosseto
Museo Archeologico Comunale
Via Mazzini 34
Open: 9am-12noon and 4-7pm.

Museo Civico di Storia Naturale
Via Mazzini (next to theatre)
Open: 4.30-7pm, closed Tuesday and Friday.

Museo Diocesano di Arte Sacra
Piazzetta del Campanile 3
Closed on Tuesday.

Lucca
Museo Nazionale di Villa Guinigi
Via della Quarconia
Open: summer, Tuesday-Sunday, 9.30am-1pm and 3-6pm, winter, Tuesday-Saturday, 9.30am-4pm, Sunday, 9am-1pm.

Palazzo Mansi
Via Galli Tassi
Open: May-October, 9.30am-4pm; November-April, Tuesday-Saturday, 9am-2pm, Sunday, 9am-1pm, closed Monday and Bank Holidays.

Palazzo Ducale
Piazza Napoleone

Lucignano
Museo Comunale
In Palazzo Comunale

Massa
Museum of the Malaspina Castle
Open: daily (except Monday) 9am-12noon and 4-7pm.

Massa Marittima
Museo del Risorgimento
6 Piazza Cavour

Museo Archeologico
Palazzo delle Armi
Corso Diaz
Open: April-October, Monday-Saturday, 10am-12noon and 4-6pm, Sunday, 10am-12noon.

Museo di Mineralogia
Viale Martiri di Niccioletta 1

Montalcino
Museum of Sacred Art
Via Ricasoli 31
Open: 9am-12noon and 4-6pm.

Civic Museum and Archaeological Museum
10 Piazza Cavour
Open: 10am-1pm and 3-6pm.

Montecatini Terme
Museo Accademia d'Arte
Viale Diaz
Open: Tuesday-Sunday, 4-7.30pm.

Information on the Thermal Cures
Direzione delle Terme
Palazzina Regia
Viale Verdi 41

Montepulciano
Civic Museum
Palazzo Neri Orselli Bombagli
Via Ricci 11
Open: 9am-12.30pm and 2.30-7pm.

Montevarchi
Museo Paleontologico
Via del Museo

Orbetello
Antiquarium Civico
Via Ricasoli 26
Open: summer, Sunday-Friday, 8am-1pm and 4-6pm, winter, Sunday-Friday, 10am-1pm and 2.30-6pm.

Lagoon of Orbetello
World Wildlife Fund Oasis
Open: October-April, Thursday and Sunday, 10am-1pm.

Pescia
Museo Comune di Pescia
Piazza Obizzi 9
Open: Monday, Wednesday, Friday, 4-7pm.

Pienza
Cathedral Museum
Piazza Pio II 1
Open: March-October, 10am-1pm and 3-6pm, November-February, 10am-1pm and 2-4pm.

Palazzo Piccolomini and Hanging Gardens
Piazza Pio II
Open: 10am-12.30pm and 3-6pm.

Pistoia
Museo Capitolare
Piazza del Duomo
Open: Monday-Saturday, 9am-12noon and 3.30-7pm.

Museo Civico
Via Curatone e Montanara 63
Open: Tuesday-Saturday, 9.30am-12.30pm, Sunday, 10am-1pm.

Museo Diocesano
Palazzo Vescovile
Via Puccini
For entrance ask custodian.

Zoo
La Verginiana
Open: all year round.

Poggio a Caiano
Villa Medici Gardens

Pontremoli
Museo del Comune
Castello del Pignaro

Populonia
Museum
Main Street
Enquire at adjoining farm.

Prato
Galleria Comunale
Palazzo Pretorio
Piazza del Comune

Museo dell' Opera del Duomo
Palazzo Vescovile
Piazza Duomo 49

Museo di Arte Murale
Church of San Domenico
Piazza San Domenico 8

Textile Museum
Viale della Repubblica 9

San Gimignano
Museum of Sacred Art
Piazza Pecori 1

Civic Art Gallery
Piazza del Duomo
Open: summer, 9am-1pm and 3-6pm, winter, 9am-1pm and 3-5pm.

San Giovanni Valdarno
Museo della Basilica
Piazza Masaccio

San Miniato
Museo Diocesano
Prato del Duomo
Open: Tuesday-Sunday, 10am-12.30pm and 3.30-7pm.

Sansepolcro
Municipal Art Gallery
Palazzo Comunale
Open: Monday-Saturday, 8am-2pm and 4-6pm.

Saturnia
Antiquarium
Villa Ciacci
Ring bell.

Sesto Fiorentino
Museo della Porcellana di Doccia
Via Pratese 31

Terranuova Bracciolini
House-Museum of the Humanist, Poggio Bracciolini

Vetulonia
Antiquarium

Vicchio
Museo di Palazzo Comunale
Palazzo Pretorio

Giotto's House
Vespignano

Villafranca Lunigiana
Museo Etnografico
Via Borgo

Vinci
Museo da Vinci
In the castle

House of Leonardo
Anchiano

Volterra
Museo e Biblioteca Guarnacci
11 Via Don Minzoni
Open: April-September, Monday-Saturday, 9am-1pm and 3-6pm, Sunday, 9.30am-1pm;
October-March, Monday-Saturday, 9.30am-1pm and 2.30-4.30pm, Sunday, 9.30am-1pm.

Museo Diocesano di Arte Sacra
1 Via Roma
Open: mid-March-mid-November, Monday-Saturday, 9am-12.30pm and 3-6pm, Sunday, 9am-12noon and 3-6pm;
mid-November-mid-March, Monday-Saturday, 10am-1pm, Sunday, 10am-12noon.

Art Gallery
Palazzo dei Priori
Open: March-October, Monday-Saturday, 10am-1pm and 3-6pm, Sunday, 9am-1pm and 3-6pm;
November-February, Monday-Saturday 10am-1pm and 3-6pm, Sunday, 9am-1pm and 3-5pm.

9 • Marche

The name Marche derives from an old German word meaning border post and has been used since the time of Charlemagne. In many ways the name is still appropriate today as the region has little in common either with the industrial north or with the agricultural south. The region is bordered by Emilia-Romagna, Tuscany, Umbria, Abruzzo and Lazio following for the most part natural features. Level ground is almost non-existent in the Marche as the hills and mountains rise straight out of the sea throughout the region. Five arched parallel chains of mountains, geologically belonging to the Apennines, give way to a group of sub-Apennine hills which, like the former, are almost always gently rounded and only rarely steep and dramatic. The mountains are mainly fairly low — the highest, Monte Vettore, is almost 2,500ft higher than the second highest.

The climate is better than that on the other side of the Apennines as the situation of most of the settlements above sea level tends to give lower average temperatures in summer, except right on the coast. The coast to the north of Ancona is of little interest in the summer months being an almost unbroken sandy beach which tends to suffer from the 'Rimini syndrome', while to the south of Ancona, the rockier nature of the coastline, while still attracting large numbers of people during the school holidays and at week-ends, is much less exploited.

A wide variety of vegetation can be seen in the region as the already large number of naturally occurring species has been increased by the activities of man, with the addition of chestnuts, vines, olives, cereals and grazing lands. The fauna of the region has not been so fortunate although wolves, foxes and eagles can still occasionally be seen up in the mountains.

Archaeological evidence shows that the region has been inhabited at least since the Stone Age, while the two warrior tribes who inhabited the area before the Romans arrived left considerable traces of their civilisations. The tribe which inhabited the south of the

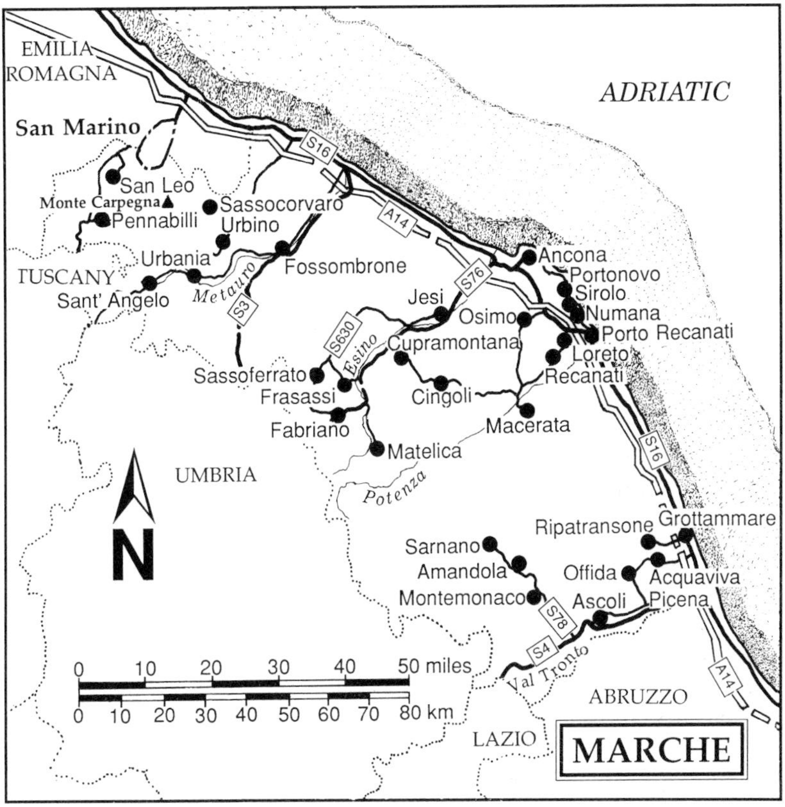

region was the Picenten, a name which survives as a component of many current place names, while the north of the region formed part of the territory of the Umbran, one of the most important tribes in Italy. After the Roman period the region's unity was fragmented with the people fleeing into the hills in the face of each successive invasion until Charlemagne made a gift of the region to the papacy. After this, different parts of the Marche were under varying degrees of papal control with large areas such as Urbino and Pesaro functioning as virtually independent duchies. These two, under the Montefeltro and the Sforza families, became great cultural centres during the Renaissance, bringing in leading artists and men of culture from Florence, Rome and the north. Under Federico da Montefeltro and his son Guidobaldo, Urbino developed into what many consider the ideal Renaissance city although later it slowly declined into provincialism. In the southern part of the Marche, which was more closely linked with Rome, all the best artists went to work in the capital and great works of art are few and far between.

One architectural curiosity which unites the region is the tendency for church presbyteries to be unusually high, inspired by the ninth-century Pieve di San Leo. The most important religious centre, however, is Loreto where thousands of tourists flock each year to see the house of the Virgin and St Anne which was supposedly brought from Palestine one night in a storm by a host of angels.

Apart from Loreto, tourism in the region is limited almost exclusively to the coast between May and September with a peak during August. Many campsites have been created on the coast and attract large numbers of foreign tourists, particularly from Germany. Inland however, camping facilities are rare and only the larger towns have any sort of adequate hotels for receiving tourists. The best places from which to start excursions in the Marche (either to visit some of the many small hilltop villages inside their defensive walls, or to visit the sandy beaches on weekdays outside the main summer season) are Fossombrone, Fabriano, Macerata and Ascoli, while an inland campsite can be found at Urbino.

The best times to visit the region are spring, autumn, and even summer if the coast is avoided, while some small ski-resorts are situated in the Sibilline mountains. Access is easy by road or rail while the nearest international airport is the relatively small one at Rimini.

Excursions from Fossombrone

Fossombrone was established on its present site in the tenth century after an earlier town established by the Romans had been devastated, first by the Goths and then by the Longobards. At the beginning of the fourteenth century, the town passed under the control of the Malatesta family of Rimini who provided it with strong new fortifications. The Malatesta sold their rights to Federico da Montefeltro, Duke of Urbino, in 1444 and under the humanist Montefeltro family and their successors, the Della Rovere, the city reached the height of its prosperity, coming under the direct control of the church in 1631.

At one time there were several ducal residences in Fossombrone, but most of them have lost much of their splendour as they have been given over to other uses over the centuries. One still worth visiting is the Corte Alta, built at the top end of the town in the thirteenth century and then modernised by Federico in the late 1460s. A fine loggia on the east side of the palace has fine views over the city and down the Metauro valley towards the sea. The palace contains the Museo Civico A. Vernarecci, consisting mainly of archaeological finds, and part of the municipal art gallery, the main part of which is housed a short distance away in Via Flaminia 32. The most interesting of the town's churches is San Filippo with its fine baroque interior. The church was erected by public subscription at the beginning of the seventeenth century to celebrate the birth of Duke Federico Ubaldo.

Five miles south-west of the city in the Candigliano valley the main road passes through the Furlo Gallery, a narrow ravine carved out of the rock by the river and then widened by the Romans. Shortly after the gallery take the right fork to **Urbania**, famous for its ceramics and porcelain. The original name of the town was Castel delle Ripe, the Castel Durante named after the French cardinal who rebuilt the city in the thirteenth century before finally taking its present name when Pope Urban VIII brought it under the direct control of the church in 1636. The points of most interest to tourists are the many fine works of art in the town's churches. Most interesting of all is undoubtedly the church of Santa Chiara with its adjacent convent. Until recently the church had a sixteenth-century aspect but large-scale restoration has taken place revealing the original thirteenth-century structure.

The Renaissance modernisation programme which gave the ducal palace its present day appearance was carried out by Girolamo Genga, one of the finest architects of the period. A hanging loggia and two cylindrical towers enliven the simple lines of the palace which contains the civic museums and art gallery. The oldest church in the town is the twelfth-century San Francesco, which although almost entirely rebuilt in the eighteenth century can still boast a Gothic portal which is believed to have been designed by the then 20-year-old Lorenzo Ghiberti (sculptor of the *Doors of Paradise* in Florence) in 1398.

Continue on the SS73 through the vines, the elms and the oaks which line the route as far as **Sant' Angelo in Vado**, birthplace of the Zuccari brothers in the sixteenth century. One of the most interesting paintings in the town is the *Madonna and Child with Saints and Taddeo and Federico Zuccari with the Children of the Latter* painted by Federico in 1603, 37 years after his brother's premature death.

A secondary road leads from Sant' Angelo north-west to **Piandimeleto**, an attractive village with a picturesque fifteenth-century castle. From Piandimeleto continue westwards for a short distance before turning right at Belforte along the beautiful twisting road leading to the monastery of Montefiorentino. The monastery was built in the thirteenth century and enlargened during the Renaissance. Of particular note is the Brunelleschian chapel of the Conti Oliva built in 1484 by Francesco di Simone Ferrucci, and decorated by the finest works of art produced by Raphael's father Giovanni Santi.

Four miles further to the north on the side of Monte Carpegna is the town of **Carpegna**, one of the best starting points in the area for mountain walkers. The summits of both Monte Carpegna and Monte Simoncello can be reached in around 2 hours from the town and both offer fine views of the surrounding hills and forests. The 6-mile drive around the base of the mountain from Carpegna to Pennabilli is spectacular, even breathtaking at times as it wends its way through woods formed mainly of oak, through which the bare rock of Monte Simoncello can at times be seen.

Pennabilli is situated in a hollow between two rocky outcrops originally known as Penna and Billi. One of the outcrops is crowned by the ruins of the medieval Castello di Billi and an Augustan monastery which incorporates the lower part of the ruined castle. The historic centre of the town is situated on the other spur where the interesting fifteenth-century church of Sant' Agostino merits a visit for its works of art and its fifteenth-century organ.

Thirteen miles north of Pennabilli is one of the area's most attractive towns, **San Leo**, which stands on top of a steep-sided hill with only one access road. The town's most impressive monument is the fortress which dominates the surrounding countryside and was cited by Machiavelli as an exemplary military stronghold. The interior of the fortress is now home to an armaments museum and the civic art gallery. The town has preserved almost entirely its original medieval structure and there is literally no part of the town which is not worth looking at. The town's *Duomo* was built in the twelfth and thirteenth centuries over the ruins of the Roman Giove Feretrio temple out of attractive golden sandstone. Another fine fortress can be seen at **Sassocorvaro**, 19 miles to the south-west. The fortress, which dates from the fifteenth century, bears some resemblance to a warship and has several imposing defensive towers. Various works of art are to be found inside the fortress which also houses a small theatre and has a number of interesting fireplaces.

Last town on this itinerary is the most important of all — **Urbino**, once one of the hotbeds of Italian culture under the Montefeltro dukes. Urbino's cultural zenith arrived under the rule of Federico and Guidobaldo da Montefeltro, the last two Montefeltro dukes. Federico greatly extended Urbino's domination of the surrounding countryside and the magnificent ducal palace was built for him. The

Ducal palace, Urbino

ducal palace was the first in the world to reflect humanist thought in its design and many of Italy's leading writers and artists attended the Montefeltro court there. Now the palace contains two very important museums — a lapidary museum and the most important art gallery in the Marche with paintings by Raphael, Titian, Paolo Uccello, and Piero della Francesca amongst others. The house where Raphael was born is also now a museum and various other important works of art are to be found in the local churches.

Excursions from Fabriano

The old centre of **Fabriano** stands on a rise in a hollow, almost completely surrounded by mountain peaks. Of the centre's original buildings only a handful remain which are of any real interest and the town can be seen fairly quickly leaving more time free for excursions into the surrounding area. The most important building is the thirteenth-century Palazzo del Podestà, a solid Romanesque-Gothic building situated in the triangular Piazza del Comune.

The *Duomo* was built in the thirteenth century but completely restructured at the beginning of the seventeenth. The painting of *St Nicholas of Tolentino in Glory* situated in the right-hand chapel is one of the earliest known works of Salvatore Rosa. During the first half of the fourteenth century Fabriano flourished as an art centre, a fact which is reflected by the quality of the exhibits in the town's Pinacoteca. The most important of all the local artists, however, Gentile da Fabriano, is unfortunately not represented in the town.

More paintings by Salvatore Rosa can be seen in **Matelica**, 11 miles to the south-east at the confluence of the Esino and the Fosso di Braccano. Examples of the Neapolitan artist's work can be seen in the baroque Suffraggio church and in the important Piersanti museum. The heart of the city is the attractive octagonal Piazza Mattei which, besides the Suffraggio church, is surrounded by a variety of buildings dating from the thirteenth to the eighteenth centuries.

Twelve miles north-west of Fabriano near the site where the Romans defeated the Sannites and the Gauls in 295BC is **Sassoferrato**. Like many Italian towns the old section is situated on a hill with more modern quarters grouped on the plain around it. Dominating the old section are the imposing remains of the town's fourteenth-century fortress now surrounded by a park. Nearby is the fourteenth-century Palazzo dei Priori which contains the town's museum and art gallery. The first of these is particularly interesting as it contains many of the findings from excavations on the site of the Roman city of *Sentinium* 20 minutes' walk outside the town by the side of the road leading back to Fabriano. The town is well provided with museums as it also has a museum of popular arts and traditions as well as a recently created botanical garden.

One mile to the east of Sassoferrato is the fine Romanesque-Lombard church of Santa Croce which was built in the early twelfth century using some of the masonry recovered from the ruins of *Sentinium*. The bell in the bell tower is one of a pair which were hung there in the fifteenth century while the other is on display on the left-hand side of the church near the main door.

Eight miles to the east alongside the river Sentino are the important caves known as the Grotte di Frasassi, the most extensive system of caves in Italy. A tourist 'walk' of 1 mile has been roped off and

The Palazzo Vescovile, Fabriano

illuminated inside the caves which are known to extend for at least 8 miles while speleologists hope to find ways through to other nearby caves giving a total length of 22 miles.

Not far from the entrance to the caves is the eleventh-century Byzantine-Romanesque church of San Vittore delle Chiuse. The ogival entrance porch is flanked on one side by a cylindrical tower and on the other by a robust square bell tower. The body of the church is unusual in having two side apses in place of the transepts, as well as three apses at the rear of the church.

Cupramontana, 11 miles to the east, is a pleasant little town which offers several possibilities to walkers in the pleasant countryside around. In the fifteenth century the town was a stronghold of the heretical sect known as the Fraticelli. From Cupramontana head north-east and then follow the Esino river as far as **Jesi** (also written Iesi) where the oldest part of the town is still enclosed by a well preserved thirteenth-century defensive wall. The centre of the town is the rectangular Piazza Federico II who is believed to have been born there in a tent in 1194. Most of the buildings around the central square are baroque but Palazzo della Signoria in the nearby Piazza Angelo Colocci is a fine Renaissance building designed by Francesco di Giorgio Martini. The large lion over the portal is the symbol of the city. Around the fine inner courtyard with its double layer of loggias are situated the town's library, historic archives, museum and art gallery, the last of which contains a painting of Mary Magdalen visited by angels, believed to have been painted by Guercino, as well as several works by Lorenzo Lotto.

Retrace your steps out of Jesi for just over 5 miles and then turn left on the minor road to **Staffolo** at the centre of the area where the greenish-coloured Verdicchio wine is produced. The village where parts of the old defensive walls are still standing is quiet and pleasant as are the walks around the surrounding vineyards.

Go east from Staffolo for 3 miles and then turn southwards on the SS502 across the Musone valley and over the hills to **Cingoli** on the eastern slopes of the mountain of the same name. Originally a Roman town and then for many centuries an independent *comune*, Cingoli has always been a fairly prosperous town and has many fine old buildings to show for it. The town's two most imposing buildings, the twelfth-century Palazzo Municipale and the eighteenth-century cathedral, face each other across the central Piazza Vittorio Emanuele, once the site of the Roman acropolis. The Palazzo Municipale contains a museum where the most noteworthy exhibits are a series of marble portraits dating from the first century AD. The great

The town hall clocktower, Cingoli

façade, which had been planned for the cathedral by the Cingolese Pope Pius VIII was never completed, work being suspended on the pope's death. At one end of the town's main street is a viewing point known as the 'Balcony of the Marche' from where a vast area of the surrounding countryside can be seen. To return to Fabriano drop back down the hill towards Jesi for about a mile and then take the first left turn for a highly scenic route.

Excursions from Macerata

Despite being a small city, **Macerata**, which is built on a hill between two parallel valleys, has always been an active cultural centre, seat of a university since 1290. The highest, oldest part of the city, which is still enclosed by the remains of the city wall, now houses only about one-tenth of the town's total population but it is in this area where the tourist will find almost all that is of interest in the town. The finest building in the city is the Loggia dei Mercanti which dates from the first years of the sixteenth century. The loggia was closed by the papal legate in 1641 to become a bedchamber reached from the adjacent Palazzo del Comune. Fortunately the three elegant arches and the open loggia above were reopened and restored to their original state in 1905. Just outside the old city wall is the magnificent

Sferisterio, a neo-classical amphitheatre built as a venue for the town's traditional ball game and for buffalo jousts. The Sferisterio also has exceptional acoustic qualities and every year is the site for a series of high-class concerts.

Most of the town's cultural institutions are situated in the old Jesuit Institute next to the seventeenth-century late Renaissance church of San Giovanni. Contained in the museum are a carriage museum, the civic museum, the civic art gallery and a museum of the Risorgimento, as well as the town's library. Particularly interesting is a collection of old photographs of Macerata in the civic museum section. Not being on the normal tourist circuit and having a high proportion of students means that eating out is normally reasonably priced in Macerata, without any noticeable lack of quality.

Drop down from Macerata to cross the river Potenza at Villa Potenza and then climb steadily northwards for 3 miles to **Montecassiano**, a small concentrical town built around a central square where the town hall and the collegiate church are situated. Both of these date from the fifteenth century as do many of the other buildings in the town, which has retained much of its original appearance and is a fine example of a typical late medieval Marche hill town.

The main road continues northwards from Montecassiano, wending its way over the picturesque hills towards Ancona. Twelve miles before Ancona, beyond the Musone valley, stands what was once one of the most important free *comunes* in this part of Italy. **Osimo** was originally a Roman town and some traces of Roman walls can still be seen while a number of Roman statues are kept in the *Municipio*. The Romanesque-Gothic *Duomo* was built in the twelfth and thirteenth centuries over a previous eighth-century church and on the site of the Roman Campidoglio. The *Duomo* is built in the form of an Egyptian cross with a Romanesque raised presbytery and a large crypt which is supported by sixteen columns originally belonging to Roman buildings. The public gardens in Piazza Gramsci have magnificent views across to the Sibilline mountains in one direction and to the Adriatic in the other.

From Osimo continue towards Ancona until just after the road passes under the motorway and then take the small road on the right to cut across to the coast at Monte dei Corvi 4 miles south of the city. Parts of the next stretch of coastline are as attractive as anything on the Riviera, but only usually attract a fraction of the tourists who flock to the better known areas. The whole stretch of coastline is known as the Riviera del Conero and some of the old fishing villages have developed into thriving resorts but there are still many quiet

Jesi

beaches, some of which can only be reached by boat. A small boat service runs from the harbours of Numana and Portonovo.

The most attractive stretch of coastline begins with the Trave cliff, a long, sheer-sided rock formation, the sides of which drop almost vertically into the sea. Slightly further down the coast is the village of **Portonovo** where the fine sandy beach is overlooked by the magnificent church of Santa Maria which while being basically Romanesque is more similar in form to churches found in Corsica and in Normandy than other Italian examples. The fine view over the village and the beach from the eleventh-century church also takes in an eighteenth-century watchtower and the small fortress built by Eugénie Beauharnais in 1808 to prevent the English from landing to take on water.

At this point the road passes round the landward side of Monte Conero but at Fonte d'Olio a side road leads off to the left, up and across the side of the hill to the Badia di San Pietro, a fine Romanesque church with an exceptional raised presbytery which was originally a Benedictine hermitage. At well over 1,600ft, the Badia has outstanding views over the coast, the Sibilline mountains and inland towns such as Osimo, Loreto and Recanati.

Legend has it that the two holm oaks in front of the ex-Franciscan monastery at **Sirolo** where the road returns to the sea were planted by St Francis. What is certain is that the Neolithic tribe who once lived on the site had good taste when choosing a spot for their villages. Were it not that here the quality of sand is much higher and there are many less tourists one could almost imagine oneself in one of Capri's most famous beauty spots when contemplating the rock formations behind the beach, culminating with the Rock of the Two Sisters.

Shortly after Sirolo is **Numana** which over the last 15 years has developed into the most popular resort on the Riviera del Conero. Outside the main school holidays and some weekends it is still, however, possible to enjoy peace and quiet there amongst the fine scenery. Numana was once an important Picentine centre with strong trading links with Greece. This has provided numerous important exhibits for the town's antiquarium. The antiquarium is set out chronologically to provide a testament to life in the area from the seventh century BC through to the Roman period.

Continue down the coast to **Porto Recanati** which is justly famous for its fine fish soup but less well known for its well stocked modern art gallery in the old sixteenth-century castle.

Three miles inland at **Loreto** is Italy's most important religious shrine. In 1291 after Palestine had been over-run by the Moslems, the house in which the Virgin Mary was said to have been born and where Jesus lived until he was 30 years old, was apparently transported by angels to the top of a hill near Fiume in the north-east of Italy. It remained there for 3 years, and then on 10 December 1294 was again miraculously transported to the middle of a grove of laurels near Recanati, from where it was again transported to its present site. A magnificent sanctuary was built around the house and a village grew up to serve the pilgrims. This was later fortified by Leo X and then raised to a bishopric by Sixtus V in 1586. Pilgrims come to Loreto the whole year round but the dates when it becomes really busy are the main festivals of the Virgin Mary: 25 March, 15 August, 8 September, 8 December and then the night of the 9-10 December. Apart from the town's fortified walls everything the visitor will wish to see is grouped around the magnificent Piazza della Madonna.

The sanctuary is a magnificent fifteenth-century Gothic cathedral which replaced an earlier building in 1468 when Paul II was cured of the plague while on a visit to Loreto and received a message from heaven informing him of his apostolic destiny. Work on the new sanctuary was not completed until the eighteenth century and involved a succession of Italy's greatest architects. 'Mary's house' itself stands at the central point of the church under the dome and is covered by a layer of bas-reliefs designed by Bramante. The church

Ancona cathedral

is full of outstanding works of art which could only be done justice in a separate volume.

Two sides of the square are taken up by the L-shaped Palazzo Apostolico. The cells on the ground floor which originally housed monks are now set aside to provide accommodation for some of the many visiting pilgrims, while the first floor houses a fine museum and art gallery.

On the top of a hill 5 miles further inland is **Recanati**, famous above all for having been the birthplace and home of Giacomo Leopardi, one of Italy's greatest ever poets. Both the *Municipio* and the monument to the poet in Piazza Leopardi were erected in 1898 to mark the centenary of Leopardi's birth. The only remnant of the previous Palazzo del Comune is the sturdy rectangular battlemented tower to the left of the new town hall which dates from the twelfth century. A room of the civic art gallery which is situated in the town hall is dedicated to Leopardi, containing his funeral mask, portraits of him and members of his family and also a collection of his manuscripts. The most important exhibits in the gallery are, however, the collection of paintings by Lorenzo Lotto in room 5. Other fine works of art can be seen in the Museo Diocesano which is situated in the old papal prison alongside the cathedral.

The house in which Leopardi was born and grew up is a large eighteenth-century building with a terracotta façade which disguises the fact that it incorporates two older houses. Descendants of the poet still live in the house but the family library is open to scholars and visitors. The new building alongside the house is the National Centre for Leopardian Studies. Those who have read Leopardi's poetry will be fascinated as they walk around the town as much of what he described has remained unchanged.

Excursions from Ascoli

Should a copy of the local tourist board's brochure come into your hands do not be fooled when it claims that **Ascoli** has no pretence to being a great monumental city (almost unique for a local tourist board to be over modest about their city). The city cannot boast a church of the stature of St Peter's or even of the *Duomo* in Florence but it does have many interesting old buildings and the centre has changed little over the last 500 years. Those wishing to search out the most important buildings should visit the *Duomo* which was built in stages between the eleventh and sixteenth centuries with its fine twelfth-century octagonal baptistry and the adjacent bishop's palace, home of an interesting diocesan museum; the thirteenth-century Gothic San Francesco; the Ponte Solesta bridge which dates from the first years of the Roman Empire; or the fine Palazzo Malaspina, formed during the second half of the sixteenth century by linking together several medieval buildings. A gallery of graphic art is housed in Palazzo Malaspina and art lovers may also like to visit the town's art gallery in Palazzo Comunale where, besides paintings by Titian, Turner and Brill, works of important but near-forgotten artists such as Elizabeth Vigée Lebrun can be seen.

The real attraction of Ascoli however is the overall atmosphere of the city, the local stone which has been used almost exclusively gives architectural unity and a great sense of character to the centre. The city is very proud of its traditions amongst which is the medieval art of flag waving. If possible try and make your visit to the city coincide with the first Sunday in August when hundreds of people dress in full medieval costume to participate in the Quintana joust or the procession which precedes it.

Take the SS4 eastwards from Ascoli as far as Sant' Antonio where a minor road runs off to the left up a tributary valley of the Tronto to the village of **Offida** which still has some remains of its fortified medieval walls. The Palazzo del Comune, which houses a museum is one of the finest in the Marche. In front of the thirteenth-century tower with its battlements is a portico surmounted by cylindrical terracotta pillars and surmounted by an open loggia. Perhaps the most interesting sight in Offida is the town's womenfolk sitting at the doors of their cottages making lace, one of the town's main sources of income since the end of the fifteenth century. Every summer a lace fair is held in the Palazzo Comunale from 20 July to 20 August.

Drop down from Offida into the Tesino valley and after crossing the river follow it for $4^1/_2$ miles towards the sea until a side road climbs up the steep hill to the left towards **Ripatransone**. Part of the town is still typically medieval in appearance within the old defensive walls and with its fine views in all directions it is a town well worth visiting. Built on top of a near impregnable hill Ripatransone was an important strongpoint during the Middle Ages yet despite being coveted by other powerful rulers it was still able to become Italy's first rural free *comune* in 1205. Despite the general medieval atmosphere most of the public buildings, with the exception of the Palazzo del Podestà, which was completed in 1304, are relatively modern. Although the town only has a population of around 5,000 there are several museums and a number of traditional folkloristic events throughout the year. Some may prefer the re-enactments of the nativity story which takes place from 24 December to 24 January. Others may be attracted by the ham and red wine festival in August.

There can be few more attractive drives than the gradual descent from Ripatransone down to the Adriatic at **Grottammare** 8 miles away. For almost the entire journey a long stretch of coast is visible as are the Sibilline mountains, the Maiella, the Gran Sasso d'Italia and the Monte dell' Ascensione.

The old medieval hill town of Grottammare stands high above its modern sea shore suburb which has now outgrown it several times over. Although one of the most popular seaside resorts in the Marche, the closeness of the hills to the sea has meant that only a thin strip has been built up and although crowded the beach never reaches the levels of other resorts further to the north. Of course if you feel you can do without a deck-chair, a shower and the constant flow of illegal immigrants selling fake African jewellery, which are a feature of most Italian beaches, one only has to move slightly up or down the coast to find much more congenial surroundings.

Follow the coast for a short distance down to San Benedetto del Tronto, and then turn inland, up into the hills again towards **Acquaviva Picena** where the main occupations are making fishing nets and working with straw. The irregular-shaped fifteenth-century fortress with its round keep and powerful corner towers is an impressive example of military architecture, as is the Gothic gateway through which one passes through the defensive wall into the town. From Acquaviva drop down to the SS4 in the Tronto valley to head back to Ascoli.

Leave Ascoli again, this time to the west on the minor road signposted Venarotta which begins with a very steep hill to climb away from the city. Turn left at Venarotta then right after 3 miles. From here the road climbs steadily for 6 miles up the side of Monte Teveraccio. At the top of the climb is a little church with a minor road running off to the left alongside it. Take this road and then follow the signs for **Montemonaco**. The second highest *comune* in the Marche is an excellent starting point for a number of walks and mountain climbs. Two of the finest excursions from Montemonaco are those to the top of Monte Sibilla and to the impressive ravine known as the Gola dell' Infernaccio which separates Monte Sibilla and Monte Priora. The ravine which is well over 2 miles long is at times no more than 10ft wide. Legend has it that Monte Sibilla was once the home of Sibilla, priestess of Apollo, while others identify the mountain with the Monte Venus of Wagner's *Tannhauser*. While none of the legends can be proved it is certain that the cave known as the Grotta della Fate, a few feet below the summit, has been used in the past by witches and members of other cults.

Another fine starting point for excursions into the Sibilline mountains is **Amandola** 9 miles to the north of Montemonaco on the slopes of Monte Rotondo. Besides being a starting point for mountain walks the town also has several interesting churches, although none as important as the Abbazia dei Santi Rufino e Vitale 5 miles to the north-east. The abbey was rebuilt in the twelfth or thirteenth century on the site of an earlier sixth-century Benedictine abbey and contains several fine thirteenth- and fourteenth-century frescoes particularly in the attractive crypt.

The most important base for winter sports enthusiasts in the area is **Sarnano** $7^1/_2$ miles to the north of Amandola and considerably higher up. An efficient network of ski-lifts and cable cars serves all the most important slopes around the town and there is also a ski-school to help beginners. The best of the facilities are to be found along the extremely attractive road which links Sarnano to the village of Bolognola. The area is also suitable for walkers in summer and one particularly interesting and not too time-consuming walk is that to the summit of Monte Castel Manardo.

Further Information
— Marche —

Tourist Information Offices

The Marche are divided into four provinces, each of which has its own tourist board.

Province of Ancona
Ente Provinciale per il Turismo
Via Marini 14
Ancona
☎ (071) 201980

Province of Ascoli Piceno
Ente Provinciale per il Turismo
Corso Mazzini 229
Ascoli
☎ (0736) 51115

Province of Macerata
Ente Provinciale per il Turismo
Viale Garibaldi 87
Macerata
☎ (0733) 40449

Province of Pesaro e Urbino
Ente Provinciale per il Turismo
Via Mazzolari 4
Pesaro
☎ (0721) 31433

The following information is set out alphabetically by town. Opening times have been given where possible but are subject to change.

Museums and Other Places of Interest

Ancona
Museo Diocesano
Duomo
Church opening times.

Museo Nazionale delle Marche
Palazzo Ferretti
Via Ferretti 6

Pinacoteca Comunale F. Podesti
Palazzo Bosdari
Via Pizzecolli 17
Open: 9am-1pm; September-June, 9am-7.30pm July-August. Closed Monday.

Apecchio
Fossil Museum
Palazzo Ubaldini

Ascoli
Galleria d'Arte Grafica Moderna
Palazzo Malaspina
Open: May-September Monday-Saturday 10am-1pm and 4.30-6.30pm, Sunday 10am-12noon all year; October-April Monday-Saturday 9am-1pm.

Museo Archeologico
Palazzo Panichi
Piazza Arringo

Museo Diocesano
Palazzo Vescovile
Piazza Arringo
Open: Monday-Saturday 10am-12noon.

Pinacoteca Comunale
Palazzo Comunale
Piazza Arringo
Open: May-September, Monday-Friday 10am-1pm and 4.30-6.30pm, Saturday 9am-1pm; October-April Monday-Saturday 9am-1pm, Sunday 10am-12noon all year.

Cagli
Museo Civico
Palazzo Comunale
Via di Porta Vittoria 2

Camerino
Museo Diocesano
Palazzo Arcivescovile
Open: Tuesday and Saturday 10am-1pm. Knock at Piazza Cavour 7 or ☎ (0737) 2611.

Pinacoteca & Museo Civico
Ex-church of San Francesco
Via Sparapani 10
Open: July-September, Monday-Friday 9am-12noon and 4-7pm, Saturday am only.

Cingoli
Museo Civico
Palazzo Municipale
Piazza Vittorio Emanuele
To visit apply to Biblioteca Comunale, Via Mazzini 1.

Civitanova Marche
Museo Polare
Via B. Buozzi 6
Open: Monday-Friday 9am-12noon and 3-5.30pm. To give prior notice ☎ (0733) 73837

Galleria d'Arte Moderna 'M. Moretti'
Ex-Palazzo Comunale
Civitanova Alta ($2^1/_2$ miles)
Open: summer 9am-12noon and 4-8pm, off-peak 8am-2pm.

Corinaldo
Museo Civico
Ex-Convento degli Agostiniani

Corridonia
Pinacoteca
Canonica
Via Cavour
See parish priest.

Fabriano
Pinacoteca Civica e Museo degli Arazzi (Tapestries)
Piazza Umberto di Savoia 4

Fano
Museo Civico e Pinacoteca
Palazzo Malatestiano
Open: summer Monday-Saturday 10am-12noon and 4-7pm, Sunday am only, winter on request.

Museo Diocesano d'Arte Sacra
Ex-church of San Domenico.

Fermo
Antiquarium (Museo Archeologico)
Largo Calzecchi-Onesti
Open: summer 9.30am-12.30pm and 5-8pm, Sunday pm only, other seasons see custodian.

Pinacoteca Civica
Palazzo del Comune
Open: Monday-Saturday 9am-2pm.

Filottrano
Museo del Biroccio
Palazzo Lucchetti
Via Beltrame
Knock.

Fossombrone
Pinacoteca Comunale
Corso Garibaldi 64
Weekday mornings, see custodians.
NB. soon to be moved to a new site.

Museo Civico A. Vernerecci
Corte Alta
For permission to visit apply to Direttore della Biblioteca Passionei, del Museo e della Pinacoteca
Via Torricelli 2.

Music making in a quiet back-street, Umbria

Gaeta, Lazio

View of Sperlonga, Lazio

Avellino, Campania

Quadreria Cesarini e Pinacoteca Comunale
Via Flaminia 32
Visit as above.

Frontino
Working example of thirteenth-century mill, access from Palazzo Malatestiano.

Gradara
Rocca
Open: winter Tuesday-Saturday 9am-1.30pm, Sunday 9am-12.30pm, summer variable.

Jesi
Museo Civico
Palazzo della Signoria
Open: Saturday 9am-1pm, first and third Sunday of month 10am-12noon, other days summer 9am-12noon and 4-6pm, winter 9am-12noon and 3.30-6.30pm.

Pinacoteca
Palazzo Pianetti-Tesei
Open: as above.

Loreto
Santuario della Santa Casa
Piazza Madonna

Salo Pio XI
Sanctuary Library
Open: 8am-12.30pm and 3.30-7pm.

Museo Pinacoteca
Palazzo Apostolico
Open: April-September Monday-Thursday and Saturday 9am-1pm and 3-6pm, Sunday 9am-1pm; October-March Saturday and Sunday 9am-1pm.

Macerata
Museo della Basilica della Misericordia
Piazza San Vincenzo
Open: 7am-12noon and 3.30-8.30pm.

Museo Civico
Piazza Vittorio Veneto
Open: Tuesday-Sunday 9am-12noon.

Pinacoteca
Piazza Vittorio Veneto
Open: as above.

Museo della Carrozza
Piazza Vittorio Veneto
Open: as above.

Museo Tipologico del Preseppio
Via Maffeo Pantaleoni 4
To visit ☎ (0733) 49035.

Museo Marchigiano del Risorgimento
Piazza Vittorio Veneto
Open: July and mid-end August 8.30am-1pm. Other times Monday-Friday 9am-1pm and 3-7pm, Saturday am only.

Maiolati Spontini
Museo Spontiniano (music museum)
Facing church of San Giovanni
Custodian at No 14 of same street.

Matelica
Museo Piersanti
Via Umberto I 11
☎ (0737) 8395
Open: Monday-Saturday 10am-12noon, notifying beforehand.

Mercatello sul Metauro
Museo della Collegiata
Collegiata church.

Mondavio
Museo di Rievocazione Storica
Rocca
Open: 8am-12noon and 2-8pm.

Numana
Antiquarium
Via La Fenice 4
Open: Tuesday-Saturday 9am-2pm (summer also 4-7.30pm) Sunday 9am-1pm.

Offagna
Rocca
Open: Saturday and Sunday 9.30-11.30am and 3.30-7.30pm.

Offida
Museo Civico
Palazzo Comunale
Open: summer 10am-12.30pm and 3-8pm, other seasons ask for permission in *Municipio*.

Pennabilli
Museo Diocesano
Near Sant' Agostino church
Ask in seminary for permission to enter.

Perticara
Museo Storico Minerario
Open: May-September Tuesday-Sunday 9am-12noon and 3-6pm.

Pesaro
Biblioteca e Museo Oliveriani
Via Mazza 97
Open: winter 9.30am-12.30pm, ask in library, summer 4-7pm. Closed Sunday all year.

Museo Rossiniano and birthplace of Rossini
Via Rossini 34
Open: April-October 10am-4pm and 2-4pm, Sunday 10am-12noon, winter pm changes to 4-6pm.

Musei Civici (Pinacoteca and ceramics)
Piazzetta V. Toschi-Mosca
Open: 9.30am-1.30pm and 4-7pm; October-March 8.30am-1.30pm, closed Sunday pm and Monday am.

Piandimeleto
Museum
Casa della 7a opera di Misericordia
Via Dante

Porto Recanati
Pinacoteca Comunale
Castle.

Recanati
Pinacoteca & Museo Beniamino Gigli
Open: Tuesday-Friday summer 9.30am-12.30pm and 4.30-7.30pm; winter 3.30-6.30pm, Sunday 10am-12noon.

Museo Diocesano
Cathedral
Open: Sunday 10.30am-12.30pm, weekdays ask Sacrestan.

Palazzo Leopardi Library
Open: winter 9am-12noon and 3-5pm; summer 9am-12noon and 3-7pm.

San Ginesio
Museo Pinacoteca
Ex-church of San Sebastiano
Open: Monday, Wednesday and Friday 5-6pm.

San Leo
Forte di San Leo
Open: 9am-12noon and 2-6pm.

San Lorenzo in Campo
Antiquarium
Church of San Lorenzo

Archaeological Museum
Palazzo della Rovere

African Ethnographical Museum
Palazzo della Rovere

San Severino Marche
Museo Archeologico e Pinacoteca
Via Salimbeni 40
Open: Tuesday-Saturday 3.30-6.30pm, Sunday 10am-12.30pm and 3.30-6.30pm.

Sarnano
Pinacoteca
Palazzo Municipale
Open: 4-7pm.

Sassocorvaro
Rocca
Open: June-September Tuesday-Sunday 9.30am-12.30pm.
Other months ask in *Municipio.*

Sassoferrato
Museo delle Arti e Tradizioni Popolari
Via Don Minzoni

Galleria Civica d'Arte Moderna e Contemporanea & Museo Civico
Palazzo dei Priori
Piazza Oliva

Senigallia
Rocca Roveresca
Piazza del Duca
Open: Tuesday-Saturday 9am-12noon and 3-6pm, Sunday 9am-1pm.

Town Archives
Palazzo Baviera

Piazza del Duca
Open: 10am-12noon and 4-6pm.

Museo Pio IX
Palazzo Mastai
Piazza Roma
Open: Monday-Saturday, June-September 10am-12noon and 4-7pm; October-May 4-7pm.

Centre for research, study and documentation of the history of agriculture and the rural environment of the Marche, ex-monastery of Santa Maria Grazie, 2 miles outside town.

Tolentino
Museo delle Ceramiche
Basilica of San Nicola da Tolentino

Museo Civico
Next to Basilica

Museo Napoleonico
Piazza Mauruzi 19
Open: 10.30am-12.30pm and 5-7.30pm.

Museo Internazionale della Caricatura
Piazza Mauruzdi 19
Open: as above.

Treia
Museo Civico Archeologico
Palazzo Municipale

Urbania
Museo Civico
Palazzo Ducale
Via Piccini
Open: every afternoon on request.

Urbino
Galleria Nazionale delle Marche
Palazzo Ducale
Open: Tuesday-Saturday 9am-12noon, Sunday 9am-1pm.

House of Raphael
Via Raffaello
Open: April-September Monday-Saturday 9am-1pm and 3-7pm, Sunday 9am-1pm; November-March Tuesday-Sunday 9am-1pm; February closed.

Oratorio di San Giovanni
Via Barocci
Open: Monday-Saturday 10am-12.30pm and 3-5pm.

Oratorio di San Giuseppe
Via Barocci
Open: as above.

Museo Albani
Via P. Maia
Open: 9am-12.30pm and 3-5pm.

Fortezza Albernoz
Open: May-September 9am-1pm and 4-7pm.

Ducal Mausoleum
Church of San Bernardino
Open: 3-7pm.

Visso
Museo-Pinacoteca
Ex-church of Sant' Agostino
For admission see priest of adjacent church of Santa Maria.

10 • Umbria

Although the name Umbria is one of the most historic Italian names, the 3,260sq miles which make up the present region correspond only roughly to the territory ruled by the pre-Roman Umbrians and to the Roman region of Umbria. The actual region has no natural geographical limits but is roughly composed of the middle Tiber valley and the side valleys which feed it. Only 6 per cent of Umbria is on level ground — mainly the Tiber valley — while the rest is hilly or mountainous with a slight dominance of the second.

To the east of the Tiber, the mountains are generally steep-sided with rounded or gently sloping grassy summits and narrow gorge-like transverse valleys. The hills to the west of the river are intensively cultivated with many small villages up to about 2,300ft. The mountains which lie in the west of the region are much more regular in shape and mostly covered by woods and forests or arid infertile soil. The region's flora is fairly standard for central Italy as is the land-based fauna. Lago di Trasimeno, however, at 50sq miles the largest lake in central Italy, supports a wide range of fish, including carp weighing up to 30kg, and attracts many migrant birds from Northern Europe.

In the pre-Roman period the area to the west of the Tiber was controlled by the Etruscans, mainly from the cities of Perugia and Orvieto, while the other half of the area was ruled by the Umbrians although Todi, which served as a kind of market place for exchanges between the two peoples, had a large immigrant Etruscan population and even took its name from an Etruscan word meaning border post. The building of the Via Flaminia by the Romans to link the capital to Rimini and the Adriatic made the region very important and during the Roman period many new towns and villas sprang up along the new route.

During the Dark Ages the region began its long history as an important centre for religion with the teachings of St Benedict ('pray and work') and the establishment in the sixth century of the first

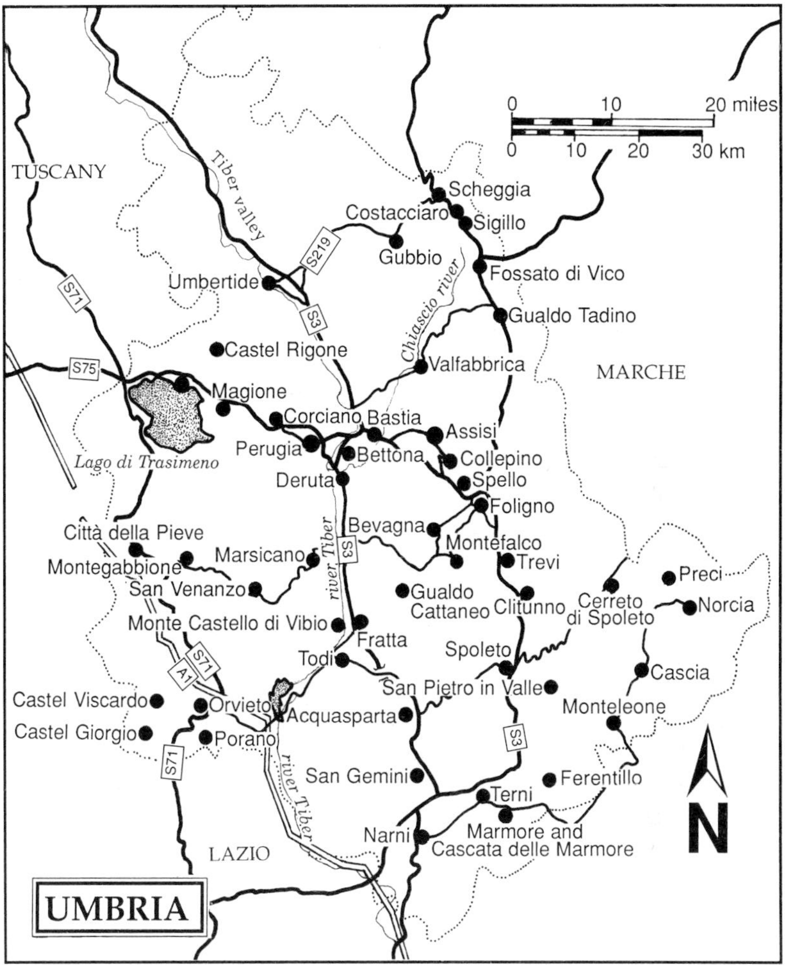

Benedictine monasteries. As St Benedict's original teaching became distorted and the order grew rich there was much discontent among the ordinary people who wanted a more popular-based religion and set up a succession of reforming movements — most of which were declared to be heretical. The last of these in the early thirteenth century deviated least from established theology and offering no direct threat was recognised by the Church as the Franciscan Order based on the principles of St Francis of Assisi.

During the Renaissance, the Umbrian School of Pinturicchio and Il Perugino was one of the most important in Italy, although after the sixteenth century only the University of Perugia could in any way be considered a major cultural force. Lack of initiative on the part of the region's papal governors and later a lack of natural resources and the fact that apart from the northern regions which border other European countries Umbria is the only region with no direct access to the sea, meant that the region stagnated economically and culturally.

In recent years there has been a concerted effort to develop the tourist industry, which while not yet increasing the number of visitors to the levels required has created an ideal atmosphere for the visitor in search of places of great interest which can be visited quietly and calmly. Fine countryside, beautiful towns with splendid architecture, sport and leisure facilities, and works of art by great artists particularly in the many historic religious centres are all waiting to be appreciated.

The region is best visited between April and October (with the exception of August) as, with the exception of a few showers at the beginning of the period, the weather is consistently good. Orvieto, Spello, Gubbio and Norcia are ideal bases from which to see the different parts of the region, while in winter Norcia is also ideally placed for the ski-runs of the Sibilline mountains.

Excursions from Gubbio

Situated at the foot of Monte Ingino, **Gubbio** developed into an important town under the Romans, but as the Roman city was razed to the ground by the Hungarians in 917 little remains today. The only important building to have escaped devastation by the Hungarians was the fine open-air theatre at the northern end of the town. The bulk of the town dates from the rebuilding which took place at the beginning of this millennium while some important public buildings were added during the Renaissance when the town was ruled by the Montefeltro of Urbino. The medieval city grew up around the cathedral and the Palatium Communis in the higher part of the town, and was enclosed by a defensive wall, much of which still remains. Palazzo Communis was incorporated by the Montefeltro within the framework of the Palazzo Ducale built by Federico da Montefeltro in 1470. Any visit to the town should include a visit to the fourteenth-century Palazzo dei Consoli, an impressive grey stone building which houses an art gallery, an archaeological museum and a fountain which predates the building itself.

Eight miles north-east of Gubbio near the Umbria-Marche border is **Scheggia**, once an important station on the Via Flaminia. A pleasant walk from this attractive village is eastwards to the pine wood of Monte Calvario where a ham festival is held every August. Head

Gualdo Tadino

south out of Scheggia on the SS3 as far as the little town of **Costacciaro**, a quiet little town perched on the top of the hill and enclosed by the remains of its medieval defensive wall. At the highest point of the town are the ruins of a medieval fortress while the fourteenth-century church of San Francesco should also be visited. The church contains some interesting frescoes and some fine sixteenth-century altar carvings. Slightly further to the south is another village with antique origins and a number of interesting churches. The churches of Sant' Agostino and of Sant' Anna in **Sigillo** are particularly worthy of attention while time should also be spared for the Spiano bridge which was constructed in the Augustan period as part of a programme for improving the Via Flaminia.

The next town along the road is composed of two parts: a new part and an older one which is built on a spur on the site of the Roman *Vicus Helvillum*. Many of the streets in the centre of **Fossato di Vico** are still essentially medieval in character. The pride of Fossato is the eleventh-century church of San Pietro, the interior of which has two naves with ogival arches. The church was restored to its original splendour in 1971. Five miles from Fossato on the side of Monte Cucco, the highest mountain in Umbria, is the Grotta di Monte Cucco, the fifth deepest cave in the world. The most impressive section of the cave is that known as the Sala Margherita which is full of stalactites and stalagmites.

Five miles further south is the attractive town of **Gualdo Tadino** which has a particularly mild climate and is a popular place for relaxing summer holidays. The centre of the town is Piazza Martiri della Libertà which is bordered by the eighteenth-century Palazzo Comunale, the thirteenth-century civic tower and the *Duomo* which was built in 1256. The remains of Fra Angelico, the important Florentine Renaissance artist, are contained in an urn in the crypt of the *Duomo*, while much of the pictorial decoration of the church was produced earlier this century. The most interesting church is the thirteenth-century San Francesco with its unusual cylindrical buttresses and poligonal apse. Part of the church houses the town's art gallery which is considered to be one of the finest in Umbria. Among the interesting paintings in the gallery is a *Family tree of the Virgin Mary* by Matteo da Gualdo. At the top end of the town is the thirteenth-century Rocca Flea which has recently become a cultural centre and the home of the town's civic museum and antiquarium.

Fifteen miles to the west along the road towards Perugia is the picturesque village of **Valfabbrica** on the northern slopes of Monte delle Croci. The town still has the remains of its thirteenth-century walls and towers as well as many buildings from the same period. Five miles after Valfabbrica a right turn leads back towards Gubbio and for those with plenty of time available, dividing this excursion into at least two sections is to be strongly recommended. The part of this excursion beyond Perugia can easily be made into another full excursion while the visitor may well wish to devote a full day to Perugia, the next port of call on this itinerary.

Originally an Umbran city, **Perugia** was later one of the twelve cities of the Etruscan Federation and then an important Roman town before being destroyed in the sixth century by the Goths. The fountain at the centre of the city's main square was erected in 1278 when a new aqueduct was built to supply Perugia. The sculptures which decorate the fountain are by Nicola and Giovanni Pisano. To one side of the square is the cathedral which has two fine cloisters and contains a museum. Across the square in the Palazzo dei Priori is the Umbrian National Art Gallery — one of the finest in Italy with works by artists such as Duccio, Piero della Francesca, Il Perugino and Fra Angelico. More of Il Perugino's work can be seen in a small chapel next to the church of San Severo, where he completed a large fresco begun by his former pupil Raphael after the latter's sudden death. The most interesting street in Perugia is almost completely underground having been built over in the sixteenth century when Pope Paul III ordered the construction of a large fort to symbolise the papal dominance over the city. One of the finest extant Etruscan gateways can be seen at the bottom of the Via Maestà delle Volte, another fine medieval street.

Nine miles west of Perugia the medium sized town of **Corciano** has retained its medieval aspect despite having a thriving modern economy. The town is built on a hill, the highest point of which is occupied by a picturesque castle from where winding streets lead down to attractive squares and the solid medieval defensive wall and towers which surround the town. The best way to visit the town is just to wander around, although care should be taken not to miss the church of San Cristoforo which is built over an Etruscan chapel and which now contains the Museo d'Arte Sacra. August is the best time to visit the town as the month is taken up by a succession of exhibitions, theatrical representations, concerts and an impressive procession in medieval costume.

A little further along the main road is the town of **Magione** whose history is tied up with that of the order of the Knights of St John of Malta. The most interesting building in the town is the Badia church which is also known as the 'Castle of the Knights of Malta'. The Badia was created in 1420 by a project which linked parts of an earlier medieval castle and a Benedictine monastery where the Templars resided. The result is a rectangular building with fortified towers at each corner and a central courtyard flanked on three sides by loggias.

Shortly after Magione the road drops down to the shore of Lago di Trasimeno, Italy's fourth largest lake. The lake, which at no point is more than 20ft deep, is quite a popular holiday place in summer and a number of hotels and restaurants are to be found around most of the shoreline. Continue westwards round the lake until **Passignano sul Trasimeno**, the largest lakeside centre, where the old town is still surrounded by medieval walls. Small boats can be hired in Passignano and organized trips on the lake are also available.

Shortly before Passignano a right turn leads up into the hills to **Castel Rigone**, a very attractive village with exceptional views. The village is famous for the terracotta earthenware produced there and, besides having the remains of a thirteenth-century castle, can also boast an exceptional Renaissance church decorated with Perugian-school frescoes. Another place with a long tradition of pottery production is **Umbertide**; several pieces of the Nero Fratta pottery produced there can be seen in the British Museum. The town is situated on the east-bank of the Tiber in one of the most attractive points of the upper valley. There are several fine churches in Umbertide but the most interesting building is the thirteenth-century Palazzo Comunale which houses a small art gallery and contains the fourteenth-century statutes governing the town of Fratta, as Umbertide was then called. Within walking distance of the town (also accessible by car) are the castles of Montaldo and Civitella Ranieri, the latter being one of the finest and best conserved in the area.

Return to Gubbio on the SS219 which passes through the attractive wooded Assino valley. Several castles and ruins can be seen along the valley as can the eleventh-century abbey of Campo Reggiano which has an extremely interesting crypt with calciferous small capitals.

Excursions from Spello

Spello on the southern slopes of Monte Subasio has had a long and varied history and consequently offers a great deal of variety to the visitor. The main testimony to the town's importance in Roman times is the ruined first-century amphitheatre which was excavated in the late 1950s and which is to be found just over half a mile outside the town. The other major Roman monument in the town is the Porta Venere gate although this has been altered somewhat by restorations over the centuries. The church of San Claudio, built at the end of the twelfth century over the ruins of a Roman building, is the most important of the many medieval buildings in the town. The graceful façade has three portals, two mullioned windows and a fine central rose window, while the main altar table is composed of the lid from a Roman sarcophagus. Although parts of the church of Santa Maria Maggiore date back to the twelfth century, most of the original church was demolished and rebuilt in the sixteenth. One of the chapels in the church, the Cappella Baglioni to the left of the nave is completely frescoed by Pinturicchio, and many consider the chapel to be his masterpiece. At the sides of the apse are frescoes by Il Perugino, but these were painted at the end of his life when his creative powers were in decline. Another of the side chapels, the Cappella del Sepolcro has been turned into a small museum. Other churches worth visiting which also provide pleasant short walks are the Renaissance Chiesa Tonda, $1^1/_2$ miles outside the town, built in the form of a Greek cross with an octagonal dome, and the fifteenth-century cloistered San Girolomo $^3/_4$ mile from the centre.

Beyond the church of San Girolomo the road climbs to **Collepino**, a fine castellated village which offers excellent opportunities for walking on Monte Subasio. Beyond Collepino the road is unmetalled, but still suitable for motor vehicles, and climbs to the top of

Porta Venere, Spello

Monte Subasio over the next 6 miles. Five miles down the track on the other side is the Franciscan monastery, Eremo delle Carceri, built near the small hermits cell where St Francis went into retreat. From there the road drops down steeply, past a pleasant camp site to **Assisi**. The top end of the town, where you arrive, is a good place to park, and is also the starting point for the track to the fine ruined Rocca Maggiore fortress which dates from the fourteenth century. The medieval streets which lead down to the cathedral of Assisi are the site of the town's most pleasant and most realistically priced restaurants. The cathedral is interesting but pales into insignificance alongside the basilica of San Francesco which consists of two fine thirteenth-century churches, one on top of the other. The lower basilica is one of the finest churches in the world with frescoes by Cimabue, Giotto, Simone Martini and Pietro Lorenzetti, while the upper church which was decorated almost entirely by Giotto is similar in style to some of the more important English cathedrals. The church of Santa Chiara is also of great importance having been built in 1257-65 by the Clarissans, the followers of Santa Chiara who set up the order of nuns to complement the Franciscans. The Corinthian façade in the main square was originally the entrance to the Roman Temple of Minerva and originally stood on a plinth above the square which has been covered up as the street level has been raised over the centuries. Excavations are being carried out under the surface of the square to throw more light on the town's Roman past and finds can be seen in the crypt of the ex-church of San Nicola which is now the civic museum.

Five miles west of Assisi is **Bastia**, which despite its generally modern aspect conserves some fine old buildings in the centre. Of these the most important is the fourteenth-century church of Santa Croce, with its pink and white stone façade and its Gothic interior. Seven miles south of Bastia, past the abbey of San Crispolto with its tenth-century apse, is the charming medieval town of **Bettona** on the crest of a hill covered with olive groves. The town was originally very much influenced by the Etruscans as a 130ft stretch of Etruscan wall demonstrates, but the bulk of the buildings date from the period immediately following 1352 when the town was destroyed by the Perugians. The centre of the town is Piazza Cavour where the most important church, Santa Maria Maggiore, contains a fine painting by Il Perugino, and Palazzo Comunale which hosts the town's art gallery and a collection of Etruscan relics.

Torgiano, across the Chiascio river, is a quiet country town with a predominantly agricultural economy. An interesting wine museum is housed in the sixteenth-century Palazzo Graziani-Baglioni. The museum has a section dedicated to the therapeutic qualities of wine, while another room contains books on wine and wine-making, the earliest of which dates from the sixteenth century.

Four miles to the south is **Deruta** which for centuries has been famous for its pottery and where an international ceramics exhibition is held once every 3 years. Examples of the town's pottery from the sixteenth, seventeenth and eighteenth centuries can be seen in the Museo delle Ceramiche on the second floor of the Palazzo Comunale, the first floor of which houses an interesting art gallery.

Fragments of masonry with Roman and medieval inscriptions

can be found in the courtyard. As well as the Palazzo Comunale, the fourteenth-century church of San Francesco containing some fine paintings should also be visited.

Follow the main road down the Tiber valley to Collepepe and then take the left turn to **Collazzone**, a quiet village on the top of an olive-covered hill. The village, which is still almost completely enclosed by its circle of defensive walls, is almost entirely unspoilt and, despite having no important monuments or churches, is a delightful place.

A few miles to the east is **Gualdo Cattaneo**, another fortified medieval town which now attracts quite a few holidaymakers in summer looking to get away from the bustle and crowds of the seaside resorts and the large cities. It is the overall atmosphere of the town rather than specific monuments which make Gualdo attractive, although the cylindrical tower built by Alessandro VI (Roderigo Borgia) in the main square is impressive. A minor road which crosses the Attone valley links Gualdo with **Bevagna**. This fine medieval town was originally a Roman settlement and there is still considerable evidence of their influence. The lower part of the thirteenth-century defensive wall is formed of the remains of its third-century Roman predecessor, while the mosaics of the Roman bath house in Via Porta Guelfa and the foundations of the amphitheatre just outside the town are well worth looking at. Within the town itself, most of the noteworthy buildings are to be found in Piazza Silvestri. Apart from the nineteenth-century fountain almost every aspect of the square is medieval, with pride of place going to the Palazzo dei Consoli, which now houses the most attractive theatre in Umbria. The Romanesque churches of San Silvestro and San Michele date from the late twelfth century. To the right of San Silvestro is the lower section of a bell tower which experts are unsure whether to class as ruined or unfinished. An interesting walk is to the north-west of the town where a small tree-lined lake is to be found beyond the Convento dell' Annunziata.

Four miles to the south is **Montefalco**, another fine medieval town famous for the quality of the frescoes in its churches. The frescoes of Benozzo Gozzoli in the churches of San Fortunato and San Francesco represent the highest level of achievement of the Umbrian school of painting and for centuries served as an inspiration for local artists. The frescoes in San Francesco are of such importance that the church is no longer used as a church but instead has become an art gallery. The nave is decorated with frescoes by many of the finest Umbrian artists but the focal point is the central apse where Gozzoli's magnificent cycle of frescoes relating major episodes from the life of St Francis can be seen. San Fortunato, which was also frescoed by Gozzoli, is situated $^3/_4$ mile outside the town and in part dates back to the fifth century. The Palazzo Comunale contains the town's library and several important paintings but the main incentive to visit it is for the excellent views to be had of the surrounding countryside from the tower.

Between Montefalco and Spello is **Foligno**, a large town, mainly modern in appearance. It is worth visiting if only for the various museums housed in the late fourteenth-century Palazzo Trinci. An archaeological museum and an art gallery are contained in the building along with the town library and archives. Besides the paintings in the gallery, the central stairway is lined by late Gothic frescoes although these are not in very good condition.

Excursions from Norcia

Besides being an attractive town set against fine countryside, **Norcia** is famous for being the birthplace of St Benedict and has a rich artistic heritage as a result. The centre of the town is Piazza San Benedetto and it is here that the town's three most important monuments, the church of San Benedetto, the *Duomo*, and the Castellina are to be found. Although the actual church of San Benedetto is only 600 years old the original church is believed to have been built over the spot where Benedict's parents lived. Some fine works of art can be seen in the interior which is built in the form of a Latin cross. The *Duomo*, which was largely rebuilt in 1730 after being badly damaged by an earthquake, is situated in the southern corner of the square and also contains some interesting works of art. Facing the *Duomo* is the square sixteenth-century castle where the town's museum is situated on the upper floor. Every July and August the rooms of the lower floor host an exhibition of works by contemporary artists, the proceeds of which go towards the upkeep of Norcia's monuments. Norcia is well placed for reaching the mountain resort of Forca Canapine, one of Umbria's main winter sports centres.

Leave Norcia westwards and then turn left along the Corno valley as far as **Cascia**, a quiet town on the crest of a hill suitable as a starting point for gentle walking excursions. Cascia was the birthplace of Santa Rita and the church of Santa Maria where she was baptised in 1381 should be visited. The basilica and monastery of Santa Rita are modern buildings which replaced the originals in the middle of this century but they should be visited as they contain relics and documents relating to the saint's life and several notable works of art and her sarcophagus in the cell where she died. Walks can be taken to the surrounding villages of Roccaporena (Santa Rita's birthplace), Logna, Poggio Primocaso, Ocosce and Piandoli with its ruined castle.

Drop down the Corno valley as far as the attractive village of **Monteleone** where a Bronze Age chariot (now in the Metropolitan Museum of New York) was found in a burial chamber. From Monteleone cross over the pass between Monte Coscerno and Monte Civitella to the Nera valley. Just down the valley, straddling both banks of the river is **Scheggino**. There are a number of interesting churches here but nothing to compare with the tenth-century abbey of San Pietro in Valle, 5 miles down the valley. This church with its single long nave is the only surviving building with direct links to the Longobard duchy of Spoleto. The frescoes which line the nave probably date from the twelfth century and seem to represent an attempt to break away from the dominant Byzantine style of the period.

Continue past Ferentillo which is overlooked by a castle and ruins, until just beyond Collestatte Piano. Leave your car here and walk to the Cascata delle Marmore waterfalls where the river Velino drops over 500ft in three steps to join the Nera. The origin of the waterfalls is to be found in Roman times when it was decided to divert the Velino in an attempt to resolve the problems of useless marshland and of the Tiber flooding Rome.

Despite being an important industrial centre **Terni** has much to offer the visitor with several fine churches and interesting museums as well as traces of the city's Roman past. The amphitheatre was built in AD32 by the Romans out of two differently coloured stone blocks, creating a fine effect which is still visible among the ruins today. Several fragments of marble Roman masonry can be seen in the walls of the nearby Romanesque church of Sant' Alò which was built in the eleventh century by the Maltese Knights. The town boasts an interesting museum of prehistory and an art gallery containing several fine paintings by Benozzo Gozzoli: both of these are situated in Palazzo Barnaba Manassei.

Take the SS3 out of Terni as far as **Narni**, the former Umbrian city of *Nequinum*. For centuries the centre of civic life in Narni has been the attractive Piazza dei Priori and in particular Palazzo del Podestà which was formed in the thirteenth century when three fortified tower houses were linked together. Various rooms in the *palazzo* are frescoed while a reasonably sized collection of Roman inscriptions has also been gathered in the building. Facing the *palazzo* is the mid-fourteenth-century Loggia dei Priori, formed of two high open arches. The Romanesque church of San Domenico has been turned into a fine art gallery where alongside the inevitable Gozzolis there is also a chapel frescoed by the Zuccaris. Gozzoli's talent was such, however, that even in such exalted company his *Annunciation* is in a class of its own. It is also worth paying a visit to the abandoned *Rocca* which has fine views in most directions, and the Ponte d'Augusto Roman bridge which was originally 400ft long and carried the road almost 100ft up over the Nera.

Due north is **San Gemini**, a well known spa centre whose mineral waters can be found in most Italian supermarkets. The town has an interesting centre which is still in part medieval but the real interest lies with the ruins of the Roman *municipio* of *Carsulae* 2 miles out of the centre. The town was established in the third century BC and is mentioned for its beauty by Tacitus and Pliny the Younger but seems to have been abandoned after its principal buildings were damaged by earth movements. The most complete of the buildings are the theatre and the amphitheatre on the eastern side of the old Via Flaminia.

Due north again on the top of a hill is **Acquasparta** which was a popular spa centre with the Romans and has recently begun again to make a name for itself in this field. There are still considerable remains of the medieval defensive system with several towers and tracts of wall defending the approaches to the town.

Spoleto, 15 miles to the north-east, can get very busy at peak times, but at others try not to pass through without visiting the town art gallery in Palazzo Comunale which contains paintings by Guercino amongst others. High above Spoleto is the holy mountain of Monteluco built around an important Franciscan sanctuary where a fresh water well is said to have been sunk by the saint himself. The slopes of Monteluco are thickly wooded and very popular with nature lovers. The very name of the mountain indicates that the woods have always been of great importance as *luco* is a corruption of the Latin *lucus*, or 'holy wood'.

Seven miles north of Spoleto are the Fonti del Clitunno, a series of natural fountains which form several crystal-clear small lakes and give rise to the Clitunno river. Among the poets who have extolled the beauty of the fountains over the centuries have been Virgil, Carducci and Byron (*Childe Harolde's Pilgrimage*). A little to the north, by the side of the main road is a small church built on the remains of the Roman Temple of Clitunno. The original Roman temple (mentioned by Pliny the Younger) was devoted to the Oracle who gave her

Le Fonti del Clitunno

prophesies at the fountains.

Trevi, situated on the top of a hill $2^1/_2$ miles to the north, is one of the most picturesque towns in Umbria as it dominates the Spoletina plain. The centre of the town is Piazza Mazzini dominated on the east side by the fourteenth-century Palazzo Comunale, site of the town's art gallery. The town passed into the papal sphere of influence at the end of the fourteenth century and the rest of the town's major monuments are all religious. The finest of the churches is the thirteenth-century Gothic San Francesco, although surrounding buildings make it impossible to see more than small sections at a time. The most important work of art, however, is the Altare del Sacramento in the church of Sant' Emiliano which was produced by Rocco di Tommaso in 1522.

Return back down the Clitunno valley until just after the fountains and take the left turn for **Campello sul Clitunno**, a small town divided into several hamlets scattered over the hillside. The highest of the hamlets is Campello Alto which grew up around a tenth-century castle. A convent in the village contains several interesting frescoes, some in the Giottesque manner. Beyond Campello, head northwards along several miles of unmetalled mountain roads until the SS319. Turn right and drop down into the attractive Vigi valley which soon brings you into **Cerreto di Spoleto**. The town is overlooked from the north by the monastic complex of San Giacomo but its chief claim to fame lies in the vast variety of herbs and spices which grow there. For centuries they have been made up into medicinal potions and sold throughout the world. Not all the potions were quite as effective as was claimed and the word charlatan comes from Cerretano (a man of Cerreto).

Preci, the last town of this excursion, is 10 miles to the north-east and appears to be a typical old Umbrian hill town. In the medieval period a fortified castle stood on the site and the village grew up within the walls of this. By the sixteenth century this little town was famous throughout Europe for the ability of its surgeons and opticians. Most of the buildings in the town date from the mid-sixteenth century as the town was destroyed by an earthquake in 1328 and then after a siege in 1528.

Excursions from Orvieto

The flat-topped volcano crowned by **Orvieto** has been inhabited since the Iron Age although after the Romans destroyed the Etruscan city in 264BC the site was relatively unimportant until the Byzantine period. By the end of the thirteenth century the city was one of the most important in central Italy but after that, internal strife and the Black Death reduced its influence until it was absorbed by the Papal States. Several popes built residences in the city which now contain the Museo dell' Opera del Duomo. The *Duomo* itself is one of the finest Gothic cathedrals in Italy although some Romanesque influence can also be detected in the nave. The finest works of art are the frescoes by Fra Angelico and Luca Signorelli which dominate the new chapel in the south transept. At the eastern end of the town behind the dismantled papal fortress is the Pozzo di San Patrizio, a 'well' down the rock face, consisting of two interlocking spiral stairways which were used for communication with the outside world during war time. The remains of an Etruscan temple and the Etruscan necropolis can be seen just outside the town.

To the east of Orvieto the SS79b passes through countryside of great natural beauty before reaching **Todi**, a medieval centre overlooking the Tiber valley. The centre of the town, Piazza Vittorio Emanuele II, has been the centre of civic life since the Roman forum stood on the spot. Now the buildings which surround it are the testaments of the thriving political life in medieval Todi. Palazzo dei Priori, Palazzo del Popolo and Palazzo del Capitano all date from the thirteenth century and form excellent backgrounds for the town's major museums. The *Duomo* was begun in the twelfth century al-

Santa Maria della Consolazione, Todi

though it was not completed until the sixteenth. There are many fine works of art in the *Duomo* and a point should be made of visiting this and the Gothic church of San Fortunato, where the fourth chapel on the right contains a *Madonna and Child with two Angels* by Masolino. Apart from the central squares and the fine churches Todi is notable for its overall medieval aspect and for its two circles of defensive walls: one having Etruscan-Roman origins and the other dating from the medieval period.

Take the road towards Perugia for 3 miles and then turn left for **Monte Castello di Vibio**. Situated on the top of a steep hill like Todi, Vibio probably has Etruscan origins. Now it is a very quiet little town, almost completely unspoilt within its medieval walls. The nearby small town of **Fratta Todina** still has much of the original walls which enclosed it when it was a castellated medieval village. The towered Palazzo Vescovile (bishop's palace) contains some interesting sixteenth-century frescoes and has an attractive courtyard. Head westwards from Fratta along roads (which at times become little more than tracks) to **San Venanzo**, an attractive agricultural centre situated on a hill covered with lush green pines. The area immediately around San Venanzo is suited for several pleasant yet not too strenuous walks.

Continuing westwards the road drops steeply down into the Fersinone valley and climbs equally steeply out of the other side

The cathedral at Todi

before finally arriving in **Montegabbione**. This village is typically medieval with its system of defensive walls, and is made particularly attractive by the copses of oak on the surrounding hillside. A few miles more brings you to **Città della Pieve** almost on the border with Tuscany. Situated on the top of a hill dominating the Chiani valley the town was known as *Castrum Plebis* until 1601 when Clement VIII turned it into a bishopric. The twelfth-century church of San Gervasio e San Protasio was turned into a cathedral although some parts such as the bell tower and the crypt are original. Many of the paintings in the cathedral are by Il Perugino who was born in the town. Another fresco by Il Perugino, considered to be the best of his works still in Italy, is to be found in the church of Santa Maria della Mercede. Of the non-religious buildings, the most notable is the Torre del Pubblico near to the cathedral dating from the tenth century.

Return back on the road towards Montegabbione until the main road bears off to the right towards Orvieto. The junction is dominated by the attractive village of **Monteleone d'Orvieto**, perched on a spur of rock high above. Much of the medieval defensive system still remains at Monteleone, the starting point for several pleasant walks into the surrounding hills. Ten miles further to the south is the active little town of **Ficulle** where many traditional crafts are still practised, and where a regular crafts fair is held. There are several interesting churches in the town and an incomplete circle of defensive walls with restored thirteenth-century towers. Three miles further towards Orvieto a right turn leads down through olive groves to the Castello della Sala which dates from 1350. The most interesting feature of the castle is the isolated cylindrical tower which was used as a last refuge if the castle itself were taken by the enemy.

After the castle the road continues over the motorway, over the rivers Ritorto and Paglia, and over the railway line to **Castel Viscardo**. This little village has excellent views over the Paglia valley. The castle has changed little since it was built by the Spada family in the fifteenth century while the parish church contains an exquisite ivory crucifix which was presented by Louis XIV to Cardinal Spada while the latter was the papal nuncio in Paris. Another attractive village which was originally a fortified castle can be seen for miles to the south. **Castel Giorgio** is very pleasantly sited in a heavily wooded area and is fairly popular with nature lovers in summer.

Follow the road from Castel Giorgio almost as far as Orvieto then take a small right turn to the village of Porano. **Porano** is a beautiful little town perched on the top of an outcrop of volcanic rock 4 miles to the south of Orvieto. Apart from a few sixteenth-century buildings everything in the village is as it was in the medieval period and the nature of the site (as with Orvieto) has prevented further expansion from taking place.

Further Information

— Umbria —

Tourist Information Offices

Umbria is divided into two provinces, each of which has its own tourist board.

Province of Perugia
Azienda di Promozione Turistica
Via Mazzini 21
Perugia
☎ (075) 23227

Province of Terni
Azienda di Promozione Turistica
Viale C. Battisti 5
Terni
☎ (0144) 43047

Other major tourist offices are sited in Assisi, Cascia, Castiglione del Lago, Foligno, Gubbio, Spoleto, Todi, Amelia, and Orvieto.

Museums and Other Places of Interest

This information is arranged alphabetically by town. Opening hours have been given where available but are liable to change.

Assisi
Tesoro della Basilica di San Francesco
Open: April-October Tuesday-Sunday 9am-12.30pm and 2.30-6pm.

Museo della Basilica di Santa Maria degli Angeli
(3 miles SW)
Piazza Porziuncola
Open: April-September Thursday-Tuesday 9am-12.30pm and 2.30-6pm.

Museo e Archivio Capitolare Cattedrale San Rufino
Piazza San Rufino
Open: 8am-12noon and 2pm-sunset.

Pinacoteca Comunale
Piazza del Comune
Open: Tuesday-Sunday, summer 9am-12.30pm and 4-7pm, winter 9am-12noon and 3-6pm, Sunday 9am-12.30pm.

Foro Romano
Via Portica
Open: Tuesday-Saturday 9am-12.30pm and 4-7pm (summer) and 9am-12noon and 3-6pm (winter), Sunday 9am-12.30pm.

Galleria d'Arte Contemporanea
Cittadella Cristiana
Via Ancajani
Open: Monday-Friday 10.30am-1pm and 4.30-6.30pm.

Galleria del Cantico
Santuario San Damiano
Open: April-September 2-6.30pm, October-March 2-4.30pm.

Bettona
Pinacoteca, Palazzo del Podestà
Piazza Cavour

Bevagna
Pinacoteca Comunale
Palazzo Comunale, Corso Matteotti
Open: Monday-Saturday 9am-1pm.

Cascata delle Marmore
Illuminated waterfalls
Open: March-April and September-October Saturday and Sunday 7.30-9pm, May-August 8.30-10.30pm.

Cascia
Monastero di Santa Rita
Open: Monday-Saturday 9am-12noon and 2.30-5.30pm, Sunday 8am-12.30pm.

Castiglione del Lago
Castle

Città di Castello
Museo del Duomo
Duomo
Via del Modello
Ask permission in Sacresty.

Museo Preistorico-Paleontologico
Piazza Garibaldi 2

Pinacoteca Comunale
Via della Cannoniera 22
Ring bell, Monday-Saturday 9am-1pm and 3-5.30pm, Sunday 9am-1pm.

Corciano
Museo d'Arte Sacra
Church of San Cristoforo
Apply to priest at Santa Maria church.

Deruta
Pinacoteca
Palazzo Comunale

Museo delle Ceramiche
Palazzo Comunale (2nd floor)

Foligno
Museo Archeologico
Palazzo Trinci
Piazza della Repubblica
Open: Sunday 9am-12noon, winter Monday-Saturday 9am-4pm, summer Monday-Saturday 9am-7pm.

Pinacoteca
Palazzo Trinci
Piazza della Repubblica
Open: as above.

Fonti del Clitunno
Fountains, 9am-12.30pm and 2.30pm-sunset.

Gualdo Tadino
Museo Civico and Antiquarium
Rocca Flea

Pinacoteca Comunale
San Francesco Church
Corso Italia

Gubbio
Museo e Pinacoteca Comunale
Palazzo dei Consoli
Open: October-March 9am-1pm and 3-5pm, April-September 9am-12noon and 3.30-6pm.

Museo di San Francesco
Piazza 40 Martiri

Museo del Duomo
Via Ducale

Montefalco
Museo
Ex-church of San Francesco
Via Ringhiera Umbra 6
Open: Monday-Saturday 9am-12.30pm and 3.30-6.30pm, Sunday 9am-12noon.

Monteluco
Santuario Francescano di Monteluco
Open: 8am-1pm and 4-8pm.

Narni
Museo di San Domenico
Ex-church of San Domenico
Ask in Communal Offices.

Nocera Umbra
Pinacoteca Comunale
Church of San Francesco

Antiquarium
Piazza Caprera

Norcia
Museo Civico Diocesano
Castellina
Open: May-September Tuesday-Sunday 10am-12.30pm and 3.30-6pm, October-April 10am-12.30pm and 2-4pm.

Orvieto
Museo dell' Opera del Duomo
Palazzo Papale
Piazza del Duomo

Opera del Duomo Archaeological Museum
Palazzo dell' Opera del Duomo
Piazza del Duomo

Fondazione Museo Claudio Faina
29 Piazza del Duomo

Pozzo di San Patrizio
Open: summer 10am-7pm, winter 9am-12noon and 2-4pm.

Perugia
Museo del Duomo
Cathedral
Piazza 4 Novembre

Umbrian National Art Gallery
Palazzo dei Priori
Piazza 4 Novembre

Galleria dell' Accademia delle Belle

Arti
Piazza San Francesco

Umbrian Archaeological Museum
Piazza San Domenico

Ipogeo dei Volumi (Etruscan tomb)
Open: Tuesday-Saturday 9am-12noon, Sunday 9am-1pm.

Ipogeo di San Manno
(Etruscan tomb)
Ask custodian.

Ipogeo di Villa Sperandio
(Etruscan tomb)
Ask custodian.

San Gemini
Carsulae Archaeological Site (2 miles north)

San Giustino
Castello Bufalini
With permission of owners.

Sigillo
Grotta di Monte Cucco
(5 miles NE)

Spello
Museo
Santa Maria Maggiore church
Piazza Matteotti
See priest.

Spoleto
Galleria Comunale d'Arte Moderna
Via Gregorio Elladio 7
Open: Wednesday-Monday 10am-1pm and 3-6pm.

Museo Civico
Piazza del Duomo
Palazzo della Signoria
Open: Monday-Saturday 10am-12noon and 3-5pm, Sunday 10am-12noon.

Raccolta Diocesana d'Arte Sacra
Palazzo Arcivescovile
Via Aurelio Saffi
Open: on request.

Basilica di San Salvatore
Via del Cimitero
Open: November-February 9am-12noon and 2-5pm, March-April and September-October 9am-12noon and 3-6pm, May-August 8am-12noon and 4-7pm.

Terni
Museo Preistorico
Via Barnaba Manassei 6
Open: Tuesday-Saturday 9am-1pm and 4-6pm, Sunday 9am-1pm.

Pinacoteca Comunale
Address and opening as above.

Todi
Museo Etrusco Romano
Palazzo del Capitano
Open: Monday 3-6.30pm Tuesday-Friday 9am-12noon and 3-6.30pm, Saturday 9am-12.30pm, Sunday 10am-12noon.

Pinacoteca Civica
Palazzo del Capitano
Open: as above.

Museo Lapidario
Address and opening as above.

Torgiano
Museo del Vino
Palazzo Graziani Baglioni
Knock at next door.

Trevi
Pinacoteca
Palazzo Comunale
Piazza Mazzini
Open: Monday-Saturday 8.30am-2pm.

11 • Lazio

The region of Lazio is divided into five provinces, based on Rome, Viterbo, Rieti, Frosinone and Latina, of which only the Province of Rome (and then only in part) is much visited by tourists. This is not because the other provinces lack interest, it is only that the overwhelming international importance of the capital throws all else into shadow. Eighty-five per cent of the tourists who visit Lazio each year are there to see Rome, not counting the millions of day-trippers.

Since the beginning of recorded history in the Western World, Rome has been a great artistic and cultural centre and this has had a strong influence on the rest of the region. Works of art by great artists can sometimes be found in the churches of smaller centres, and their influence can almost always be seen in the works of lesser known artists. Numerous Roman remains are to be found throughout the region while evidence of a strong Etruscan presence can be seen in the north. Some of the larger towns such as Viterbo are of great historic interest with large medieval sections while the fortifications of many of the smaller towns reveal that they were once on fiercely disputed borders with other states.

Lazio does not have obvious geographical boundaries, including part of pre-unification Tuscany, part of Campania, and almost the whole of the province of Rieti (belonging geographically to Umbria). Geologically it can be divided into two — the older part, a broken line of calciferous mountains which run roughly parallel to the main Apennine chain at first following the course of the Tiber and then moving slowly seawards until reaching the Tyrrhenian at Terracina; and the new, formed by hills and coastal plains, first flanked then divided by the course of the Tiber. This part of the region was thrown up from the sea bed by a series of great volcanic eruptions centred on the Albani hills. The presence of many spas in this part of the region is evidence of continuing subterranean secondary volcanic activity.

Long stretches of sand dunes tend to form along the coastline, particularly in the southern part of the region, which for centuries

was uninhabitable because of the vast areas of marshland which resulted from the inability of the rivers to reach the sea. It was only in the 1920s and 30s that an adequate irrigation system was developed — the one great achievement of the fascist regime. The land recovered, however, and the three new towns of Latina, Pomezia and Aprilia are of interest only to those interested in irrigation schemes and, like Rome, will not be dealt with in this guide.

Although never extensive enough to be classed as a forest, roughly 20 per cent of the region is covered by natural growth, the most common in the form of mixed woods (oak, cork oak, and holm oak) while up in the mountains beech predominates. The pine woods along the coast are almost all the result of plantations established in previous centuries while the chestnut woods on the Albani hills have also been cultivated by man. Until fairly recently bear, wolves and lynx were common in the mountains of Lazio but all are now believed to be extinct or virtually extinct and only a handful of wild boar and deer now remain despite recent attempts to protect them.

Viterbo, Rieti, Fiuggi and Terracina are four towns ideally placed to serve as starting points for exploratory excursions into Lazio. Autumn is the best period to visit the region, with spring and its slightly more unpredictable climate a close second. The mountains can be visited without discomfort in summer and in winter offer a few winter sports centres, mainly in the province of Frosinone.

Excursions from Viterbo

Seat of the papacy for most of the second half of the thirteenth century, much of the centre of **Viterbo**, particularly the San Pellegrino quarter, is still typically medieval, having been built between the twelfth and fourteenth centuries when the city rivalled Rome in importance. Much of the medieval city was built in the same local stone which further enhances the city's charm.

Any visit must begin in Piazza San Lorenzo where the magnificent papal palace (1255-66) stands alongside the restored twelfth-century cathedral. The cathedral contains many fine works of art including the funeral monuments of John XXI (the only Portuguese pope) and of Letizia Bonaparte. After the damage suffered in the last war, the cathedral was restored to its original Romanesque style, with the exception of the façade. To the right of the papal palace is an elegant loggia added in the fifteenth century containing a fountain made up of fragments from earlier fountains.

The centre of the medieval quarter of San Pellegrino, is Piazza San Pellegrino which is the best preserved medieval square in Italy with its dark tower-houses, loggias, covered walkways and Romanesque mullioned windows. The whole quarter is gently illuminated at night. The whole of the old centre is surrounded by the 3 miles of city wall roughly triangular in shape. The city contains many fountains and at one time was known as the city of beautiful women and fountains.

Six miles to the north are the ruins of *Ferento*, established by the Etruscans, destroyed and then rebuilt by the Romans. The town flourished for several centuries and rivalled Viterbo for influence. In 1172 the Viterbesi destroyed the city because the citizens had allegedly erected a heretical crucifix where Christ's eyes were open instead of closed. The best preserved Roman building is the restored theatre which hosts classical plays during the summer. Much of the rest of the town is still being excavated.

To the north-east is **Montefiascone**, an attractive old hill town

Palazzo Farnese, Caprarola

overlooking Lago di Bolsena, famous for its white wine and interesting church built on two levels in the eleventh and twelfth centuries. From Montefiascone drop down to the lake and follow the shore clockwise until the **Capodimonte** promontory. Here, the medieval town which gives its name to the promontory (best avoided during busy periods), is dominated by the fine octagonal castle designed by Antonio da Sangallo the Younger for Pier Luigi Farnese in the sixteenth century. The Bisentina Island has more fine buildings by Sangallo. To visit the island from Capodimonte it is necessary to obtain permission from the Princes of Drago, in nearby Bolsena.

Near where the main road turns away from the shore are the ruins of *Bisentium*. Built by the Etruscans, destroyed by the Longobards, rebuilt in the tenth century, destroyed in the thirteenth by the pope, rebuilt again by the Counts of Bisenzio it was finally abandoned because of the high-level of malaria in the early nineteenth century.

Fifteen miles to the south is **Tuscania**, once one of the most important Etruscan cities, now a small centre with little industry and depopulation problems. The town itself has a typical medieval section and another which is decidedly Renaissance, but most interesting are the many Etruscan necropoli dating back to the seventh century BC. An important museum of Etruscan and medieval art is being set up in the fifteenth-century ex-monastery, Santa Maria del Riposo, and may open soon. The town has a great deal of interest and yet is virtually ignored by tourists.

South again is **Tarquinia**, another of the twelve main cities of the Etruscan Federation. The Etruscan town and necropoli were situated to the east of the hill where the present town is sited and include some of the most important tombs yet to be discovered. Many of the tombs were decorated with fine paintings. Several of the tombs are open to visitors during the opening hours of the Museo Nazionale Tarquinese in the nearby town. The museum contains one of the world's most important archaeological collections. Until Tarquinia fell into the possession of the Church in the sixteenth century it had a flourishing maritime trade which allowed many different architectural influences to leave their mark on the medieval town.

Other necropoli and medieval ruins can be visited at **Blera**, just to the south of Vetralla, while returning to Viterbo. **San Martino al Cimino**, a good base for the chestnut-covered slopes of the surrounding hills, is 4 miles south of Viterbo. It grew up around a fine early thirteenth-century abbey in Gothic-Cistercian style. Much of the monastery which once adjoined the church has disappeared but the magnificent church is still virtually intact.

Caprarola to the east of Lago di Vico is the starting point for many walks in the woods covering the slopes of the Cimini mountains. It is the site of the Palazzo Farnese, the finest piece of mannerist architecture. The two-storey pentagonal building is designed and decorated as a celebration of the power of the Farnese family. Most of the rooms are filled with frescoes by Federico and Taddeo Zuccari.

Sutri, 7 miles to the south, is an interesting town incorporating fragments of buildings from the Etruscan to the medieval periods. Just outside the town is an Etruscan amphitheatre carved out of the soft local rock and nearby a semi-underground chapel which was adapted from a much earlier tomb in the medieval period (to visit ask for permission in the town's cathedral). Further to the south are the ruins of the Etruscan city of *Veio* which was a strong rival of Rome until the crushing victory of the latter in 396BC. Systematic excavations have only been undertaken in this century and important discoveries are still being made fairly regularly.

Excursions from Rieti

One of the most important cities of the Sabines in the Roman and pre-Roman periods, **Rieti** was an important centre of the Church in the

The amphitheatre at Sutri

medieval period. Most of the interesting buildings date either from this period or from the rebuilding programmes which were undertaken in the Renaissance and baroque eras. Piazza Vittorio Emanuele II, 10ft above the level of the Roman forum, is the centre of the city. On one side of the square in the old Palazzo Comunale is the civic museum which houses an interesting collection of paintings, mainly by local artists. The building dates from the thirteenth century but underwent alterations in the eighteenth.

Very close by is the city's other main square, Piazza Battisti, where the Renaissance governor's palace, the twelfth-century cathedral (which underwent major structural changes in the seventeenth century) and the interesting cathedral museum should all be visited. The finest building in the square, however, is the magnificent thirteenth-century bishop's palace. Two of the columns supporting the preceding loggia and the fountain to the left of the building date from the Roman period. The imposing archway to the right of the building was erected by Boniface VIII at the end of the thirteenth century and gives onto a street lined with Renaissance buildings.

Just to the north of the centre it is possible to walk along a considerable section of the city's wall which has been well preserved. The wall dates from the twelfth century and is periodically broken by square or semi-circular towers. There is a good view of the city from the top of the Cappuccini hill, a mile outside the city's eastern gate.

Take the SS4 to **Cittaducale**, an attractive town founded in the early fourteenth century to protect the northern border of the kingdom of Naples. Much of the town is unchanged from its late medieval aspect although some buildings were added and others modernised in the neo-classical and baroque periods. Parts of the city's defensive walls are still intact, and these, along with the churches of Santa Maria delle Grazie and Santa Maria dei Raccomandati, are the main monumental attractions.

A secondary road winds 14 miles to the south-east through beautiful countryside to the medieval village of **Petrella Salto**, built on a spur of rock overlooking Lago di Salto. The ruined castle above the town was the site of the assassination of Francesco Cenci in 1598 by mercenaries hired by Cenci's daughter with the connivance of her mother and brothers. The story has inspired works by Shelley, Dumas and Stendhal amongst others.

Follow the road around the shore of the lake until the turning for Rocca Sinibalda. **Longone**, 7 miles before Rocca Sinibalda, is another old hill town which, apart from still having much of its defensive wall standing, is completely unchanged within the walls. The village is suffering from the movement of people from the countryside to the cities but it still manages to maintain its old traditions, such as the lamb chop festival in mid-August and a 3-day-long festival to celebrate its patron saints, Damian and Cosmo, 26-8 September. Four miles to the north just off the road to Concerviano are the ruins of the eighth-century monastery of San Salvatore Maggiore, suppressed by Urban VIII in the seventeenth century. At one time the monastery was under the direct protection of Charlemagne.

There has been a castle or *Rocca* at **Rocca Sinibalda** since the tenth century if not longer, but the present building dates from the sixteenth century when Paul IV was planning to drive the Spaniards out of the kingdom of Naples. It is a typical Italian Renaissance fortress, the village which surrounds it having grown up along with the staffing needs of the fortress. Seventy-two of the several hundred rooms and the hanging gardens have been well restored.

Monteleone, 9 miles to the south-west, was built in the medieval period on the highest part of the site of the large Sabine-Roman town of *Trebula Mutuesca*. Thorough excavations have yet to be carried out but many fragments of Roman buildings can be seen in the fields around the town. The tenth-century bell tower of the interesting church of Santa Vittoria contains one of the oldest bells in Italy (1223). The church was built on the site of previous ones in the eleventh century and it is thought that there are Palaeo-Christian catacombs

Classical sculptures, Gaeta, Lazio

Market in Tropea, Calabria

Bagnara Calabra, Calabria

somewhere underneath.

Seventeen miles west-south-west is another typical hill town. Like many other small towns in the Rieti area **Fara Sabina** is interesting and unspoilt without having any buildings which particularly stand out. It does however have an interesting history as most of the medieval and Renaissance popes tried to sieze towns in the area to create estates for relatives and illegitimate children. Try the *Fettucine alla Burina* as your first course in one of the town's small restaurants.

Just to the west of Fara is the abbey of **Farfa**, which was the most important monastic centre in Italy before going into decline in the twelfth century. The actual building, which now has less than ten monks, dates from the Renaissance although there have been religious buildings on the site since the pre-Roman era. In the Roman period the emperor kept a villa next to what was then the Temple of Diana. Much of the stone was reused in the building of the later churches but a team of English archaeologists has been working on the site since 1977. Many of their finds are on display in the abbey museum in the Great Cloister. The abbey contains many fine works of art and at one time possessed a great treasure. Two long secret passages were constructed during the Dark Ages for removing the treasure in emergencies. It is not known exactly where these passages came out, but one is believed to have led to one of the many caves on the side of Monte San Martino which separates Farfa from Fara. In the eleventh century an abbot decided to build a basilica on top of the mountain. Building was discontinued after his death in 1093 but the ruins of the incomplete church remain as his memorial.

Head north to visit the old medieval centre of **Poggio Mirteto** then westwards over a steep hill before dropping down into the Tiber valley and turning towards **Stimigliano**. The town on the top of a long, narrow hill is typical of the Sabine hill towns containing very few straight roads. The most imposing building is the attractively restored baronial castle with its interesting 'grotesque' ceilings. The baroque parish church containing a painting of the *Massacre of the Innocents*, by a follower of Caravaggio, is also worth visiting.

Four miles north-west, the Roman Ursacia family is said to have offered hospitality to St Peter. A church was built on the site, of which the oldest part is the semi-circular ninth-century crypt. The rest of the church was rebuilt in the form of a Latin cross in the eleventh century. The frescoes in the single nave were painted by an early fourteenth-century Byzantine artist.

Extremely beautiful is the little hill town of **Roccantica** 12 miles to the east on the foothills of Monte Pizzuto. At the highest point of the town, which is surrounded by olive groves, is a sixteenth-century Clarissan convent built onto the ruins of the baronial castle. A circular tower and part of the external wall of the castle can still be seen.

Head north to **Contigliano**, one of the largest towns in the province of Rieti. A local society has carefully restored many of the buildings in the older, upper part of the town. One-and-a-half miles to the north of the town on the road to Greccio is the abandoned abbey of San Pastore. Since the last century the abbey has been left to rot, a shame as the visitor who fights his way through the weeds will find traces of fourteenth-century frescoes and trabeated stone work.

The town of **Greccio** with its magnificent surroundings, excellent summer climate and its mineral springs attracts quite a few visitors in peak periods but it is more important for its connections with St Francis of Assisi. At Christmas 1223 St Francis led a procession of people from the town to the top of a nearby hill and recreated the nativity scene. This was the first time such a thing had been done and was the beginning of a practice that is the basis of Christmas as we now know it. Greccio is officially twinned with Bethlehem.

Six miles north of Rieti on the west side of Monte Terminillo, popular with skiers, is **Cantalice**, formed by the fusion of three castle villages in the twelfth century. The del Cassero tower at the highest point of the town has recently been restored. North again is **Poggio Bustone**, a small medieval town which like Greccio has strong connections with St Francis. When the saint first arrived in the town he said 'Good day fine people' before ascending the mountain where he lived for a time as a hermit in a small cave. The event is celebrated on the 4 of October each year when the town's drummer goes to each house to wish the occupants 'Good day'. A small chapel has been built on the site of the cave and is reached up a very steep stony path through the woods.

Five miles to the west, **Labro** is a fine example of a medieval hill town. Nothing has changed except that the feudal castle, which once stood at the highest point, was partially demolished and partially altered in the Renaissance period to become a church. The ruling family built a more comfortable, less fortress-like castle just inside the old walls to replace it.

Return towards Poggio Bustone for 2 miles then turn left on the main road towards **Leonessa**, which crosses the Reatini mountains. Leonessa grew up between the twelfth and fourteenth centuries and maintains a typical medieval appearance. The town can be quite busy during peak periods as it is well placed both for walking and skiing. A number of fine churches in the town are worth visiting, particularly the late thirteenth-century Santa Maria del Popolo.

Drop down to the Velino valley and head for Amatrice in the north-west corner of Lazio. **Amatrice** is an attractive town surrounded by wooded mountains. Most of the buildings date from the sixteenth, seventeenth and eighteenth centuries as the town was destroyed by the imperial troops of Charles V in 1528. The town's main churches escaped the devastation and contain some fine works of art.

Head south to Montereale and then turn on the SS471 towards **Antrodoco**. Situated at the confluence of two steep-sided Apennine valleys the town's Roman name was *Interocrium* ('between the mountains') and the view in any direction explains why. The summit of Monte Giano can be reached in about $4^1/_2$ hours although the track is not clearly marked and at times disappears. The remains of a Roman spa centre can be seen near the station while up-to-date facilities for thermal cures are available in July and August.

Excursions from Fiuggi

The town of **Fiuggi** is divided into two distinct parts — the old town on the side of the hill, where most of the population live, and a new town which grew up around the thermal springs below at the beginning of this century. The baths which have been renowned for centuries in the treatment of gout and renal problems are busiest in July and September so, unlike most places in Italy, August is one of the best months for visiting the town. Parts of the old defensive wall can still be seen around the medieval centre, and a thirteenth-century fresco can be seen in the church of San Biagio. Two pleasant walks from Fiuggi are to Lago Canterno, 3 miles to the south, and to the Capuchin monastery 2 miles north-west of the centre.

Continuing past the monastery and across the 'High Plains of Arcinazzo' the scenery is at times breathtaking. Half a mile before Subiaco are the remains of a Roman villa built by the Emperor Nero. Near the villa is the monastery of Santa Scolastica, the only one of the twelve original Benedictine monasteries to have escaped destruction by the Saracens. St Benedict (San Benedetto) was a local boy who withdrew into a cave to meditate for 3 years. When his sister persuaded him to come out of the cave he gathered a few followers and divided them into twelve small monasteries. Hostility from the local priest forced Benedict himself to leave the area and he established his headquarters on Monte Cassino. **Subiaco** itself has a lively medieval centre clustered around the eleventh-century castle. In the fifteenth century the castle was the home of Cardinal Rodrigo Borgia (later Alessandro VI) and in 1480 saw the birth of his daughter Lucrezia. Now the castle is a Benedictine study centre and permission to visit the interior must be obtained from the abbot of Santa Scolastica. There are excellent skiing facilities on Monte Livata, 10 miles east of Subiaco.

Head south-east along the road which twists along the side of the Aniene valley, past the Trevi waterfall and climb up to the village of **Filettino**. There are thirteenth-century frescoes in the cemetery church of this village which, owing to rural depopulation, is like a ghost town for much of the year. During holiday periods many of the village's former residents return for the skiing and the excellent walking possibilities in the surrounding hills.

Drop back down the valley again until a left turn just after Trevi nel Lazio leads you back onto the 'High Plain of Arcinazzo'. Ten miles to the east is the town of **Guarcino** which has a well preserved medieval quarter. Fifteen minutes' walk brings you to the source of the river Filette where the water emerges at a constant 12 °C (53.6 °F) and aids the digestive process with its mineral content. From there another 4 hours' walk will take you past the ruins of an old monastery to the summit of Monte La Monna.

South of Guarcino turn left to reach **Collepardo** on the road signposted Vico nel Lazio. Collepardo is a typical old depopulated village with part of its defensive wall still standing. Twenty minutes' walk to the south on a small rough track brings you to the Grotta dei Bambocci, a large cave with a vast array of stalactites and stalagmites. Four miles east of Collepardo next to the ruins of a Benedictine monastery abandoned in the twelfth century is the Cistercian Certosa di Trisulti. Built in the early thirteenth century and extended in the seventeenth the monastery has a fine pharmacy and library. The library is situated in the Palazzo di Innocenzo III where soon after the monastery was built Innocenzo wrote his *De Contemptu Mundi*. Herbal liqueurs made by the monks are on sale.

Four miles south of Collepardo is **Alatri** on the site of one of the most important towns of the Ernici mountains. A well preserved polygonal wall fortified with medieval towers surrounds the town. Most of the buildings on the main streets are characterised by fine Gothic arches while those of the side streets are mainly Romanesque in style. The acropolis which lay outside the original city once had a wall of its own, and parts of this still survive from the fourth century BC. See also the thirteenth-century Santa Maria Maggiore church which stands where the Temple of Jove once stood.

A side road climbs gently to **Veroli**, 6 miles south-east, where John X and John XII were both held prisoner in the old ruined castle above the oldest part of the town. From the castle it is possible to look across the valley to the abbey of Casamari, 5 miles south-east. The abbey, which dates from the twelfth century, is one of the best examples of the Cistercian-Gothic in central and southern Italy. The monastery which now houses a theological institute contains a small museum and the monks are usually available to give guided tours through the rest of the buildings. A liquoreria sells the drinks made by the monks while the old pharmacy sells other herbal products.

Continue eastwards and cross the Liri valley with its many waterfalls to **Arpino**, birthplace of the artist Giuseppe Cesari (Cavalier d'Arpino, several of whose works can be seen around the town) and possibly of Cicero. The town is built on two hills, a lower one where most of the medieval and later buildings are to be found and a higher one where the original town was situated and where the remains of many Roman buildings are to be seen.

Frosinone to the west is the provincial capital but has little of interest for the visitor other than the remains of the Roman amphitheatre. The road to the town, however, passes through attractive scenery as does that which leads from Frosinone to **Ferentino**, 6 miles away on one of the first foothills of the Ernici mountains overlooking the Latina valley. Most of the old defensive wall built between the fifth and the second centuries BC is still in existence as is the old covered market, the theatre and a water tank. An austere eleventh-century cathedral on the site of the Roman acropolis is the most important of many medieval buildings in the town. The picture of St Ambrose (Sant' Ambrogio) in the sacristy is by the Cavalier d'Arpino but the finest artwork is the stone floor of the central nave and parts of the side naves, laid by members of the Cosmati family in the twelfth and thirteenth centuries.

The ex-church of Santa Lucia not far from the Roman theatre has a crypt which is believed to have been the first Christian church in the town and is a fourth-century adaptation of part of the Roman bath house.

Return to Fiuggi by way of **Anagni** where there are several interesting medieval buildings including the thirteenth-century *palazzo* known as Palazzo Bonifacio VIII. On 7 September 1303 Pope Bonifacio, a native of the town, was captured in the building by French troops after he had announced a decision to excommunicate the French king. The town's medieval churches are particularly rich in fine works of art as Bonifacio was the third pope to come from the town in little over half a century.

Excursions from Terracina

The origins of **Terracina** are not certain although it is known to have been an Etruscan city before the fifth century BC. The medieval centre was built on a hill in the thirteenth and fourteenth centuries slightly set back from the sea and the remains of the Roman town below. Many stones from the previous town were used in the new buildings and this, along with the building of a new centre in this century, has erased most of the traces of the Roman town. What Roman remains there are are completely overshadowed by the remains of the Temple of Giove Anxur high on the mountain above the town facing out to sea. The rectangular Corinthian temple was built in the first century BC on a plinth so that it would be visible not only from the sea but also from the beach.

The finest of the medieval buildings is the cathedral, built in the eleventh century over an old Roman temple and modernised in the twelfth. The central nave and the floor of the raised presbytery are both covered with twelfth-century mosaics as is the architrave. On one side of the cathedral is a very attractive twelfth-century Gothic *palazzo* while on the other a medieval tower house is incorporated in the modern town hall which houses an archaeological museum.

Follow the coast road to **San Felice Circeo**, on the tip of the peninsula west of Terracina. The town, at the foot of Monte Circeo (at one time an island) is mainly modern and during the summer school holidays and at weekends can be very busy. It is worth a visit outside these periods as the mountain and part of the plain behind have been designated a national park to protect the area. There are also some exceptional beaches around the peninsula.

The coast road runs northwards for several miles along a narrow strip of sand dunes between the sea and the elongated Lago di Sabaudia, very popular for watersports before reaching **Sabaudia** itself. The town is an example of rational town planning, having been developed in the 1930s after the draining of the marshlands.

Drive inland through the national park and then continue in a straight line across the Via Appia and up into the hills to the abbey of Fossanova. Built by the Cistercians in the twelfth century it is the earliest example of Cistercian architecture in Italy. The monastery was closed by Napoleon and for several years the church was used as a stable for buffalo before the building was reconsecrated in 1826.

Hilltop town of Priverno

On the first floor of the *Foresteria* behind the church is the room where St Thomas Aquinas died in 1274.

Just to the north is **Priverno**, partially medieval in a fine elevated position above the valley. The town was moved to its present hilltop site from the plain below in the ninth century when the risk of Saracen raids was at its greatest. The site of the old town was discovered in 1899 near the church of the Madonna di Mezz' Agosto and excavations have continued since then.

Continue up the valley to Roccagorga and then head west to **Sezze** high on a promontory above the railway. Traces of the Roman city wall can still be seen and several medieval towers and other buildings of the same period can be seen in the centre. The old Palazzo della Pretura now houses an antiquarium which, apart from archaeological finds from the Roman period and a medieval section, also has a very important prehistoric section. Caves in the nearby hills have revealed bones and fossils of prehistoric animals, and one, known as the 'Cave of the Buffalo', contains a cave painting reminiscent of the Mesolithic paintings found in Spain.

Twelve miles to the north on the other side of Monte Acquapuzza is **Sermoneta**, a small medieval hill town which still has its old defensive wall. In 1500 Alessandro VI siezed the town for his son Cesare Borgia and a new section was added to the already impressive castle. Besides the castle the thirteenth-century Romanesque cathedral, which contains a *Madonna of the Angels* in the first chapel on the right, should be visited.

The abbey of Valvisciolo was built in the eighth century by Greek monks and then rebuilt by the Knights Templars in the thirteenth century. The abbey is situated on high ground 2 miles north of Sermoneta and some interesting, fairly easy walks can be taken in the surrounding countryside.

Another interesting walk can be taken from the little hill town of **Norma**, 4 miles further on, to the ruins of the Roman town of *Norba*. The foundations of the town and many of the buildings can be seen very clearly and recent restoration work has made the site very interesting to visit. After visiting the site drop down to the Via Appia and then another 25 minutes brings you back to Terracina.

The coast road south of Terracina is magnificent with large bays separated by rocky headlands through which tunnels have been bored to take the road. Many of the smaller bays have been turned into expensive bathing establishments but other parts of the coast are open to everyone. Before taking the coast road however, cut inland on the Via Appia immediately south of Terracina and pass between the mountains and Lago di Fondi to **Fondi** itself. Still maintaining its original Roman street plan within the rectangular fourth-century BC walls, the town contains several interesting medieval buildings, although some of them are suffering from neglect. Perhaps the most interesting is the fifteenth-century Palazzo dei Principi which fuses several different architectural styles. The town's three-towered castle was built in the late thirteenth century and in 1378 was the site of the election of Clement VII.

Rejoin the coast road again between the two small lakes at the foot of Monte Lauzo and head east to **Sperlonga**. The original town where the locals live consists of white medieval fishermen's houses on a spur protruding into the sea. Most of the houses in the new part of the town are second homes and are usually only occupied during peak periods. Sperlonga (Latin for 'place of pleasure') was a popular resort with important Romans, many of whom built villas in the area and turned the many caves into pleasure parks. The most important of these, Tiberius' Grotto, had been used for centuries by fishermen before archaeologists began a systematic exploration in 1957. A museum was established half a mile south of Sperlonga to house the finds but there are so many that the museum is too small to display everything. The cave is sometimes open to the public.

Continue along the road below Monte Moneta and Monte Cristo to **Gaeta**, one of the most interesting towns in Lazio. During the

GESÙ MUORE IN CROCE
Veder l'orrenda Morte
Del suo Signor non puole;
Onde si copre il Sole,
E mostra il suo dolor.
Trema commosso il Monte
Il Sacro Vel si spezza;
Piangon per tenerezza
I duri marmi ancor.

Fresco, Gaeta

medieval and Renaissance periods Gaeta changed hands often between the papacy and the kingdom of Naples before being developed by the latter as a virtually impregnable fortress. During the 1848 revolutions the castle, built by Frederick II in 1227 and enlarged in 1289, 1436 and 1536, sheltered the King of Naples, the Grand Duke of Tuscany and Pius IX after each had been forced to flee from their capitals. Despite heavy damage during the last war Gaeta preserves many other fine old buildings, particularly the twelfth-century cathedral bell tower which incorporates fragments of several Roman buildings, and the picturesque medieval quarter, parts of which are in urgent need of restoration. Next to the cathedral is the cathedral museum containing works of art from several churches in Gaeta. At the tip of the small peninsula is the cylindrical mausoleum of Lucio Munazio Planco erected in 22BC. A similar mausoleum at the northern end of the town is dedicated to the commander of Mark Antony's fleet in the 21BC African campaign.

Facing Gaeta across the bay is **Formia**, the birthplace of Vitruvius and scene of Cicero's death. Roman remains between Gaeta and Formia are claimed to be Cicero's tomb. A cart track which starts in Piazza Sant' Erasmo, above the old castle leads up into the Aurunci mountains past the remains of a thirteenth-century Benedictine monastery. Formia is also the departure point for the **Pontine Islands**, a small archipelago of beautiful islands in crystal clear water well away from the pollution of the mainland. The ferries only serve Ponza and Ventotene, the largest of the islands. On Ponza the taxi service, which is the only means of transport from the small port, is fairly expensive, but worth investing in at least once. All parts of Ventotene are accessible on foot.

From Formia a new *superstrada* avoids the congestion of the small towns along the coast in taking you to the Roman remains of *Minturno*. The town, which was abandoned at the end of the sixth century is situated on the old Via Appia just before it crosses the Garigliano river. Of the buildings so far excavated the most impressive is the theatre which in summer is illuminated and hosts ballets and representations of classical plays. Near the town are the considerable remains of the aqueduct which once brought water to the city.

When the old town was abandoned the inhabitants established a new town on a hill just behind the coastal plain. The town has a characteristic medieval section and a fine eleventh-century cathedral. In July a large procession on allegorical themes takes place in the town to celebrate the Corn Festival.

Ten miles inland along an attractive route which follows the Garigliano is the spa of **Suio Terme** where the waters are used in cures for skin diseases, respiratory illnesses and as diuretics. Con-

Remains at Minturno

tinue along the Lazio bank of the river and when the road leaves the river head due north until reaching **Cassino**. The famous abbey of Montecassino was at the centre of some of the fiercest battles of the last war and was totally destroyed. Since the end of the war the magnificent headquarters of the Benedictine movement has been reconstructed exactly as it was before, although the frescoes and larger paintings were completely lost. Around the abbey are military cemeteries for several nationalities, a memorial to the more than 30,000 soldiers who died in the fighting.

A few miles to the west is the small medieval-looking town of **Aquino**, birthplace of St Thomas Aquinas. The fine Santa Maria della Libera church was built in 1125 over the ruins of a Roman temple by one of the saint's ancestors. Ruins of the Roman town of *Aquinum* can be seen on the western bank of the small river which runs alongside the town.

Continue on the SS6 to Ceprano and then take the SS82 southwards into the Aurunci mountains. Shortly after passing the highest point at San Nicola a small road off to the right leads to the sanctuary of the Madonna della Cività. It is said that the picture of Mary in the church appeared mysteriously on top of Monte Cività in 796 and the people of nearby Itri then built a small church on the spot.

Itri itself, 5 miles north of Formia on the Via Appia consists of a lively market town and a ruined medieval castellated village. The town is well situated for walking as it is surrounded by the Grande, Ruazzo, Orso, Cefalo and Marano mountains.

Further Information

— Lazio —

Airports

Rome 'Fiumicino' (Leonardo da Vinci)
☎ (010396) 60121

'Ciampino'
☎ (010396) 4694 (most charter flights)

Tourist Information Offices

Lazio is divided into five provinces, each of which has its own tourist board.

Province of Frosinone
Ente Provinciale per il Turismo
Piazzale de Matthaeis
Frosinone
☎ (0775) 851750

Province of Latina
Ente Provinciale per il Turismo
Via Duca del Mare 19
Latina
☎ (0773) 498711

Province of Rieti
Ente Provinciale per il Turismo
Via Cintia 87
Rieti
☎ (0746) 41146

Province of Rome
Ente Provinciale per il Turismo
Via Parigi 11
Roma
☎ (06) 461851

Province of Viterbo
Ente Provinciale per il Turismo
Piazza dei Caduti 16
Viterbo
☎ (0761) 226161

Museums and other Places of Interest

This information is arranged alphabetically by town. Opening times are given where possible but are subject to change.

Alatri
Museo Comunale

Albano Laziale
Museum of Apennine and Latin Civilisations
Open: mornings and Monday, Wednesday, Thursday afternoons. Sunday only 1st and 3rd of the month.

Allumiere
Communal Museum
Closed Monday, open 10am-12.30pm other days.

Barbarano Romano
Antiquarium
Open Thursday and Sunday 10am-12noon and 3-5pm.

Bracciano
Military Aviation Museum

Open: summer 9am-4pm, winter 8am-6pm.

Cerveteri
Museo Nazionale Cerite
Closed Monday, summer 10am-4pm, winter 10am-7pm.

Civitacastellana
Museo Nazionale Falisco
Open: 9am-1pm, closed Monday.

Formia
Antiquarium

Gaeta
Cathedral Museum (Diocesano)
Open: May-September 9-10am and 5-7pm, October-April 3.30-4.30pm. Closed Sunday morning.

Galleria Palazzo de Vio
Antiquarium

Ischia di Castro
Antiquarium
Open: 9am-1pm and 3-6pm.

Licenza
Horatian Museum
Open: 9am-4pm (ask in *Comune* (town hall) for museum to be opened).

Minturno
Antiquarium

Nemi
Museo Nemorense

Orte
Museo Diocesano di Arte Sacra
Open: 9am-1pm and 4-7pm, closed Sunday.

Ostia Antica
Museo Ostiense
Open: 9am-1pm, closed Monday.

Palestrina
Museum
Open: 9am-hour before sunset, closed Monday.

Rieti
Museo Civico
Open: 8.30am-1.30pm.

Sabaudia
Museo Circeo
Apply to National Park Offices
Via Carlo Alberto 107
☎ (0773) 57251

Sezze
Antiquarium
Open: 8.30am-12.30pm Wednesday, Saturday, Sunday.

Sperlonga
Museo Archeologico Nazionale
Open: April-September 10am-6pm, October-March 9.30am-4pm, closed Mondays all year.

Tarquinia
Museo Nazionale
Open: 9am-2pm, closed Monday.

Terracina
Museo Archeologico
Open: April-September, Monday-Sunday 9am-1pm and Tuesday-Sunday 4-6pm, October-March, Tuesday-Sunday 9am-1pm.

Tolfa
Antiquarium

Velletri
Museo Comunale
Open: Monday-Friday 9.30am-12noon, Thursday also 3.30-6pm.

Viterbo
Museo Civico
Open: April-September 8.30am-1.30pm and 3.30-6.30pm, October-March 9am-1.30pm, closed Monday.

Vulci
Museo Nazionale
Open: April-September 9am-1pm and 3-5pm, October-March 10am-4pm, closed Monday.

12 • Abruzzo-Molise

Until 1963, the two regions of Abruzzo and Molise were officially considered as one, having the same natural boundaries with the rest of Italy. To the north, the river Tronto and its valley mark most of the region's border with the Marche, while in the south, the same function is performed by the Fortore, this time dividing the region from Puglia. Eastern and western limits are the Adriatic coast and three Apennine sub-chains (or rather elongated groups) which tend to close up forming a single mass in the south-west. Of these mountains, which are mainly calcareous, the Gran Sasso d'Italia, at over 9,500ft is the highest in Italy outside the Alps. The great height of the mountains and the channelling effect they have on the winds means that the temperature in the mountainous zone of Abruzzo-Molise is generally much lower than in other areas on the same latitude. L'Aquila, the region's capital for many centuries, is situated in a long hollow high up between the eastern and central chains.

To the east of the mountains, occupying most of the remainder of the regions, are a series of sandy sub-Apennine hills created by a raising of the sea bed in prehistoric times. In general, these hills decrease gently in height as they near the coast but in places, the effect of wind and water has created much variety on the easily eroded surface. South of Francavilla only a thin strip of sandy coastline separates the hills from the sea, while to the north, an alluvial plain, often culminating in a series of sand dunes, distances the sea from the higher ground. Unlike the mountains, the coast enjoys very mild winters with temperatures rarely falling below 4°C (39°F).

The nature of the flora in the valleys depends greatly on the direction in which the various valleys face, with maritime species such as holm oak often penetrating high into favourably placed valleys. From 2,000ft to 4,000ft many chestnuts have been planted alongside the indigenous species, although from 3,500ft upwards the mantle of trees rapidly becomes almost exclusively beech. High up, parts of the original forests have been cleared over the centuries

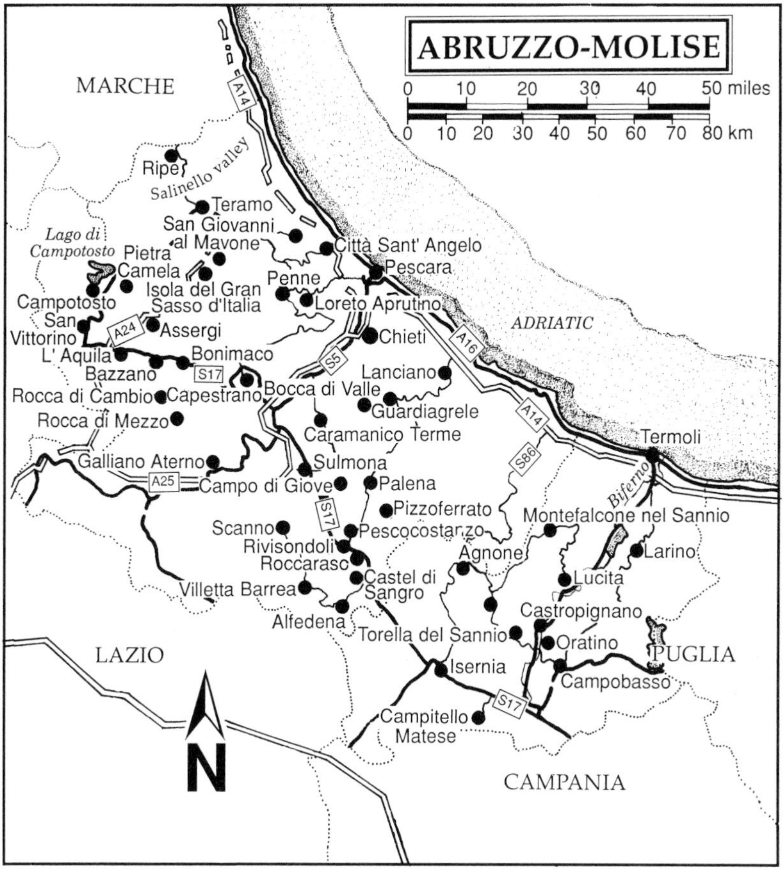

to create grazing land although this is now little used. Various types of rare mountain flowers and an interesting selection of medicinal herbs (mentioned by Ovid) make walking in the mountains a rewarding experience for the botanist.

Part of the region was designated a national park in 1923 and although the lynx has since become extinct it is still possible to see the chamois, fox, wild cat, wolf and brown bear as well as the royal eagle and other species of hawks and falcons.

Little is known of the region's early history, until, as *Sabina* and *Samnium* it became the Fourth Roman Region. A number of towns of medium importance were built by the Romans but outside these administrative colonies very little changed in the region owing to the tribal nature and relative backwardness of the inhabitants. However, although the Romans contributed relatively little to the region, during the Roman period two of the most important and progressive

'Roman' writers were born here: the historian Sallust and the poet Ovid.

In 1140, Roger II annexed the region to the 'Kingdom of the Two Sicilies' and it began to gain some importance as a border state with the papal dominions. Another stimulus to development was the spreading southwards of the Franciscan movement which began in the thirteenth century. In 1254, the city of L'Aquila was founded, although it is disputed whether by the pope or by the emperor, and despite being destroyed by Manfred soon after, had become by the fifteenth century, the second most important city in the kingdom and a great cultural centre.

With the change of dynasty in Naples in the sixteenth century, L'Aquila slowly declined in importance as first Chieti and then Pescara were favoured by the government. Although originally developed for its defensive possibilities, Pescara with its port and easy lines of communication with the north has, in this century, become the leading city in the region, particularly since World War II. Only the province of Pescara has gone against the general trend in the region by increasing its population, while some inland areas have seen reductions of around 50 per cent, with many of the higher villages and the poor quality farming land around them being completely abandoned.

In recent years there has been some attempt to open up the region to tourism, but apart from the coastline above Pescara and the mountain resorts, Abruzzo-Molise still attracts very small numbers compared with other Italian regions.

The region is, however, very interesting, despite the absence of great artistic centres. The landscape is varied and often beautiful; good beaches are only rarely crowded, and there are many interesting small towns and villages to be visited. In some of the higher villages which are now inhabited only by a handful of older people it is often possible to get a fascinating insight into a bygone way of life.

Because of the effect of the mountains on the temperature the region can be visited without discomfort even in summer although to miss the traffic on the roads, August is best avoided if possible. In this chapter the suggested itineraries are based from L'Aquila, Sulmona and Campobasso although it may be easier to move on to a new destination every day or so rather than make a series of circular excursions, as some of the roads are rather primitive.

Excursions from L'Aquila

Until the last war, **L'Aquila**, or 'the Eagle' had remained almost completely enclosed by the old city walls. Since then, however, there has been much new building around the old centre and unfortunately several sections of wall have been dismantled to facilitate this. There are, however, many old buildings in the centre of great interest. One can still see many houses which obviously date from when the city was founded in the medieval period alongside a few typically Renaissance buildings and a much larger number representative of the baroque.

A visit to the city is extremely rewarding for those interested in religious architecture as the city boasts many fine churches. The cathedral in the fine central square is relatively modern having twice been completely rebuilt after earthquakes, although some of the sarcophagi and memorials inside were salvaged from the earlier buildings. The finest of L'Aquila's churches is without doubt Santa Maria di Collemaggio with the pink and white marble fourteenth-century façade providing a fitting setting for a splendid rose window. The church was built in the thirteenth century by Pietro di Morrone for his coronation as Celestine V. He later abdicated and returned to his life as a hermit being condemned to hell by Dante and immortalised as '*Colui che fece il gran rifiuto*' ('he, who from cowardice made the great refusal') in the *Inferno*. Celestine is buried in a fine tomb within the church and his story is told in a series of frescoes.

Like Santa Maria, the church of San Silvestro is also Romanesque-Gothic and is particularly important for a fine series of fifteenth-century frescoes in the apse (anonymous artist). It once held an altarpiece by Raphael but this has now been replaced by a copy.

The basilica of San Bernardino was built in the sixteenth century although the interior was rebuilt in the baroque style after an earthquake. The mausoleum in the right aisle, which contains the body of the saint, was built by Silvestro dell' Aquila, a pupil of Donatello, as was the tomb to the left of the main altar.

The thirteenth-century Romanesque Santa Maria di Paganica is noteworthy above all for the fine carved portal where the bas-relief of *Christ Blessing with Six Apostles* bears the date 1308. The bell tower, which was built of stones from the historic destroyed city of *Amiternum*, was reduced to its present height by the Prince of Orange in 1529 to provide stone for the castle. Built to strengthen the Spanish hold over the area by the architect responsible for Castel Sant' Elmo in Naples, the castle has, since the last war, contained the Museo

Nazionale dell' Abruzzo and, with fine collections from medieval times onwards, it is one of the finest museums in Italy outside Rome, Venice and Florence. One of the bastions contains a million-year-old Mediterranean elephant, found near L'Aquila in 1954.

The other main civil monument in the city is the 'fountain with the ninety-nine spouts'. This is to be found by the Porta Rivera in the old city wall. The fountain consists of ninety-nine faces, each emiting water, which represent the lords of the ninety-nine castles which contributed to the foundation of the city. The only other monument of comparable value is the Monumento Camponeschi in the church of San Giuseppe. The monument, which celebrates one of L'Aquila's leading medieval families, is surmounted by an equestrian statue.

Two miles north of the city, the church of San Giuliano is of great interest despite its modern rebuilt exterior. Inside are many fine works of art, both Renaissance and baroque while a small museum contains archaeological and ethnological exhibits as well as religious relics and works of art. Another interesting church is to be found at **San Vittorino** 6 miles further to the north-east where the irregular-shaped church, which shows the architecture of each of its many restorations, has a large underground cemetery or catacomb. Immediately to the north of San Vittorino is the plain where *Amiternum* once stood. Parts of the city have been excavated and at times the excavations may be visited.

From San Vittorino take the SS80 northwards over the spectacular Capannelle Pass until Cant. At Cant turn left and then left again after 3 miles keeping the Campotosto reservoir on the right until reaching **Campotosto** which is a pleasant winter sports resort and in summer a point of departure for walks into the surrounding mountains. Back on the SS80 continue northwards down the Vomano valley, flanked on one side by the river and on the other by the steep rocky slopes of the Gran Sasso. After 13 miles, a twisting, steep road up to the right leads through a beautiful wooded valley, with occasional spectacular views of the Gran Sasso, to the small village of **Pietracamela**. This is an ideal departure point for walks on the Corno Grande and the Corno Piccolo. The woody hollow where the Arno torrent has its source can be reached in $1^1/_2$ hours on an easy-to-follow track. Beyond Pietracamela are the ski-runs of the Prati di Tivo from where several other mountain walks can be undertaken in good weather.

Six miles further along the main road is another right turn leading up into the mountains to a number of small villages of interest, near the **Isola del Gran Sasso**. The windows of many of the small medieval houses in Isola, which is the main starting point for ascensions of

'Fountain with the ninety-nine spouts', L'Aquila

the Gran Sasso, are inscribed with phrases in Latin advocating prudence or recalling the readers to religious morals. One-and-a-half miles to the north is the sanctuary of San Gabriele established by St Francis of Assisi in 1215 which attracts many pilgrims. Monte Prena and Monte Infornace, the Corno Grande and the Corno Piccolo can all be reached from Isola in around 6 or 7 hours of walking. There are various *rifugi* along the routes.

Leave Isola down the Mavone valley, which, apart from the exceptional scenery, contains two more churches of great interest. Your first view of San Giovanni al Mavone will be the apse but the most exceptional part of the church is the façade with its mixture of architectural and sculpted decoration. Alongside the church are the ruins of the old monastery which give an idea of the former importance of the church. The second church, Santa Maria di Ronzano, an almost rectangular-shaped Romanesque building facing the Gran Sasso, was also alongside a monastery until 1183 when this was destroyed by fire. Part of the church was also damaged but the frescoes which had been completed two years earlier in the transept and two of the apses survived. These are particularly interesting because rather than showing Byzantine influence they seem to reflect a continuation of Palaeo-Christian traditions.

The city of **Teramo**, 15 miles to the north, is notable for several fine medieval churches including the cathedral with its fine portal and magnificent sixteenth-century decorated silver screen. Near the cathedral are the remains of the third- or fourth-century Roman theatre and amphitheatre. At the start of Viale Bovio facing a curious group of mock medieval buildings known as the Castello della Monica, an interesting collection of local and Neapolitan paintings can be seen in the town's art gallery.

At **Ripe**, 10 miles to the north of Teramo is a group of thirty caves of great interest to those interested in geology or palaeontology. An interesting $3^1/_2$-hour walk takes the visitor through the Salinello gorge to the source of the river of the same name.

For those particularly interested in winter sports the following excursion will be of great interest as it takes the visitor to some of the best equipped ski-slopes near L'Aquila. Leave the city to the south-east as far as **Bazzano** where the columns of Santa Giusta church appear to rest on human and animal heads. Inside the church the small brick archway to the left of the altar is said to have originally been part of the oven where Santa Giusta was roasted for 3 days before walking out alive! Soon after Bazzano turn right, crossing the railway line and the river Aterno until reaching the church of Santa Maria delle Grotte and then after the village of Fossa take the small unmetalled road over the hill to the SS5b. Santa Maria delle Grotte is a thirteenth-century Gothic church with well preserved frescoes by Benedictine monks of the same period and later ones by artists of the Florentine school. Before reaching the SS5b the track passes by the ruined Castello d'Ocre and the monastery of Santo Spirito d'Ocre.

Rocca di Cambio was already a favoured holiday resort at the beginning of the millennium when the Emperor Ottone II passed most of his summers there. The summit of Monte Rotondo can be reached in $3^1/_2$ hours, and the return made by chair-lift. In winter, skiers will want to take the chair-lift up to Monte Rotondo in order to gain access to the sixteen ski-runs of Campo Felice. Access to these runs which are colour-coded for degree of difficulty, can also be gained from **Rocca di Mezzo**, the highest part of which still nestles inside its medieval walls. In summer numerous tracks lead up into the mountains to mountain *rifugi* for a number of difficult climbs. After Rocca di Mezzo continue south-east for 12 miles amidst attractive scenery until Secinaro and then take the minor road to the right to visit (from the outside only) the castle at **Gagliano Aterno**, well preserved amongst the pines and beeches on the eastern slopes of Monte Sirente. In the village the convent of Santa Chiara and the church of San Martino with its fine Gothic portal are also worth going out of the way to see.

After Gagliano continue towards the SS261 and then turn towards L'Aquila. Sixteen miles later a right turn leads to the village of **Bonimaco** where the two fine churches above the town and the ruined castle inbetween them were once the main buildings of an important monastic community until 1423 when the castle was destroyed after the monks had rebelled against Neapolitan rule. Join the SS17 and continue towards L'Aquila until the turning at Castelnuovo for **Peltuino**. The church of San Paolo di Peltuino was built in the medieval period from stones recovered from the old city of *Peltuinum* destroyed at some time in the Dark Ages. The actual building has been restored several times after earthquakes but is worth a visit for its fine views and the possibility of exploring the site of nearby *Peltuinum*, originally the major town of one of the local pre-Roman tribes.

The third excursion from L'Aquila leaves the city eastwards on the SS17b as far as **Assergi**, a small medieval town, still surrounded by its defensive walls. A few remains of the old pre-Roman town of *Prifernum* can be seen around a spring in the area known as Il Forno. The Grotta a Male cave 50 minutes' walk to the west of Assergi reaches 300ft into the mountainside and has produced relics of the second Iron Age (now in the archaeological museum at Chieti). Just north of Assergi at Fonte Cerreto is the lower station of the Funivia del Gran Sasso which carries visitors up to the Rifugio Duca degli Abruzzi and many interesting walks and climbs on the Corno Grande and the Campo Imperatore.

From Assergi take the road eastwards until finally, after passing through 30 miles of ruggedly beautiful countryside, dropping into **Penne**. This is one of the most attractive towns in the region, as not only the buildings but also the majority of the road surfaces are made of local bricks giving an unusual uniformity of colour. The city is also unusual in that it has no regular street plan despite having been under Roman rule at one point. Many of the buildings date from the late medieval period while the bulk of the others were either built or adapted to the baroque in the seventeenth and eighteenth centuries. The brick ramps leading up to the *Duomo* and the Annunziata church are particularly attractive, as is the Romanesque courtyard in Via delle Rimesse.

Atri, 20 miles to the north, is another historic town although this time the influence of the Romans on the street plan is very noticeable. Most of the town dates from the twelfth and thirteenth century when an increase in importance led to an increase in building and the filling up of many of the spaces between the primitive nucleus and the

View of Penne

churches which surrounded it. The most impressive building is the cathedral, built between 1223 and 1305; the internal decoration consists of good quality work from all the major thirteenth-, fourteenth-, fifteenth- and sixteenth-century styles.

To the south-east of Atri is the interesting small town of **Città Sant' Angelo** standing on a spur with fine views all around. The collegiate church and some of the medieval houses and courtyards along the Corso Vittorio Emanuele are worth looking at before driving southwards to join the SS151 for **Loreto Aprutino** at Cappelle sul Tavo. In Loreto the old Roman layout is immediately evident with the well ordered streets dominated by the religious site known as the Matrice where the acropolis once stood. The centrepiece of the Matrice is the fourteenth-century San Pietro Apostolo church with its Renaissance portal and Romanesque loggia with large three-lighted mullioned windows.

From Loreto cross the river Tavo and after passing the fine church of Sant' Angelo at Pianella continue southwards and join the SS602 at Cepagatti. From here the route back to L'Aquila is at times tortuous but the magnificent scenery makes it well worthwhile. The area between Offena and Capestrano has been the site of many important archaeological finds particularly around the tiny Lago di Capestrano where in 1934 the Picentan 'Warrior of Capestrano' statue, now in the

Loreto Aprutino

Archaeological Museum of Chieti was found.

Excursions from Sulmona

The birthplace of Ovid, **Sulmona,** is situated towards the south-western edge of the basin of the same name. The original town which still remains to a large extent intact as the historical centre was built on a small steep-sided plateau between the rivers Gizio and Vella. Modern development on the plain around the plateau has allowed the establishment of tourist and commercial facilities without harming the old centre. Although Sulmona was one of the few towns in Abruzzo to survive the Dark Ages more or less intact, almost all the town's buildings were rebuilt or at least modernized during the twelfth and thirteenth centuries, beginning with the cathedral, to the north of the town which was originally built in the eighth century. Much of the thirteenth-century building has survived, particularly the crypt and the double row of columns although other parts have been rebuilt after the earthquakes which have several times devastated the town. An example of how this has led to an interesting mixture of styles is the thirteenth-century aqueduct which ends in a Renaissance fountain in the main street. Perhaps the best idea of medieval Sulmona can be gained from the narrow Vico dei Sardi which has survived intact. The finest Renaissance building is without doubt the Palazzo dell' Annunziata which houses the civic museum, while the adjacent baroque church is also a fine example of its period.

Leave Sulmona on the SS479 and continue until reaching the town of **Scanno** where, in recent years, a modern area has grown up around the interesting old centre to cater for the walkers and winter-sports lovers who come to the town for the local ski-runs and the varied walking possibilities. Walking to the peaks of most of the nearby mountains presents no great technical difficulties but all of them require several hours. After Scanno the road continues to climb fairly steeply for several miles before dropping down to **Villetta Barrea** with its attractive reservoir, another starting place for walks. The ascension of Monte Marsicano is to be particularly recommended.

From Villetta Barrea the road descends gradually to **Alfedena**, a fairly quiet mountain resort where the old castle has an imposing octagonal tower. Fifteen minutes' walk to the north are the remains of the pre-Roman city of *Aufidena*. The town is also well placed for walks on Monte a Mare and Monte Metuccia. Moving northwards, **Castel di Sangro** is a pleasant town with some interesting medieval and Renaissance buildings. These are mainly private houses as the majority of the public buildings were blown up during the war. Twenty minutes' walk from the town are the ruins of the castle from which the town takes its name, and nearby are traces of megalithic defensive walls.

Roccaraso has been completely rebuilt after the last war and has become one of the leading mountain holiday resorts in southern Italy. The town is well provided with winter sports facilities and a number of interesting walks begin there but it tends to get very crowded in winter, summer and at weekends in other periods.

Rivisondoli also attracts a fair number of tourists but does not give the same impression of being crowded. In the old part the parish church contains a beautiful 1557 silver cross used to lead the procession on 6 January every year. The ski-slopes of Monte Pratello are within easy reach of the town as are those of Pescocostanzo. **Pescocostanzo** itself may be reached on foot by ascending Monte Calvario (1 hour) and then making the short (30 minutes) descent on the other side. The town has often been described as a miracle as from the fourteenth to the seventeenth centuries it was a flourishing artistic and cultural centre despite being apparently a typical mountain town. This was because at that time it was situated at a key point on one of the main routes linking Naples with northern Italy. The

Scanno

best view of the whole town is from the spur of rock where the original tenth-century settlement was built. The magnificent sculpted, gilded and painted wooden baroque ceiling in the collegiate church is one of the finest in Italy. From Pescocostanzo to Sulmona the road is fairly unspectacular except for a brief stretch 6 miles north of Pescocostanzo where the road climbs up to the hermitage of Sant' Antonio.

The second excursion from Sulmona takes the visitor first eastwards and then north on the SS487 past the ski-runs of the San Leonardo Pass and those of Sant' Eufemia a Maiella to **Caramanico Terme**. Caramanico still has part of its old defensive wall standing around the town which is built on a steep slope. The thermal springs from which the town takes its name are still used to treat a variety of illnesses. After visiting the fifteenth-century ogival-Romanesque church of Santa Maria Maggiore the visitor should walk north-west for half an hour to see the 160ft-high Orfento waterfall in its wild rocky valley.

After Caramanico continue northwards on the SS487 and then take the SS5 towards Chieti (if Chieti is to be the final destination for the day other smaller roads make a more interesting albeit more time-consuming route). Nine miles before Chieti a small turning to the right leads to the basilica of Santa Maria Arabona, the first church in Abruzzo to be built in the Cistercian style. The church was built in 1208 and accurately restored in the 1950s after almost 400 years of neglect.

Known as *Teate* in the Roman period when it was a town of some importance, **Chieti** took its present name when reconstructed after the ravages of the Barbarians. It is a pleasant lively city with an important archaeological museum, interesting remains of the Roman period and fine medieval cathedral. The archaeological museum is housed in two adjacent buildings, one of which contains the prehistoric and protostoric sections, the other housing the archaeological section. In room ten of this latter building is the famous pre-Roman statue *The Warrior of Capestrano* from the sixth century BC. Not far from the museum in Via Porta Napoli are the remains of the Roman theatre which is still only partially excavated. More Roman remains can be seen in Piazza dei Templi Romani, much of which is occupied by three buildings which were originally part of the temple on the north side of the forum. The cathedral underwent the first of several rebuilding programmes in the 1840s although the oldest visible parts of the present building date from the twelfth and thirteenth centuries. Many of these older parts, including the frescoes and some Romanesque brickwork, were rediscovered earlier this century when the baroque decorations were stripped off during restoration work. The Costantino Barbella provincial art gallery in the ex-Jesuit college is also worth a brief visit before leaving Chieti, as is the museum of sacred art in the seventeenth-century church of San Domenico.

From Chieti take the road eastwards to Ripa Teatina and Miglian-

Lanciano

ico and then south-east along the slow twisting road which crosses six parallel valleys before reaching the main road from Ortona to **Lanciano**. In the lower newer section of Lanciano the only building of any great interest is the cathedral. In 1088 when the townsfolk were restoring a Roman bridge, damaged by an earthquake, a statue of Mary was found under one of the arches. A chapel was built next to the bridge and gradually enlarged becoming the town's cathedral in the fourteenth century. The other main religious building is the church of Santa Maria Maggiore built in 1227 in the Burgundy-Cistercian style. Note the tripartite façade and entrance portal and particularly the cross-shaped pillars separating the naves strengthened by four slim columns. The fifteenth-century walls built by the Aragonese still protect the south-west corner of the old town while the high tower behind them is even earlier, dating from the late tenth or early eleventh centuries. The other sight which should not be missed is the six-mouthed Fontana del Borgo in Piazza Pietrosa which dates from the thirteenth century.

Fourteen miles to the east at the head of the Dentolo valley is **Guardiagrele** with several interesting churches and the remains of a medieval castle. From Guardiagrele take the road west to Bocca di Valle and then south around the base of the Montagna della Maiella until joining the SS84 at Corpisanti. Three miles to the south a track leads off to the right to the magnificent Grotta del Cavallone with their stalagmites and stalactites. Another 3 miles brings the visitor to **Palena**, 75 per cent of which was destroyed in late 1943 when it was the site of fierce combat. Many of the buildings have been rebuilt in the original styles and many of the delicate wood carvings in the churches were recovered. Monte Porrara to the north and the Pizi mountains to the south are both easily accessible from the town.

More tracks into the Pizi begin from **Pizzoferrato**, a pleasant little town surrounded by pines and dominated by the ruins of an old castle. Return to Sulmona along the minor road which runs along the side of Monte Pizzalto through the shallow valley which separates it from Monte Porrara. **Campo di Giove** has a number of excellent ski-slopes and is the starting point for a footpath which in 5 hours will take the visitor over the Tavola Rotonda mountain to the Grotta del Cavallone.

Excursions from Campobasso

The capital of Molise, **Campobasso**, is situated on the side and at the foot of a hill dominated by the Castello Monforte. The castle was built in the Longobard period but was almost completely rebuilt and strengthened after strong earthquakes in 1349 and 1546. There are excellent views from the rear courtyard although parts of the interior are used by the Ministry of Defence and not open to the public. Just below the castle is the church of San Giorgio, the oldest in the city, where the architrave of the decorated portal carries the date 1382. While many of the city's buildings are interesting few are outstanding and if time is limited the visit can be concluded by a look at the Museo Sannitico in Palazzo Mazzarotta.

Leave the city on the SS87 northbound for $2^1/_2$ miles and then turn left and head for **Petrella Tifernina** built on a hill overlooking the Biferno valley. Look at the fine Romanesque church of San Giorgio before heading northwards again and crossing the main road at Ponte Morgia Schiavone to reach **Lucito** and its fifteenth-century castle. Continue along the same road, past the fourteenth-century castle of Cività Campomarano with its two well preserved cylindrical towers to the town of **Montefalcone nel Sannio**. Montefalcone is situated at the north-western end of a small chain of mountains and has been inhabited since the pre-Roman period, as the remains of the defensive wall erected by the Sannites on the nearby Monte la Rocchetta demonstrate. In the town itself the round tower next to the ducal palace is a remnant of the old medieval castle while apart from the sixteenth-century bell tower the parish church probably dates from the fourteenth century.

Follow the main road alongside the Trigno river until it reaches the sea, then take the coast-road to **Termoli**. Termoli has three fine sandy beaches which are to be highly recommended in June and October during the week, before and after the school holidays. The town is also the only port in Molise and the ferry for the Tremiti Islands (Puglia region) leaves from here. The old, original part of the town is built on a rocky promontory protected by the thirteenth-century castle and walls erected by Frederick II. The impressive central tower which rises out of the steep-sided, round-cornered square base is a superbly functional piece of military architecture making no concessions to comfort but ably defending the town from attack by land or sea. Much of the old town consists of fishermen's homes and small workshops for many of the old traditions which have been 'Riminized' further to the north are still alive here even though the tourist industry has the upper hand in the newer parts of the town. The old cathedral was built in the sixth century over the ruins of a Roman temple. It was rebuilt in the eighteenth century after being sacked by the Turks and again in the 1930s but sections of the original building can be seen in the crypt.

Take the main road south, up the Biferno valley until the beginning of Lago di Guardialfiera and then turn left to **Larino**. The town has had a troubled history; from being important in the Roman period it was devastated by a combination of earthquakes and Saracens in the fourteenth century and for a while completely abandoned. After being rebuilt the plague of 1656 reduced the population from over 10,000 to around 350. Despite this, or possibly because of it, much of the town has preserved a medieval look. The fourteenth-century cathedral is the finest surviving medieval building while the adjacent castle dates from the Renaissance. The main area of archaeological interest is situated a mile to the south of the town where a small museum contains finds from the nearby ruins.

Slightly further to the south on a rise beyond the Cigno which runs alongside the road, are the very limited remains of the second-century BC town of *Gerione*. Also of interest, shortly before reaching Campobasso again, is the twelfth-century abbey of Santa Maria della Strada isolated on a rise to the right of the road. Particularly interesting is the bas-relief on the portal on the right-hand side which shows Alexander the Great being carried up to heaven by two hippogriffs.

The second excursion from Campobasso leaves the town on the SS618 passing below, the hill town of **Oratino** with the remains of its ducal castle and the ruined medieval tower, La Rocca, high on top of a hill overlooking the Biferno valley, before reaching **Castropig-**

nano, another interesting hill town with the ruins of a Norman castle overlooking everything.

A little further on another fine old castle can be seen at **Torella del Sannio**, although much of the present structure dates from an eighteenth-century restoration. The town's parish church, San Nicola was built in the middle of the sixteenth century. Another interesting castle is to be found on top of a rocky outcrop which rises out of the village of Bagnoli del Trigno a little further on. Half a mile to the south of the interesting town of **Pietrabbondante** are the archaeological excavations which have brought to light the most important Sannitic remains yet discovered. The temple and the theatre are the most impressive of the many buildings which have come to light in the last hundred years.

The easternmost point on this excursion is represented by the town of **Agnone**, on a hill overlooking the river Verrino. The façade of the Sant' Antonio Abate church, with its ogival portal, was erected in 1118 while the interior was 'modernized' in the early eighteenth century. From here take the road to **Pescolanciano** where the old part of the town inside its defensive wall is linked by a bridge to a well preserved castle.

After a succession of earthquakes and heavy wartime bombing, **Isernia** is a fairly modern town although the odd treasure has survived, such as the fine fourteenth-century Fraterna fountain in Piazza Celestino V. The town deserves visiting, however, for its fine museum which is particularly strong in its pre-Roman sections. Apart from being at the centre of Sannitic civilisation the valley is the site of intelligent *Homo erectus*' first known settlements in Europe.

From Isernia it is worth making the short trip north-west to **Cerro al Volturno** where the fifteenth-century castle seems to grow out of the rocky outcrop which dominates the town. Nearby is the abbey of San Vincenzo al Volturno which has recently been restored by the abbot of Montecassino abbey after lying in ruins for several centuries. The abbey was built in the eighth century and in its early years played host to such as Charlemagne and Ludwig the Pious.

Just to the south-west of Campobasso, **Campitello Matese** is a well equipped and well known winter sports centre, while **Bojano** is a good starting place for walking in the Matese mountains. Just to the south-west around the village of **Altilia** are the ruins of the Roman city of *Saepinium* which has gradually been excavated over the last 40 years. Many of the buildings along the Decumano have already been fully excavated, such as the basilica, the slaughterhouse and the theatre in the north of the town.

Further Information
— Abruzzo-Molise —

Tourist Information Offices

Abruzzo is divided into four provinces and Molise two, each of which has its own provincial tourist office.

Province of Campobasso
Ente Provinciale per il Turismo
Piazza della Vittoria 14
Campobasso ☎ (0874) 95662

Province of Chieti
Ente Provinciale per il Turismo
Via B. Spaventa 29
Chieti ☎ (0871) 65231

Province of Isernia
Ente Provinciale per il Turismo
Via Farinacci 11
Isernia ☎ (0865) 3992

Province of L'Aquila
Ente Provinciale per il Turismo
Piazza Santa Maria di Paganica 5
L'Aquila ☎ (0862) 25140

Province of Pescara
Ente Provinciale per il Turismo
Via Nicola Fabrizi 171
Pescara ☎ (085) 22707

Province of Teramo
Ente Provinciale per il Turismo
Via del Castello 10
Teramo ☎ (0861) 51357

Museums and other Places of Interest

This information is arranged alphabetically by town. Opening times have been given when available but are liable to change.

Agnone
Biblioteca Emidiana Museum
Corso Vittorio Emanuele

Albe
Excavations of Alba Fucens (Sannitic city)

Alfedena
Archaeological Excavations

Amiternum
Archaeological Excavations

Archi
Archaeological Excavations (*Pallanum* on Monte Pallano)

Atri
Museo Capitolare
Cloister of cathedral
Open: June-September 9.30am-12.30pm and 4-8pm, October-May on request.

Avezzano
Museo Comunale
Palazzo del Comune
Via Vezia
Provisional site, visitable on request.

Balsorano Vecchio
Castello Piccolomini, used as a hotel.

Baranello
Museo Civico
On request in *Municipio.*

Sannitic Archaeological Site.

Campli
Archaeological Museum
Ex-monastery of San Francesco

Campobasso
Museo Sannitico
Palazzo Mazzarotta
Via Anselmo Chiarizia

Chieti
Museo Diocesano d'Arte Sacra
San Domenico church
Corso Marrucino
Open: when church is open.

Museo Nazionale di Antichità
Via Villa Comunale
Open: Tuesday-Sunday 9am-1pm.

Pinacoteca Provinciale 'C. Barbella'
Palazzo Martinetti
Corso Marrucino
Open: Monday-Saturday 9.30am-1.30pm.

Corfinio
Museo delle Antichità Corfiniesi
Ex-Seminario Valvense

Fossacesia
Neolithic village (2 miles outside village)

Isernia
Museo Comunale
Ex-church of Santa Maria Assunta

L'Aquila
Museo Nazionale d'Abruzzo
Castle
Open: Tuesday-Saturday 9am-12noon, Sunday 9am-1pm.

Museo di Speleologia Vincenzo Rivera
Via del Cembalo di Colantonii 21
Open: Thursday 4-8pm.

Larino
Biblioteca Comunale (with archaeological exhibits)
Palazzo Comunale
Piazza del Duomo (See librarian).

Lettomanoppello
Grotta delle Praie Cave
Ask for keys at Comune di Lettomanoppello.

Loreto Aprutino
Galleria delle Antiche Ceramiche Abruzzesi, ☎ (085) 826325

Ortona
Museo Capitolare
Cathedral
Open: when cathedral is open.

Penne
Museo Diocesano
Palazzo Vescovile

Pescara
Mostra Archeologica Didattica Permanente
Casa di Gabriele d'Annunzio
Corso C. Gabriele Manthoné
Open: Tuesday-Saturday 10am-12.30pm and 5.30-8pm.

G. d'Annunzio Museum
Casa di G. d'Annunzio
Open: Tuesday-Saturday 9am-2pm, Sunday 9am-1pm.

Museo delle Tradizioni Popolari
Casa di G. d'Annunzio
Open: Tuesday-Saturday 10am-12.30pm and 5.30-8pm.

Museo Civico Basilio Cascella
Viale Marconi
Museo Ittico
Via Raffaele Paolucci

Pietrabbondante
Bovianum Archaeological Excavations

Prata d'Ansidonia
Peltuinum Archaeological Site

San Giovanni in Galdo
Tempio Italico Archaeological Site

Sulmona
Museo Civico
Palazzo dell' Annunziata
Corso Ovidio
Open: Tuesday-Sunday 10am-12noon and 3-6pm.

Teramo
Museo Civico e Pinacoteca
Viale Bovio
Closed Monday.

Vasto
Birthplace of Gabriele Rossetti
Behind Santa Maria Maggiore church

Museo Civico
Palazzo d'Avalos
Piazza Lucio Valerio Pudente
Open: Wednesday-Monday 9am-12noon.

Venafro
Museo Nazionale
Ex-monastery of Santa Chiara

Scilla, Calabria

Greco-Roman remains at Tindari, Sicily (top)
and at Selinunte, west of Sciacca, Sicily (bottom)

13 • Campania

Naples, Capri, Ischia, *Pompei, Herculaneum* and the Amalfi coastline are justly famous throughout the world and as such are beyond the scope of this guide. Besides these well known centres, however there are many other places of great historical and cultural interest in Campania. At 5,250sq miles the region is one of the smallest in Italy, but the vast number of people living in and around Naples make it the second most densely populated after Lombardia. Despite this, large areas suffer severely from rural depopulation and even before the earthquake of 1980 several smaller centres were all but abandoned.

Before the unification of Italy in the 1860s, Naples was the capital of one of the peninsula's most powerful states and the inland towns had an important role to play in the then agricultural economy. The shifting of the centre of power away from Naples and the industrialisation of Italy which favoured the northern cities with their easier access to the main European markets, however, sent the region's economy into a seemingly irreversible decline.

Although in many ways tragic, this situation has created one of the most fascinating areas in Europe for the tourist who really wishes to get off-the-beaten-track. The reduction in population has meant that no new building or even modernisation of existing buildings has taken place. The interior is characterised by poor roads leading to small mountainside towns, grouped around a baronial castle or small cathedral and subsisting on an agricultural and artesan economy. This is not a region where one will come across works of art by Leonardo or Michelangelo in the parish churches but rather lively works of art by local artists which reflect the lifestyles of the periods rather than historical concepts and subtle religious messages. Alongside these fascinating examples of folk art the churches are decorated with beautiful carvings diligently sculpted by forgotten craftsmen.

With the exception of the Tyrrhenian Sea, the region does not have well defined geographical boundaries although the Apennine crest can be seen as a rough guideline. Thirty-five per cent of the region is formed by mountains while another 50 per cent is formed by hills reaching out from the mountains to the coast and often forming rocky peninsulas. The hills and mountains were once thickly wooded but now only a replanting programme lifts the surface area covered back up to 20 per cent. High up in the mountains the occasional wolf can still be seen and even more rarely a wild cat.

Despite the economic problems of the interior, some of the larger provincial towns have much of genuine artistic interest in them. Campania was one of the first parts of Italy to be colonised by the Greeks, and Etruscan settlers also exerted an influence on parts of the region. During the Roman period the region maintained its importance and many important Roman ruins can be seen besides the more celebrated ones at *Pompei* and *Herculaneum*.

The visitor wishing to visit the region without having to face the chaotic Neapolitan traffic will do best to base himself in Capua, Benevento, Avellino, Salerno or Vallo di Lucania, each of which is well placed as a starting point for seeing large areas of Campania. The best periods for visiting the region are spring and autumn for the whole region, summer for the mountains and the lesser known stretches of coastline, and winter for the Amalfi coastline as the weather is generally mild and the normal crowds of tourists are absent.

Excursions from Capua

Although **Capua** is partly surrounded by fifteenth-century walls, its origins are much earlier. The Etruscan city of Capua was situated slightly to the south of the present city which stands on the site of *Casilinum*, a small Etruscan/Roman port on the Volturno estuary. *Casilinum* was abandoned in the sixth century but when Capua was destroyed by the Saracens in AD841 the survivors moved to *Casilinum* to rebuild their city. Since then the most notable event in the city's history occured on 24 July 1501 when Cesare Borgia massacred more that 5,000 of the population during a supposed truce in his siege of the city.

Great damage was caused to the city during the last war but many of the most important buildings have been restored to a high standard giving the city an interesting antique appearance. The baroque *Duomo* and the Annunciata church should not be missed, but the city's greatest treasure is the Campano museum which contains an excellent collection of Roman, Etruscan and pre-Etruscan exhibits, supplemented by interesting medieval and Renaissance sections

Punta Sant'Angelo

including a group of sculptures from the castle of Emperor Frederick II.

Just north-east of Capua is **Sant' Angelo in Formis** which takes its name from one of the finest medieval basilicas in Campania. Built on the site of a Roman temple, the basilica was completed in 1073. The four columns which support the portico are relics of the original Roman construction as is the floor inside, which bears an inscription dating from AD74. The frescoes in the church are extremely important, having been painted by local Byzantine artists in the late eleventh century.

The peak of Monte Tifata can be reached from Sant' Angelo in 90 minutes and there the visitor will find the ruins of a church and the Roman Temple of Jove. Another interesting walk leads to the top of Monte Maggiore, up a track which begins where the road from Formicola, a pleasant town surrounded by chestnut woods, ends. The walk is most rewarding in April and May when the orchids and narcissus are in flower.

From Formicola head north to **San Giorgio** where a marble Roman font and a fine sixteenth-century wooden organ can be seen in the Annunciata church. From there head north-west and then west across the motorway to **Caianello Vecchia**. This is an extremely attractive medieval hillside village dominated by the ruins of a thirteenth-century castle with a cylindrical tower.

Another attractive medieval town is nearby **Roccamonfina** at the foot of Monte Santa Croce. Numerous pleasant short walks can be made in the chestnut woods which surround the village including one to the fifteenth-century monastery of Santa Maria with its beautiful cloister and works of art.

From Roccamonfina take the road north around the base of Monte Santa Croce alongside a small river until the old village of Sipicciano from where a long, twisting road descends slowly through exceptional scenery to **Sessa Aurunca**. Once the capital of the Aurunci tribe the town has noteworthy remains of the Roman and medieval periods. The early twelfth-century cathedral stands out among the surrounding buildings, most of which are roofed with local green and yellow tiles. It is particularly important for the numerous fine medieval bas-reliefs with which it is decorated. The other main medieval monument is the ruined castle on the outskirts of the town, dominated by its square tower. At the western edge of the town near the public gardens are the remains of several Roman buildings, including the theatre and the bathhouse. More important is the Ponte degli Aurunci Roman bridge, 2 miles south of the town. Those wishing to spend time on the beach can easily reach Baia Domizia from Sessa. Once there, 20 minutes' walk northwards along the beach will leave the crowds far behind even at the height of summer.

Four miles south of Sessa is **Carinola** where the fifteenth-century cathedral owes much of its architectural inspiration to the famous abbey of Monte Cassino just over the border in Lazio, and yet is virtually ignored by tourists. The town's other main monument is the fifteenth-century castle.

Just outside **Teano**, 8 miles north-east, are considerable remains of the town's amphitheatre built in the period after Hannibal had devastated the town in 334BC. The town itself is attractive and an interesting collection of works in marble can be seen in the crypt of Santo Paride church.

The next place on this itinerary is also of interest for its Roman remains: *Cales* flourished from the pre-Roman period until the ninth century when it was destroyed by the Saracens. The town was later rebuilt as **Calvi** and regained its former importance as the fifteenth-century cathedral and partially ruined castle testify. Near the cathedral are the bulk of the ruins of the original town and most of the basic pre-Roman and Roman town plan can be easily identified. Smaller finds from the site can be seen on request in the old seminary, which will eventually be organized into a museum. From there, Capua is easily reached on the Via Appia.

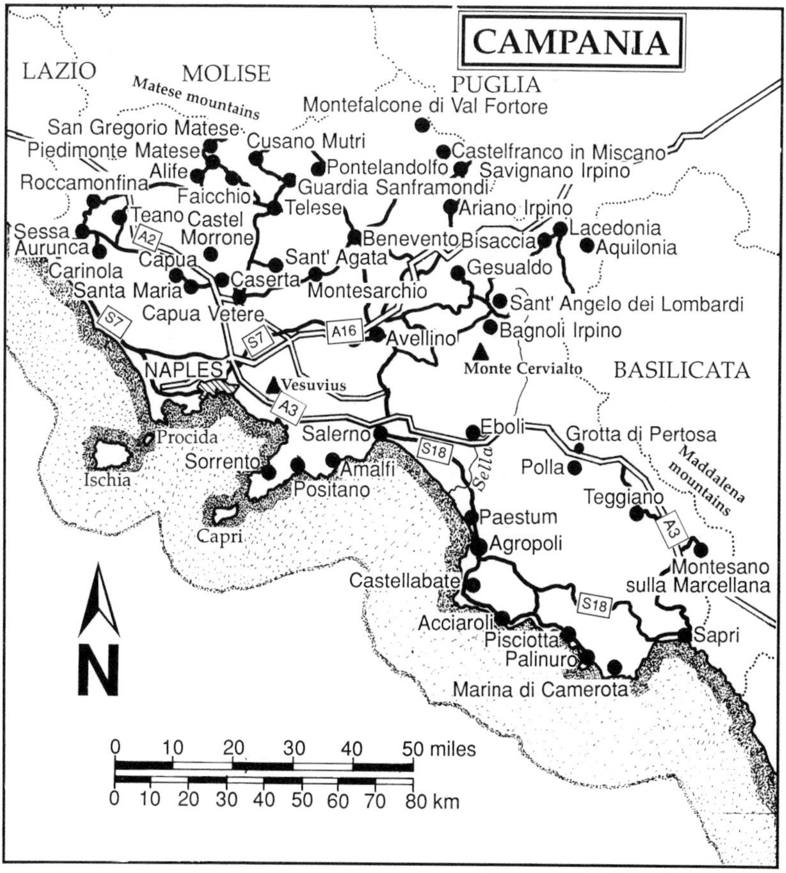

First port of call on the second itinerary from Capua is **Santa Maria Capua Vetere** on the site of the old Roman Capua. The finely frescoed underground Temple of Mitreo is one of the best preserved monuments relating to the cult of the Persian god and in most towns would be the main attraction. In Santa Maria, however, it is overshadowed by the great first-century amphitheatre which is only slightly smaller than the Colosseum itself. The nearby village of **San Prisco** has two major attractions; the eighteenth-century parish church, built by Vanvitelli, one of the century's greatest architects, and the nearby Santa Matrona chapel where the splendid mosaics date from the beginning of the sixth century.

Caserta is the local provincial capital although it did not exist until Vanvitelli built a royal palace there in the second half of the eighteenth century for Charles the Bourbon. As well as the royal

The royal palace at Caserta

apartments the palace also contains a well stocked art gallery. One of its most impressive features is the gardens which once rivalled Versailles. The gardens now, however, give the impression of having just enough spent on them to stop them decaying but not enough to bring out their full splendour.

Caserta Vecchia is a fine medieval hill town, 6 miles to the north-east, founded in the eighth century by the Longobards whose ruined castle stands at the edge of the town. The interesting cathedral in the central square was built in the twelfth century and fuses together elements of Romanesque, Arab and Benedictine architecture.

Slightly south-east of Caserta is **Maddaloni** at the foot of Monte San Michele. The oldest part of the town on the first part of the slope contains several interesting churches and a small museum containing finds from the Roman town of *Calatia*. This stood on the plain below the mountain until being destroyed by the Saracens in 862. Much of the site is now covered by new buildings.

Leave Maddaloni eastwards on the SS7 until Messercola where a small road leads up into the hills to the semicircular town of **Sant' Agata dei Goti**. The town was established by the Goths in the sixth century on the ruins of a Roman town, of which many reminders are still visible. The whole town is attractive but as is usual the outstanding buildings are the churches: the *Duomo* with its magnificent twelfth-century crypt, San Menna with its early twelfth-century

Roman theatre at Benevento

mosaics, the Annunziata with a series of sixteen stained glass 'history' windows, and the ex-church of Santa Maria del Carmine which now houses the town's museum.

From Sant' Agata take the road which runs alongside the Isclero river and then the Volturno until Limatola where a left turn leads to **Castelmorrone**. This scattered town is situated around Monte Castello (1,600ft) which is surmounted by the remains of a large medieval castle and much older dwelling places. There is also a memorial to the members of Garibaldi's thousand who fell in a nearby battle. A pleasant 10-mile drive brings the visitor back to Capua.

Excursions from Benevento

Built on a hill in a large hollow surrounded by mountains, **Benevento** is believed to have been founded by the Sannites before becoming an important Roman city. On 26 February 1266 Benevento saw one of the most important events in the struggle between Church and Empire when the Emperor Manfredi was killed in the Battle of Benevento by Charles of Anjou who restored the city to the pope. The city has been devastated several times by earthquakes over the centuries and over 60 per cent of its buildings were destroyed during the last war. However, four of the finest reminders of its great past have survived — Traiano's Arch is over 50ft high and has an opening almost 30ft wide. It was built in AD114 at the start of the Via Traiana linking Benevento with Brindisi and is the best preserved of the Roman triumphal arches. The bas-reliefs have earned its executor recognition as one of the finest sculptors of the Roman period ('Master of the Arch of Benevento'). The fine Roman theatre has recently been restored and in summer is the venue for a series of concerts and recitals. The church of Santa Sofia which has been restored to its original eighth-century state is one of the best examples of medieval architecture in Europe. A central hexagonal area which supports the dome is surrounded by a ten-sided area surrounded in turn by a series of side chapels which use geometric aspects to create a series of optical and spatial illusions. A well stocked museum and art gallery around the cloister of the adjacent monastery was originally founded by Talleyrand when Prince of Benevento in 1806. The lapidary section of the museum is now housed in the Rocca dei Rettori castle which dates from 1321.

Campolattaro, north of Benevento on the SS88 consists of two sections, a small old medieval centre with narrow streets separated from a slightly later section by a forbidding twelfth-century castle. The town is famous for its mimes which are performed at the end of August. Nearby **Pontelandolfo** has an attractive central square with a seventeenth-century fountain and the polygonal walls of a fourteenth-century castle providing a fine backdrop.

The castle which dominates **Guardia Sanframondi**, 10 miles to the west, was built by the Normans in the twelfth century. This medieval village has always been dominated by the church and every 7 years in August, almost all the town's population takes part in a large procession known as the Penitential Rites in Honour of the Assumption. A small museum in the Casa dei Filippini contains precious objects from the many local churches.

After Guardia the road drops down to the baroque town of **Cerreto Sannita** which was totally rebuilt after the earthquake of 1688 with a typical sixteenth-century street plan. A complete contrast is the village of **Cusano Mutri** reached after a 5-mile drive through the attractive valley separating Monte Erbano and Monte Cigno. Cusano is still essentially a quiet medieval village although some of the buildings have been given baroque embellishments. From Cusano head first north-east and then almost due west through the magnificent foothills of the Matese mountains. At the Miralago Pass junction, the right-hand fork quickly leads to Lago Matese where fishermen fish for trout in the water which reflects the surrounding mountains. **San Gregorio Matese** 5 miles down the left-hand fork is an attractive little hillside village handily placed as a stárting point for walks into the mountains and in winter, for the nearby ski-runs.

Piedimonte Matese, just to the south, has several interesting churches, including the fifteenth-century St Thomas Aquinas church with its excellent frescoes. Also of interest is the civic museum in an old monastery next to the church, with a wealth of archaeological and palaeontological collections. The Sannites established the small town of **Alife**, $3^1/_2$ miles to the south but the most important surviving features are the complete rectangular Roman walls and the eleventh-century cathedral which has an unusual crypt with three apses.

Take the minor road eastwards from Alife to the Madonna della Libertà church and then turn right along the main road to **Faicchio**. The fifteenth-century castle with its four cylindrical towers has been refurbished with medieval furniture and turned into a hotel and restaurant. Pleasant walks can be taken through the pine wood above the village on the slopes of Monte Monaco di Gioia.

Head southwards alongside the base of Monte Acero to the thermal station of **Telese**. Just over a mile outside the town are the ruins of a Roman city of *Telesia*. The complete circle of walls with the four gates and alternate circular and pentagonal towers can be seen, as can the remains of the amphitheatre, the baths, the theatre and other important buildings. The town was rebuilt after being sacked by the Saracens in 847 and 863 but was finally abandoned after an earthquake in 1349.

After Telese head for Solopaca, pass through the town and continue slowly through the fine scenery until Cautano and then turn up to the right towards the hilltop town of **Tocco Caudio**. There is nothing outstanding about Tocco and because of this it is an ideal place to visit to get an idea of a typical Campanian village. Parts of the village are medieval while others have been rebuilt after various earthquakes.

Montesarchio, 10 miles to the south, is built on the site of the Roman city of *Caudium*, founded by Hercules whose baroque fountain is to be found in the attractive central square. The oldest part of the town is clustered around a central spur of rock on which a well preserved fifteenth-century castle stands. The old Roman baths have been excavated and the finds will eventually be housed in an aquarium. From Montesarchio, Benevento is easily reached in 15 minutes but before that the visitor may wish to make the 3-hour ascent of Monte Taburno on a track which starts from the hamlet of Cirignano, 2 miles north of the town.

The second itinerary from Benevento leaves the city in a north-easterly direction on the SS212. **San Giorgio La Molara** had many of its finest buildings badly damaged in the 1962 earthquake but is still well worth a visit for the magnificent views it enjoys from its hilltop position. Further to the north is the attractive small town of **Montefalcone di Val Fortore**, where traditional costumes of great interest can be seen during the several fairs, of which the most important is the Festival of Hospitality in August. The ruined castle was destroyed in 1809 after becoming a stronghold for bandits.

The road continues to the south-east at an altitude of around 3,000ft with views of higher mountains in all directions until **Castelfranco in Miscano** appears on a spur in a hollow. The oldest part of the town lies virtually abandoned around the ruined castle after being severely damaged in 1962. The hills around the town are well stocked with game and many hunts begin from the town. Shortly after Castelfranco the road turns southwards and after passing along the side of Monte Rovitello reaches the village of **Savignano Irpino** where the ruins of the castle built by the Anjou dynasty can be visited.

Head southwards from Savignano on the SS90 which passes through some exceptional scenery before reaching **Ariano Irpino** which has been largely rebuilt after the 1980 earthquake. Many fifteenth-century elements can still be seen in the restored cathedral. The Norman castle was ruined during an earlier earthquake in 1732. During the summer Ariano is a good starting place for walking in the surrounding mountains.

Excursions from Avellino

Avellino has been hit hard by the many earthquakes which have struck the region and as a result is a modern-looking city. It does have, however, two important museums which should not be missed. The Museo Irpino consists of an archaeological section which covers the period from the Stone Age to the late Roman period, and a modern section which includes a fine collection of late eighteenth-century pottery. The site of the city was originally 2 miles to the east of the present centre and excavations which have brought to light the Roman theatre, bathhouse and several private houses can be visited beyond the ring-road near the station.

Leave Avellino to the east for **Chiusano di San Domenico** from where it is possible to ascend Monte Tuoro. After Chiusano head north through the mountains to the **Passo di Mirabella** where the ruins of the Roman city of *Aeclanum* may be visited. The bathing

Piazza della Libertà, Avellino

house, the market place, several private houses and parts of the city walls have been excavated and a small antiquarium has been established to house finds from the city and from nearby necropoli.

Gesualdo is an attractive little town on the crest of a hill dominated by a medieval castle with four towers which was transformed into a noble dwelling in 1582 by Carlo Gesualdo. The town's monastery was also founded by him as a penance for killing his wife and her lover. An interesting painting in the church shows Carlo being pardoned by Jesus after the requests of several saints, including Mary and Carlo's maternal uncle San Carlo Borromeo.

The scenery along the road after Gesualdo is impressive as was the next town, **Sant' Angelo dei Lombardi**, until it found itself at the epicentre of the 1980 earthquake. All the most important buildings were destroyed except the sixteenth-century cathedral which was badly damaged. Attempts are being made to rebuild the town more or less as it was. Five miles to the south, the ruined twelfth-century abbey of San Guglielmo al Goleto is being restored and already houses the library of the Benedictine monks who are restoring it.

Bisaccia, 20 miles to the north-east of Sant' Angelo is a pleasant village on a spur between two side valleys of Monte Calvario. Excavations have produced evidence that a settlement existed on the site in the Iron Age and it is believed that a Roman town once stood on the site, although archaeological work has been halted since the earthquake. Shortly after Bisaccia a road to the left leads to the attractive town of **Lacedonia**, believed to be the site of the Roman city of *Aquilonia*. After the 1930 earthquake the cathedral was slowly restored to its previous splendour, a process which is now again taking place. The town is well situated for walking into the surrounded hills.

The modern **Aquilonia** is to be found on the other side of Monte Arcangelo, along the next turning to the left off the main road. The town itself is modern, having been built after the 1930 earthquake, but it is interesting to walk the $1^1/_2$ miles north-east to see the ruins of the old town which was completely abandoned at that time. Back on the main road again the next stopping point is **Calitri** with its triangular street plan. The most interesting buildings have disappeared after the earthquakes but those prepared to walk to the tops of the surrounding hills will be rewarded by excellent views in all directions.

The road then cuts across a corner of the Puglia region alongside the river Guana until re-entering Campania at Sant' Andrea di Conza and climbing up to the Sella di Conza junction. From here the road descends tortuously through fine scenery for almost 10 miles to the confluence of the rivers Temete and Sele. Turn right here and begin to climb again to the famous sanctuary of San Gerardo Maiella at **Materdomini**. The main church contains some fine sculptures by Tommaso Gismondi while there is an outstanding view of Monte Cervialto and the Sele valley from the square outside.

Take the unmetalled road which leads off to the left a mile north of Materdomini and follow the signs for Bagnoli Irpino. Four miles before Bagnoli is the Piano Laceno, a picturesque wooded plain at well over 3,000ft with a small lake. The plain is quite popular at weekends throughout the year as many pleasant walks can be taken from there. In winter the surrounding hills are popular with skiers and a few small hotels operate around the edge of the plain.

Bagnoli Irpino is a lively attractive town with considerable artistic merit. The Assunta church contains a beautiful wooden choir which represents 7 years of work by a local school of craftsmen: the church of San Domenico incorporates parts of older churches in its basically sixteenth-century structure including a sturdy medieval bell tower with octagonal battlements, and a Renaissance cloister, the only remnant of the monastery which at one time adjoined the church. The whole town is overlooked by the ruins of a fifteenth-century castle.

From Bagnoli there is a choice of attractive routes for returning to Avellino but the finest is the SS574, reached after first following the signs for Montella. The SS574 wends its way between the Felascosa, Terminio and Faggeto mountains before running into Avellino along the river Sabato valley. A short diversion off to the left at the beginning of the valley allows the visitor to see the town of **Solofra** with its fine late-Renaissance ducal palace. The town once belonged to the powerful Orsini family and Vincenzo Maria Orsini (Benedict XIII) once lived in the palace.

Three miles west of Avellino is **Mercogliano**, a pleasant town at the foot of Monte Partenio. The town, which is popular with walkers in summer, is dominated by the ruins of the feudal castle of the abbot of the sanctuary of Montevergine. The sanctuary can be reached by funicular in 7 minutes from the town or in about half an hour by car on the mountain road. It is also possible to walk up a track to the sanctuary which consists of two churches, a monastery and a museum. The sanctuary's greatest treasure is the Madonna di Montevergine painting dating from the second half of the thirteenth century. An exquisitely carved twelfth-century abbot's chair is the best of many fine exhibits in the museum and art gallery. The monastery itself may only be visited by males. In winter the abbot and most of the monks transfer to the much lower Palazzo Abbaziale di Loreto just outside Mercogliano. The pride of the *palazzo* which was constructed in the eighteenth century is its pharmacy which contains a vast collection of herbal vases. The archives contain papal bulls dating back as far as 947.

Campania's better known attractions are all easily reached from Avellino, to the west: Capri and Ischia, *Pompei* and *Herculaneum*, the Costiera Amalfitana, Sorrento and of course, Naples itself.

Excursions from Salerno

In many respects **Salerno** cannot be regarded as off-the-beaten-track as its easy accessibility from Naples means that crowds of people flock to the sea there in good weather. The city does, however, have an interesting medieval centre which tends to be forgotten by the masses. Until the twelfth century Salerno was the most important mainland city of the kingdom of Sicily and this importance was reflected by the establishment of the Salerno Medical School in the eleventh century, which for 300 years was the most important in the world. One of the teaching centres of the school is believed to have been in the Sala San Lazzaro, on the right-hand side of the square in front of the eleventh-century *Duomo*.

Two lions flank the main entrance to the large atrium, which has an early thirteenth-century Romanesque bell tower on the right-hand side. The main body of the cathedral is divided into three naves leading up to a raised transept above the crypt and backed by three apses. The cathedral was badly damaged in 1688 and much of the rear of the church was redone although most of the fine works of art which are in the church are original. Many more works from the cathedral are to be found in the Museo del Duomo at Via Mons. Monterisi 2, along the left-hand side of the building.

The provincial museum is situated in the new (fifteenth-century) castle and contains varied and interesting collections from the pre-historic period onwards. The museum has plans to expand into the nearby Norman castle and the ex-monastery of San Benedetto. The rest of the town with its typical narrow medieval alleyways should be explored slowly on foot as even the smallest side street can produce surprises of great interest.

Leave Salerno southwards on the coast road and head towards *Paestum*. The road is mainly dual carriageway so even the first section which gives access to the many bathing establishments does not often become blocked. *Paestum* is always busy at weekends and is quite often the destination for school trips during the week. *Paestum* is one of the most awe-inspiring archaeological sites in Italy, in many respects putting even *Pompei* into shadow. Excavations are still continuing but amongst the many buildings which have so far been completed are four magnificent temples; three Doric and one Italic. The smaller finds from the excavations are exhibited in a well laid-out museum opened near the Temple of Cerere in 1952. Also contained in the museum are articles found in a prehistoric necropolis, a mile north of the city. This necropolis is believed to be that of a tribe who immigrated from Asia Minor more than 2,000 years BC. By the sea to the west of *Paestum* is the Tower of Paestum, a medieval watchtower erected to defend the coast against the Saracens.

Six miles to the south the ground rises sharply as the Cilento mountains reach right up to the sea. On one of the foothills is the pleasant fishing town of **Agropoli**. A ruined castle stands behind the town and there is a view of the whole of the Bay of Salerno and even Capri.

It is pleasant to explore some of the mountain roads which snake through the woods, the olive groves and the sparsely populated villages, often dominated by the ruins of feudal castles. This is also a good area for pleasant, relatively short walks.

Continuing along the mainly rocky coastline with its many small sheltered sandy beaches the next town of interest is **Santa Maria di Castellabate**. The architectural aspects of the old fishing port have been maintained despite the development of facilities for receiving tourists in summer. The town has a fine sandy beach and an interesting twelfth-century church is best avoided at peak periods. Two-and-a-half miles inland up a steep road with many hairpins is Castellabate upon which the church of Santa Maria originally depended. The town is quiet and unspoilt around its twelfth-century castle.

The village of San Marco is situated at the beginning of the Licosa Point Peninsula. A track follows the base of the peninsula for 4 miles on the seaward side passing the ruins of two medieval towers before reaching Ogliastro Marina on the other side of the peninsula. On the small island which faces the peninsula the remains of pre-Roman walls have been found.

The scenery is magnificent along the coast road around the rest of the tip of the Cilento. About half way round this stretch is the small resort of **Acciaroli** which was often visited by Hemingway. A thirteenth-century defensive tower and a twelfth-century church provide the historical interest.

Just to the south of the Alento estuary at the junction of the coast road and the SS18 are the ruins of the Greek-Roman city of *Velia* where excavations began in the 1920s. So far the perimeter wall and part of the southern side of the city have been brought to light. The outstanding building so far uncovered is the magnificent fourth-century BC Porta Rosa gate at the north-west corner of the city. Much of the acropolis to the west of the city has also been excavated and the Velia museum is sited in several of the buildings here.

At this point it is worth making a deviation 20 miles inland to visit the sanctuary of the Madonna di Novi Velia at the top of Monte Sacro. It is known that the church existed in the early fourteenth century but its earlier history is wrapped in mystery and legend. The mountain is the highest for many miles at 5,600ft and very few other places in southern Italy can offer such a spectacular view. The village of **Novi Velia** is very characteristic with a picturesque castle and two interesting churches.

Back on the coast road the next small town of interest is **Pisciotta**, where the medieval *palazzo* of the Marquis of Pappacoda can still be seen. An attractive side road descends through the olive groves to the sea at Marina di Pisciotta. Two camp sites cater for summertime visitors here.

Palinuro, 6 miles down the coast, has been developed into a modern resort and is to be avoided during school holidays. A ruin near the end of the Palinuro promontory is said to have been the cenotaph where Aeneas buried his pilot Palinurus in Virgil's epic poem. The promontory is riddled by caves, most of which are only accessible from the sea. Evidence that they were once inhabited by cavemen has been found.

More caves of great interest to the palaeontologists are situated further down the coast, particularly on the stretch around **Marina di Camerota**. An archaeological museum has been established in **Camerota**, 4 miles inland where the remains of a town dating from the fourth century BC have been found. The area has been developed to cater for a fairly high-class tourism with three special holiday villages, so prices may tend to be higher than in other towns a few miles away.

After Marina di Camerota the coast road climbs steeply and moves inland for 10 miles until dropping down to the sea again after the village of San Giovanni a Piro. Another 4 miles along the coast and then take the left-hand turn which leads up into the hills from Villammare. Seven-and-a-half miles after Sanza cross the motorway and head for **Montesano sulla Marcellana**. Montesano is a well equipped spa centre and is also a good place from which to begin walking in the Maddalena mountain range.

Drop down into the Diano valley again and head north on the SS19 until **Teggiano** appears on the signposts to the left. This attractive old town on a hill dominating the valley has much of historical interest. Many medieval buildings, and several Roman remains set the scene for the fine twelfth-century cathedral and the fourteenth-century castle which stands above the town. The ex-church of San Pietro now houses a museum of Roman marble sculptures.

Polla, at the northern end of the valley, is another similar town although not quite as impressive as Teggiano. Just to the north of Polla, however, is the magnificent Grotta di Pertosa with its wide variety of rare geological features. The caves were inhabited for thousands of years before the early Christians consecrated them and set up a statue of San Gennaro inside.

The drive back to Salerno can either be done quickly by taking the motorway from Polla, or in a more relaxed way along the picturesque state road through the hills. Just after the two routes meet again to finish the journey alongside each other, is the flourishing town of **Eboli**, made famous by the author Primo Levi's *Christ Stopped at Eboli*. The older, higher part of the town still maintains much of its original medieval appearance and is worth a quick visit. The cylindrical towers and battlements on the fifteenth-century Castello dei Colonna were added by Vanvitelli in the eighteenth century. Although in excellent condition the castle cannot be visited internally as it is used as a prison.

Further Information

— Campania —

Airports

Naples, 'Capodichino'
☎ (081) 7092815

Tourist Information Offices

Campania is divided into five provinces, each of which has its own tourist board.

Province of Avellino
Ente Provinciale per il Turismo
Piazza della Liberta
Avellino ☎ (0825) 22626

Province of Benevento
Ente Provinciale per il Turismo
Via N. Sala 31
Benevento
☎ (0824) 21960

Province of Caserta
Ente Provinciale per il Turismo
Palazzo Reale
Caserta ☎ (0823) 322233

Province of Naples
Ente Provinciale per il Turismo
Via Partenope 10/a
Napoli ☎ (081) 418988

Province of Salerno
Ente Provinciale per il Turismo
Piazza Ferrovia
Salerno ☎ (089) 224322

Museums and Other Places of Interest

This information has been arranged alphabetically by town. Opening times have been given in most cases but are liable to change at short notice.

Acerenza
Museo Diocesano
Vescovado (Opening 1988 or 89)

Amalfi
Chiostro del Paradiso
Cathedral
Open: 9am-7pm.

Museo Civico
Municipio
Piazza del Municipio
Open: Monday-Friday 8am-2pm, Saturday 8am-12noon.

Museo della Carta
Valle dei Mulini (above Amalfi)
Open: Tuesday, Thursday, Saturday 10am-1pm.

Grotta di Smeraldo
6km towards Positano.

Avellino
Museo Irpino
Palazzo della Cultura
Corso Europa
Open: Monday-Saturday 8.30am-2pm; Monday-Friday also 4-7pm.

Museo Diocesano
Duomo
Open: 9am-1pm Tuesday, Thursday and Saturday also 4-8pm.

Aversa
Museo di San Fancesco
Ex-monastery
Strada di San Francesco

Bacoli
Cento Camerelle
161 Via di Cento Camerelle
Leave tip.

Piscina Mirabile
Via A. Greco 16
Leave tip.

Baia
Parco Archeologico
Open: 9am, closing time depends on season.

Castello di Baia Archaeological Museum

Benevento
Museo del Sannio
Ex-monastery of Santa Sofia
Open: Monday-Saturday 9am-1pm.
Roman Theatre, 9am-dusk.

Capua
Museo Campano
Palazzo Antignano
Open: Tuesday-Saturday 9am-2pm, Sunday 9am-1pm.

Caserta
Palazzo Reale
Palace
Open: Tuesday-Sunday 9am-1.30pm.
Gardens, 9am-variable.

Castellammare di Stabia
Antiquarium Stabiano
Via Marco Mario 2
Open: Tuesday-Saturday 9am-2pm, Sunday 9am-1pm

Cava de' Tirreni
Abbazia della Trinità di Cava
Corpo di Cava ($2^1/_4$ miles SW)
Open: Monday-Saturday 9am-12noon, Sunday 8.30-10.30am.

Ercolano (*Herculaneum*)
Archaeological Site
Open: variable.

Ischia
Castle
Ischia Ponte
Open: March-October.

Villa Arbusto
Archaeological Museum
Lacoo Ameno

Maiori
Santa Maria a Mare Museum

Marina di Ascea
Museo di Velia

Minori
Villa Romana
Open: 9am-12noon and 4-6pm.

Montevergine
Abbey Museum
Open: 9am-12noon and 4-6pm.

Nocera Inferiore
Museo dell' Agro Nocerino
Convento di Sant' Antonio
Open: 8am-2pm and 5-8pm.

Nola
Complesso delle Basiliche
Cimitile (1.2miles)
Open: Tuesday, Thursday, Sunday 9am-12noon and 2-5pm.

Museo Culturale del Nolano
Cicciano (1.8miles)

Padula
Certosa di San Lorenzo
Open: 9am-1 hour before sunset.

Museo Archeologico della Lucania Occidentale
Open: 9am-1pm and 4pm-1 hour before sunset.

Paestum
Archaeological Site

Open: 9am-dusk.

Archaeological Museum
Open: Tuesday-Saturday 9am-1.30pm, Sunday 9am-12.30pm.

Palinuro
Antiquarium
Next to church

Passo di Mirabella
Excavations of *Aeclanum.*

Pertosa
Grotte di Pertosa
Open: 9am-5.30pm.

Pozzuoli
Flavio Amphitheatre
In high part of town
Open: 9am-variable.

Ravello
Villa Rufolo
Open: 9.30am-sunset.

Villa Cimbrone
Open: 9am-sunset.

Roccamonfina
Sanctuary of Santa Maria dei Lattani

Salerno
Museo del Duomo
Open: 9.30am-2.30pm.

Museo Provinciale
Ex-monastery of San Benedetto
Open: Monday-Saturday 9am-1pm and 5-8pm, Sunday 9am-1pm and 5-7pm.

Pinacoteca-Museo
Santa Maria delle Grazie church
Open: 7am-1pm and 4-8pm.

Castello di Arechi
Open: 9am-1pm and 3-6pm.

Santa Maria Capua Vetere
Campano Amphitheatre
Open: Tuesday-Sunday 9am-4pm (or 6pm).

Santa Maria di Castellabate
Underwater marine park
Sea behind Santa Maria Assunta church.

Sarno
Museo della Valle del Sarno
Open: 10am-4pm.

Telese
Telesia Archaeological Site (1.2miles)

Torre Annunziata
Villa Romana di Poppea
(wife of Nero)
Via dei Sepolcri
Open: 9am-variable.

Torre del Greco
Museo del Corallo
Piazza L. Palomba
Open: Monday-Saturday 9am-1pm.

Vallo della Lucania
Museo Diocesano
Open: Monday-Saturday 9am-2pm (summer also 4-8pm).

Vesuvius
Chairlift
Open: 9am (variable).
Closed most of November.

Vico Equense
Antiquarium
Open: summer 9am-1pm and 6-8pm, winter 9am-2pm.

Vietri sul Mare
Museo della Ceramica
Villa Guariglia
Raito (0.7miles)
Open: Tuesday-Sunday 9am-1pm (also 5-7pm Thursday and Saturday in spring).

14 • Calabria

Calabria forms the 'toe' of the boot of the Italian peninsula and is mountainous, lush and thickly forested in many parts. The wealth of archaeological sites have attracted tourists to Sicily since the early decades of this century but Calabria has remained relatively undiscovered until very recently. The Italians are now trying to promote tourism in Calabria as part of the scheme for the development of the south but few if any places could truly be described as 'developed'.

The opening up of Calabria to national and international tourism has given rise to a cultural movement which aims to preserve the wide variety of genuine popular traditions and skills which the region has retained. This isolation has in the past produced the unwelcome consequence of extreme poverty and unemployment with subsequent depopulation. Education, and communication with the more industrialised north, has been minimal with the result that the 'forgotten south' has remained culturally isolated. Although this has had an undesirable effect on the health, prosperity and morale of the region's population it has meant that the Calabrians have clung firmly to their own traditions.

The rich heritage of arts and craftmanship includes a vast range of shepherd's carvings, widespread spinning and weaving, and the various productions of wicker articles, terracotta and ceramics. A characteristic of typical Calabrian crafts is the frequent use of symbols — magic, ritual and talismanic images. There is an interesting association in southern Italy between the pagan and the Christian, a strong belief in the 'evil eye' and the double nature of both people and everyday objects. Many of the inland towns and villages perform Passion Plays at Easter, according to a precise script often written by the inhabitants themselves, with the whole community taking part.

Tradition has been enriched by the presence of ethnic and linguistic minorities — Grecian, Waldensian and Albanian. The Greeks live

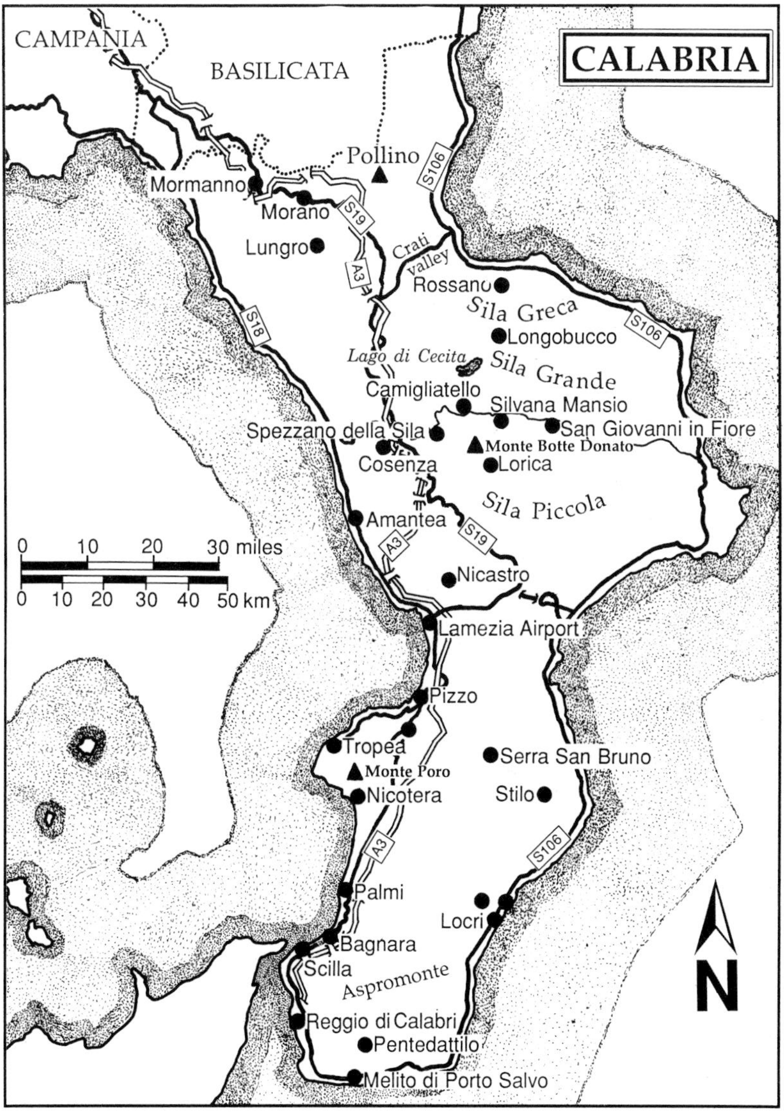

in the wildest area of Calabria in a highly inaccessible area encompassed, more or less, by the towns of Bova, Condofuri, Roccaforte del Greco and Roghudi. They are essentially herders and farmers, speaking Ancient Greek and conserving many interesting customs and traditions.

The Albanians, who form a close knit community in the province of Cosenza, also speak their own language and preserve their own religion, literature and traditions. The weddings are particularly impressive with the couple, wearing splendid costumes, being crowned several times with garlands of flowers. In a number of towns such as Savelli on the Sila, the bride's trousseau is carried through the streets for all to see.

Calabria has much to offer. Its beaches have been described as the best in Italy, and a recent study by the Ministry of Health declares that they are also the least polluted. The mountains provide a spectacle of extreme natural beauty; they give refuge from the heat and humidity of the coast and have facilities for walking and climbing in summer, and skiing in winter. There are many interesting and picturesque towns and villages to discover both inland and on the coast. Only in July and August do any parts of the region even approach the definition of crowded, and the remote interior remains practically devoid of tourists for the whole year.

The Pollino

The northernmost region of Calabria is known as the Pollino. It is a beautiful area which may well become a National Park, and it can be reached by leaving the Autostrada del Sole at the 'Lauria South' exit and heading in the direction of Rotondo, Castelluccio Superiore, the upper part of the Peschiera river valley and the Mangano forest.

The area is thickly wooded, the main trees being beech and the Calabrian pine which has a silvery-scaled bark giving the trees a very soft appearance. This pine is also found in the Balkans and there may well be a connection between its presence in the north of Calabria and the Albanian settlers who arrived here in the late Middle Ages. Only about 2,000 of the trees, nicknamed the 'Sentinels of Pollino' remain, and they are heavily protected. A few wolves also remain, which, together with the otter and the golden eagle make up the rarer wildlife of the region. Towards the eastern side there are lush meadows filled with flowers such as crocuses, daisies, bluebells, violets and cyclamen.

It is possible to climb in the Pollino, starting from Morano, Mormanno or San Lorenzo Bellizzi. **Morano**, as well as being a base for walks and climbs is an interesting place to visit. It is built on a hillside in the upper Coscile valley and has steep, narrow streets. One leads to the remains of a Norman castle rebuilt in the 1500s. Also worth visiting is the church of San Bernardo which has been recently and carefully restored to its original fifteenth-century state. Both the façade and the interior have fine frescoes, though some are in a rather poor state of preservation. Better is the artwork, including an excellent fifteenth-century polyptych by Vivavini. Note too the woodwork, a good tenth-century ceiling and a crucifix from the eleventh century. The cloisters, too, are of fifteenth-century construction. Also to be visited are the churches of the Maddalena (sixteenth century), San Pietro and San Paolo which has a baroque interior, Purgatorio and San Nicola which has a fifteenth- to sixteenth-century crypt.

Lungro, south of Morano, is a notable centre of Albanian traditions: a carnival parade at Easter takes place in full traditional Albanian costume. The Greek-rite cathedral has the remains of a medieval chapel where traces of Byzantine frescoes can still be seen.

The Sila

The Sila Massif, which forms a large part of central Calabria, is divided into three areas, the Sila Grande, the Sila Piccola and the Sila Greca, the latter named for the large number of Albanian settlements. The Sila Grande, Sila Piccola together with the Aspromonte in the south, constitute the National Park of Calabria established in 1968. The Massif is an area of great natural beauty with a wide variety of plant and animal life.

The Sila used to be totally covered by forest but large areas have been cleared for pasture. To avoid total deforestation, there is now a careful replanting programme. On the lower slopes there are olive, oak, poplar and fruit trees as well as vineyards and typical 'Mediterranean scrub'. Above the 2,300ft contour these are replaced by chestnut and turkey oak, while the chief arable crop is cereal. Above 3,900ft the vegetation takes on an almost alpine appearance, with Calabrian pine, silver fir, beech, alder, aspen and maple. The area is beautiful in the autumn, the colours of the deciduous trees contrasting with the dark green of the pines.

Wild flowers include snowdrops, in February and March, followed by daffodils, jonquils, violets and small orchids in April, May and June. The pine forests are thick with wild strawberries in June and July and with mushrooms in the autumn. At Fallistro (near Camigliatello) there is a group of about fifty huge pines and sycamores, locally known as the 'Giants of the Sila', some of which reach a height of 130ft.

The Apennine wolf tops the list of protected species to be found in the Sila. Although they are reputedly ferocious the wolves are also extremely shy and it is highly unlikely that a visitor to the area would have the fortune (or misfortune!) to come across one. Visitors to mountain camp sites, however, especially in the nature reserves, may hear the howls of a pack at twilight. In the winter when the Sila is covered by snow, their tracks are easily distinguishable and occasionally a hungry pack may visit lower ground for food.

Other mammals include the now rare wildcat, badgers, martens, otters, roe and fallow deer. Wild boar have been introduced and are extensively hunted. Squirrels are common, as are hares and foxes. Birds, resident and migratory, are more numerous than mammals, and the visitor may see a wide variety of forest species including the pied woodpecker, nuthatch and jay, together with many birds of prey, some of them rare. There are long-eared owls, goshawks, sparrowhawks, red kites and even a few eagle owls. Wildfowl include an interesting native species of partridge. In the wilder areas it is possible to find the southern viper, and the rare spectacled salamander is sometimes to be seen. Additional information about the National Park can be obtained from the Ufficio Amministrazione Demaniali in Cosenza.

It is difficult to know which route to take through the Sila. Because it is so mountainous, distances on the map seem deceptively short and so it is advisable to allow a longer time than you might if you were only taking note of the number of miles. Numerous villages of interest lie scattered amongst the vast pine and beech forests and there are also a number of scenic reservoirs, used to generate hydro-electric power.

Leaving **Cosenza** from the east, the road quickly climbs the west slope of the Sila. The first village of particular interest is **Spezzano della Sila**, built in a panoramic position on the slopes of a spur. The parish church still has parts of the original fifteenth-century building and a fine wooden statue of San Biagio. The San Francesco sanctuary has an interesting cloister, and from near it there is a beautiful view over the Crati valley. Beyond Spezzano the road runs through a series of tunnels and gradually penetrates the forest.

Continuing, the visitor reaches **Camigliatello**, a summer and winter sports resort, set in the conifer forest. In summer, it provides an excellent base for walks and excursions and in winter it is one of the most important ski-resorts in the region with several lifts. In October a mushroom festival takes place in the town.

Just before Camigliatello, near the Monte Scuro Pass, is a turn off onto a panoramic side road (the Strada delle Vette) that twists and turns up to Monte Botte Donato through fine beech woods. The views are spectacular on the descent towards Lago Arvo, which offers a fine shoreline drive and good fishing for trout. There is another ski-resort at nearby **Lorica** set in a beautiful wooded area on the north-eastern shore of the lake. Beyond the lake is the spectacular

Ascione Pass with breathtaking views westwards to the Tyrrhenian sea and eastwards over Lago Arvo.

Taking the road in the opposite direction one reaches Rovale, from where one can follow the road north through the picturesque village of **Silvano Mansio**.

Continuing north, and then eastwards along highway 107, the chief town of the Sila, **San Giovanni in Fiore**, is reached, a town built round an abbey founded in the twelfth century. The surrounding landscape is dominated by dark granite rocks and the whole place has a slightly depressing air, an air certainly helped by the many half-built houses, abandoned by emigrants, and such slogans as 'The only alternative to boredom is revolution' plastered on the walls. The women are famous for their attractive costumes, however, and the town is further enlivened by the colourful textiles made locally. Bright fabrics and rugs with oriental designs are on offer, the rugs being woven using a recently imported Armenian method and the fabrics being hand embroidered. The town also has a very colourful procession on Good Friday. It is possible to visit the abbey begun in 1191-2 by Gioacchino da Fiore, although little is left of the original structure of the convent and cloister. The church was restored during the baroque period.

Returning to Camigliatello and taking highway 177 reach Lago di Cecita, the largest of the artificial lakes in the Sila, and surrounded by an almost lunar landscape. At the eastern end of the lake the road enters the Gallopane forest and winds uphill, then descends in a series of hairpin bends with splendid views to Longobucco in the Sila Greca.

Longobucco has a distinctly alpine character. It is a bustling little town, and like San Giovanni in Fiore, is a centre for textiles, hand-woven to traditional designs. Weaving in Calabria is of very ancient origin. During the long winters, when the rivers were in spate and roads almost non-existent, every town and village had to be self sufficient in cloth, and excavations, at Amendolara for example, have unearthed ancient loom weights. Fabric dyes are obtained from local herbs, the work being done exclusively by the women. At one time silkworms for the splendid silks of the east left from here for Constantinople.

Continuing past Longobucco into the heart of the Sila Greca one reaches the town of **Rossano**, built on a sandstone cliff that dominates the coastal plain, that is characterised by steep, narrow streets. It was one of the main centres of Byzantine civilization in Calabria and for this reason is called 'Little Ravenna'. There is a beautiful

Byzantine fresco in the cathedral and other Byzantine buildings include the church of San Marco with its eleventh-century dome. The diocesan museum contains a valuable sixth-century Greek gospel.

Nearby is the basilica of Santa Maria del Patire which is reached along a road built by Austrian prisoners of war in 1916-17. It is an outstanding monument, clearly showing the high standard of architecture which the Basilian monks succeeded in maintaining even under Norman rule. The church was, at first, attached to a monastery which for three centuries, from around 1100 to the fifteenth century, was renowned throughout Italy. Of the original Norman complex only the basilica now remains, though this required restoration in the seventeenth and eighteenth centuries.

The Serre

Soriano, Serra San Bruno and Stilo are three interesting towns which lie within 30 miles of each other in the picturesque Serre region.

Soriano Calabro is built on a slope on the Tyrrhenian side of the Serre. The ruined church originally was built in 1655 but was destroyed by an earthquake. The large baroque façade is still standing and is most impressive. You can also visit the convent beside it which has been rebuilt and restored on numerous occasions. It used to contain some fine works of art, some of which have been transferred to the local parish church. Elsewhere a small exhibition of the wicker and cane work of local craftsmen is worth a visit.

Serra San Bruno, lying in a hollow surrounded by woods and mountains, is the main town of the Serre region. Here it is hard to believe one is in the southern Mediterranean, ash and birch trees forming the thick woods more typical of northern Europe, occasional fresh green meadows with splashes of yellow broom adding to the illusion. But if you are walking in the woods it is as well to watch out for snakes, which can sometimes be found coiled up in the middle of the path.

In the town itself one can visit the main church, built in the late eighteenth century, but which contains seventeenth-century statues, sixteenth-century paintings and a pulpit by Scaramuzzino. The church of the Addolorata has a striking baroque façade and inside, at the high altar, is a ciborium designed for the monastery of La Certosa in 1631.

La Certosa, a Carthusian monastery lies slightly south of the town Serra San Bruno, within walled gardens, overtopped by fifteenth-century cylindrical corner towers. It was reconstructed in 1595 and again after an earthquake in 1783. With its pastoral setting it exudes an atmosphere of peace and tranquility. If you are a man it is possible to visit the monastery in the company of a monk. Women are not admitted.

Stilo is built against the rocky slopes of Monte Consolino, on the south-east side of the Serre half-way up the Stilaro valley. The road from Serra San Bruno to Stilo runs across the Pietra Ospada Pass (4,380ft) and through the Santa Maria and Stilo woods. The little town is beautiful, with a wealth of art and architectural work.

Of principal interest is the Cattolica, a well preserved Byzantine church dating from either the seventh or tenth century, the exact date of its foundation being disputed. It is built to a traditional design still found in Asia Minor, corresponding to the shape of the Greek Orthodox cross. The floor plan is square with four marble columns dividing it into nine smaller squares, five with cylindrical cupolas and four that are barrel vaulted. There are some Byzantine frescoes but unfortunately these have been badly damaged.

One can also see the medieval cathedral with its well preserved exterior, the church of San Domenico and the church of San Francesco which has a typical curved centre façade and two setback wings, a fine example of the eighteenth-century style. Close by is the church of San Giovanni Vecchio built in the eleventh century. In the area there are many grottoes, once Basilian churches, with remains of Byzantine frescoes.

The Ionian Coast

The Ionian beaches begin south of Reggio. They are wide, baking hot and as far as Locri in the north, practically deserted except in high summer. The inland scenery is more arid than the Tyrrhenian coast with startling rocky outcrops instead of the green mountains. There is a coastal plain and inland amongst the hills, are numerous old villages, once the refuge for shore dwellers from Saracen raiders.

Pentedattilo, inland from Melito di Porto Salvo, is a charming hamlet with an interesting legend surrounding the origin of its name. Pentedattilo means 'the five fingers' as it clings to a five-pointed sandstone cliff, Monte Calvario. These are said to resemble five fingers stained with blood, shed during the torture of a local baron who was forbidden to marry the Lady Alberty, sister of the feudal lord of Pentedattilo. In the village you can see the ruins of a medieval castle rebuilt in the sixteenth century and there are other interesting medieval buildings. The church of the Candelora has a sixteenth-century marble statue and next to this church are the ruins of a Dominican monastery.

Gerace cathedral door

About 2 miles from **Locri** lie the excavations of ancient Locri, a vast area containing the remains of walls, a Greek-Roman theatre and several temples. There is the Ionian Temple of Masara, the Doric Temple of Marafioti, the little Temple of Athena Pramachos, the underground sanctuary of Pan and the Nymphs, and the sanctuary of Persephone.

Gerace

Inland from Locri the town of Gerace is perched on the top of a plug of rock. It is a picturesque little place, dominated by a ruined castle, which, sadly, is not open to the public. There are magnificent views over the surrounding countryside, which is unusual and striking rather than beautiful, from the grassy area beside the castle. Other remains of the complex medieval defence system include the ruins of a fortress and tower.

The eleventh-century cathedral, restored in the thirteenth century, has remarkable elegance and simplicity, and an atmosphere of peace. The nave is outstanding in its dimensions 240 x 85ft and it seems surprising to discover such an imposing building in such a

Pizzo

humble town. It is the largest church in Calabria, built to the plan of a Latin cross, and with an interesting transept and apses, and a Byzantine crypt. Also worth visiting is the church of San Francesco which contains the fourteenth-century Ruggo tomb, a seventeenth-century baroque chancel screen and, adjacent to it, the remains of a cloister. It is said that the area around Gerace is ruled by outlaws and this is not hard to believe given the wildness of the scenery.

Pizzo

South from Lamezia airport, following the coast road, lies the fortified clifftop town of Pizzo. It is a lively and interesting town both in terms of history, art and natural beauty. Viewed from a distance it has similarities to the town of Tropea further down the coast but whereas the latter is impressive because of the tall elegance of the houses Pizzo has a smaller, more intimate charm. The fifteenth-century Aragon castle stands at the head of the promontory and the little houses spread back from it, following the line of the cliff. Some of the most delightful streets lie off Via San Francesco, which runs parallel to, but above the main route for traffic passing through the town. Walking up the Via San Francesco to the church at the end there are small alleyways on the left sloping down steeply to the main road below. The houses are crammed one on top of the other with stone steps leading to entrances on all levels. Wrought iron lamp holders cling to the walls, and the balconies are covered with pots of trailing geraniums. It is a shame that on reaching the end of Via San Francesco (where there is a small *piazza*) the view back towards the little town clustered around the castle is marred by an ugly modern building. The skyline too is spoilt by a modern block of flats. Happily there are few examples of this type of thoughtlessness in Calabria. Returning to the centre of the town there is a small market selling excellent quality fruit and vegetables and a large range of fish. Tuna fishing can be viewed from the cliffs, and boats, still built by local craftsmen, can be seen in the boatyards.

The Marina has a cramped stony beach and is worth visiting only for the excellent restaurant, La Madonnina, where good value Calabrian home cooking is prepared and served in a delightful setting under a large rubber tree. A more attractive place for a swim in the area would perhaps be from the rocks beside the little church of Piedigrotta, hollowed out of the tufa, just beyond the water's edge.

Tropea

Half an hour's drive south of Pizzo lies the town of Tropea. The older part ot the town is built on a cliff, the houses rising straight out of the rock, as if forming part of the natural sandstone. The approach to the town, on the road from Pizzo, provides a spectacular introduction. The houses are tall and elegant, their green shutters contrasting gently with the mellow stone. Many houses have carved granite doorways often crowned with family crest or a grotesque mask to ward off the 'evil-eye'.

The cathedral is of Norman or pre-Norman origin but has been often restored, especially after the 1783 earthquake. Extensive work in 1926-9 restored it substantially to its original eleventh- to twelfth-century form and also brought to light the arches and the fine inlaid work along the left side; the interior is divided into three naves by octagonal columns and contains a beautiful woodcarving, the 'black' crucifix, probably dating from the fifteenth century. One sees many crucifixes in Italy but rarely one in which the Christ figure appears so human and so moving in his pain. There is also a painting on wood in the Byzantine style (thirteenth or fourteenth century) a marble statue by G. Montorsoli (1555), a marble ciborium of the fifteenth century, several pieces of Tuscan art and the Madonna delle Libertà,

Grotticelle beach

a sixteenth-century sculpture.

A beautiful portico with fourteenth-century pointed arches unites the church and the episcopal palace. In the palace chapel are frescoes from the late 1400s and the treasure includes a precious fourteenth-century bishop's crozier and a pre-eleventh-century bronze statue.

Opposite the cathedral is an excellent restaurant, Il Normano. Not only is the food well cooked and delicious, but one eats in a walled courtyard, surrounded by exotic plants and with views over the side of the cliff to the countryside and coast. The food in this area of Calabria is outstanding. There is a wide variety of fish and seafood and even the smallest and most unostentatious restaurant seems to produce an appetising dish of home-cooked pasta typically followed by whole prawns, swordfish or fresh tuna, and usually at a very reasonable price. One can find light and tasty pizzas at La Pergola on the road to Capo Vaticano to be eaten under a canopy of vines.

The coast around Tropea is wild and rugged with beaches separated by outlying rocks. The sand is coarse and white, and the sea clear, clean and buoyant. There are many holiday villages and camp sites in the area but these are only visited by great numbers of visitors in July and August. Travelling south from Tropea one reaches the scenic area of Capo Vaticano. The prettiest beach in the area is known as Grotticelle and is clearly marked from the main road. There is a shady camp site right on the beach which, again, is only full in July and August.

Nicotera

Driving south from Capo Vaticano one finds the hilltop town of Nicotera on the flank of Monte Poro. Besides wandering around the narrow streets admiring the quaint houses, many of which have eighteenth-century wrought iron balconies, the visitor can visit the castle, constructed in 1763 on the site of a Swabian-Angevin castle. Nicotera is an episcopal seat, with a cathedral, of medieval origin, rebuilt and restored in 1785 and containing fifteenth-century tomb fragments, a baroque bishop's throne, a painting from the late 1400s, a beautiful mosaic altar, a sixteenth-century crucifix of the Neapolitan school and precious furnishings and vestments from the 1700s. The bishop's palace has a fifteenth-century marble high relief.

South of Nicotera Marina lies the 'Violet Coast', said to get its name from the sunsets. South of Rosarno the coast road winds through ancient olive groves, perhaps amongst the most renowned in Italy. This area is of considerable archaeological interest. There are Roman ruins at La Timpa and Badia, near Nicotera and the site of the Greek colony of *Medma* is to be found on the Rosarno plain. This was founded by the people of Locri in the sixth century BC, and among the archaeological finds from here are the famous *Medma* terracottas, now housed in the museum at Reggio Calabria.

Monte Sant' Elia rises a few miles away from Taureana, the site of the ancient *Tauroentum*. It is covered with pine forests and has a delightful camp site. There is a beautiful view up to Nicotera in the north, out to sea as far as the Aeolian Islands with, behind it, the Aspromonte. The cove of Sant' Elia at Melicucca is very interesting and is only 2 miles away. At the foot of the mountain is the small beach of Marinella, surrounded by jagged rock formations and practically deserted. It has a freshwater spring and is surrounded by fishermen's houses, most of which are abandoned.

Bagnara Calabra

Bagnara is an attractive seaside town, tumbling down steep hills to a shingle beach. It is famous for the swordfish, still hunted by a method that resembles an ancient rite, probably brought by the Phoenecians. When a swordfish has been chased by the *'passerella'* (nowadays a motor boat) and harpooned, silence falls over the boat. The fish is hauled on board and laid under a type of scaffold. The skipper makes ritual marks, similar to small squares, on the gills of the dead fish and mutters a few words over the corpse. There is a swordfish festival at Bagnara in July.

It is difficult to find a restaurant in which to eat unless you visit Bagnara in July and August when a few tourists, mainly expatriates, rent accommodation in the town. There are two hotels, both of which appear closed, and only lengthy enquiries reveal a restaurant ready to switch on its lights and serve delicious bowls of home-cooked pasta. Truly off-the-beaten-track.

The esplanade is deserted except in the season, and rather bleak. It is the upper, older part of the town, which is most picturesque. Although built on a steep cliff, every available square inch of land is cultivated. Terraces, retained by stone walls, are overrun with vines and any remaining space between the villas is occupied by gardens where colourful roses, camellias, bougainvillaea and hibiscus run riot. One can visit the church of the Confraternity of the Rosary, built in eclectic style with a fine three-naved interior with beautiful seventeenth-century paintings, an interesting twelfth-century carved column and a sculpture of the sixteenth-century. If one takes the elevated *autostrada* rather than the coast road one has a magnificent view down onto the towns of Bagnara and Scilla. Given the terrain it seems remarkable that they have been built at all.

Scilla

Scilla has slightly more facilities for tourists than Bagnara although it is still delightfully unspoilt. Like Bagnara it slopes steeply towards the sea but it has the added character and interest of being built around a promontory. At the end of the promontory is a little har-

Scilla

bour, dominated by the castle.

The castle, originally late medieval, has been rebuilt at various times and now houses a youth hostel, open from April to October. It is an idyllic place to stay, with wonderful views on either side of the headland and across the Strait of Messina to Sicily. Below the castle, the church of the Spirito Santo is eighteenth century and has a graceful façade and, inside, paintings from the same period. There is a square opposite the church and from there steep steps lead to terraces overlooking the town. The views are breathtaking. There is luxuriant vegetation and fine splashes of colourful bougainvillaea. Beyond is the light shingly beach and curving coastline.

Further Information

— Calabria —

Calabria National Park
Ufficio Amministrazione
Foreste Demaniali
Cosenza

Reggio Calabria
Museo Nazionale della Magna
Grecia
Piazza de Nava
Open: Tuesday-Saturday, 9am-1pm, 4.30-7pm, Sunday 9am-1pm.

Scilla
Ostello della Gioventu
Open: April-October.

15 • Sicily

The ferry from Villa San Giovanni to Messina takes you from Italy to Sicily, the largest of the Mediterranean islands, with a history and culture distinct from that of the country to which it officially belongs. Sicily forms the 'football' of the Italian peninsula. It is more of a miniature continent than an island — for thousands of years it has had its own history and culture and although it has failed to achieve independence it has been granted regional autonomy, a gesture at least towards an acknowledgement of the Sicilian's strong feelings of having a separate identity. It is a grave mistake to describe a Sicilian as 'Italian'.

From the eighth century BC Sicily was part of Magna Graecia, when Syracuse became the rival of Athens. The Phoenicians felt threatened by the Greek colonists and the rivalry came to a head in 480BC in the first Punic war. After the fall of Carthage most of Sicily was seized by Rome but later it was invaded by the Barbarians. In the ninth and tenth century AD the Saracens founded a great civilization in Sicily. They were driven out by the Normans in the eleventh and twelfth centuries.

In Sicily one can find Greek theatres, temples and citadels, Roman bridges and aqueducts, Saracen mosques, houses and towers and Norman churches, castles and palaces. There are many fascinating and characterful towns, villages and monuments to be discovered which do not lie on the recognized tourist circuit and can often be explored in peace and tranquility or at least with only the native Sicilians for company.

A casual tourist is unlikely to come into contact with the Mafia. These gangsters still have their strongholds in the hills of western Sicily where they make a living from extortion and protection rackets as well as drug dealing in recent years. However, there has lately been more open public feeling against the Mafia, especially in Palermo. The island is gradually becoming more prosperous thanks to various schemes set up by La Cassa per il Mezzogiorno (the Fund for

Olive collecting

the South) and there is a new upsurge of interest in the island's culture and heritage.

Tindari

Arriving at Messina may provide an unfortunate introduction to the island. The traffic is indescribable and parking virtually impossible. Even escaping from the noise, fumes and heat may prove difficult as signposts are unclear and it is only too easy to get in the wrong lane and end up in a slow moving traffic jam travelling in the wrong direction. The motorway exits lie to the north of the town so if in doubt, head directly away and 'upwards' from the port.

Happily, within an hour it is possible to reach Tindari, one of the most beautiful settings for Greco-Roman remains anywhere in Sicily. Take the motorway in the direction of Palermo, leave at the 'Falcone' exit and head in the direction of the 'Chiesa della Madonna' which sits on a headland, Capo Tindari, dominating the skyline. This sanctuary attracts many pilgrims at the ceremony in early September in honour of the black-faced icon of the virgin.

Beyond the church lie the ruins of the ancient *Tyndaris*, founded in 396BC by Dionysius of Syracuse to protect Sicily's northern coast from the Phoenicians. As the town was vulnerable from the south-west the walls had to be particularly strong there and these can still be seen today to the left of the road approaching the main archaeological area. Near the entrance there is a little museum with models and finds from *Tyndaris*, including a reconstruction of some of the original scenery.

Down the path and to the right there are the remains of Roman houses, some with mosaics which have been excavated only comparatively recently. The most imposing ruin is that of the basilica, thought to have been built shortly after the town's resettlement by Caesar Augustus, perhaps in the early first century AD. It is an interesting building, incorporating Greek influences in the Roman style of construction.

Turning left at the end of the path from the entrance is the Greco-Roman theatre. The site is superb, perfectly positioned with a backdrop of the sea. It was built by the Greeks in the late fourth century BC but was completely reconstructed by the Romans for gladiatorial and circus spectacles. There are classical drama performances in the theatre every June.

Besides being a site of immense archaeological interest and great beauty, the views from the headland are breathtaking. On a clear day the Aeolian Islands break the horizon and one can see the whole of the Gulf of Patti. To the south lie mountains rising towards Etna. Even in high summer there are rarely more than a dozen or so people about.

The amphitheatre at Tyndaris

For those wanting to eat, the restaurant Agora is tastefully furnished, cool, and good value for money.

The Aeolian Islands

Returning along the coast from Tindari to Messina, the port of Milazzo stands on a narrow promontory and is the main embarcation point for visits to the Aeolian Islands. You can either take a steamer, which costs less and allows the beautiful island scenery to creep up on you gradually, or a hydrofoil which is more expensive and quicker.

Lipari is the largest island of the group and makes a good base for visiting the others. It is also the only island with a bank so it is as well to exchange money before you visit the others. Lipari town is an attractive place with cafés lining the waterfront. The hydrofoil port lies between the walls of the castle, the site of which has been inhabited since Neolithic times, and a natural rocky breakwater.

The Corso Vittorio Emanuele has most of the shops and the tourist office and is a delightful street. Besides the castle there is an interesting museum containing one of the best Neolithic collections in the world and the cathedral of San Bartolomeo, patron saint of the Aeolian Islands (and a common name there). Inside there are eighteenth-century frescoes and a silver statue of the saint, who suffered martyrdom by being skinned alive.

If you have not brought a car over on the ferry it is possible to explore the island by local bus. One can see the white slopes of Monte Pelato, white because of the pumice which is mined here. Pumice, the lightest rock in the world, floats on water so do not be alarmed whilst having a swim to see strange little lumps floating around you; for those with experience of the polluted northern Mediterranean beaches these are not what you might think!

From Pianoconte there is a path winding up to the crater of the extinct volcano, Monte Sant' Angelo (1,950ft). It is a steep climb but well worth it for the strange sight of the pumice quarries, two veins of obsidian (volcanic glass) and the magnificent view of the entire island. Near Pianoconte, at Bagno Secco, you can visit the little volcanic steam kettles or fumaroles. On the south side of Pianoconte is the Belvedere Quattrocchi with a spectacular view of Vulcano and the four Faraglione in the sea between the islands.

Vulcano is a strange island reeking of sulphur and composed of many colours. You can take a sulphur bath in the hot springs of Acqua del Bagno or Acqua Bollente — a bath which is meant to be good for you, although you have to put up with smelling like a rotten egg afterwards! You can walk to the summit of the volcano (it takes about an hour and you need proper shoes) to discover a near lunar landscape, but apart from the area around Vulcano Piano in the centre of the island, walks around Vulcano should really only be attempted by serious hikers.

Stromboli is the furthest north and east of the group of islands. It is composed entirely of the cone of an active volcano which is in constant mild eruption, exploding and sending puffs of smoke into the air at 10-minute intervals. The scene is particularly impressive at night when you can also see the showers of red sparks. The climb to the top is difficult and should be made with a guide.

It is impressive to see all these islands by boat and if time is limited one can do a day trip with a quick stop at Lipari and a view from the sea of the others. This is well worth it although a longer stay on the islands gives one time to appreciate their strange and unique characters. The islands are a Mecca for sub-aqua enthusiasts, the marine life being quite outstanding. One can find flying fish, swordfish, turtles, sea horses and hammer fish. There is a diving air-bottle service on all islands except Alicudi.

Forza d'Agro

South from Messina is the pretty medieval village of Forza d'Agro, near to which is the Norman church of San Pietro and San Paolo, said

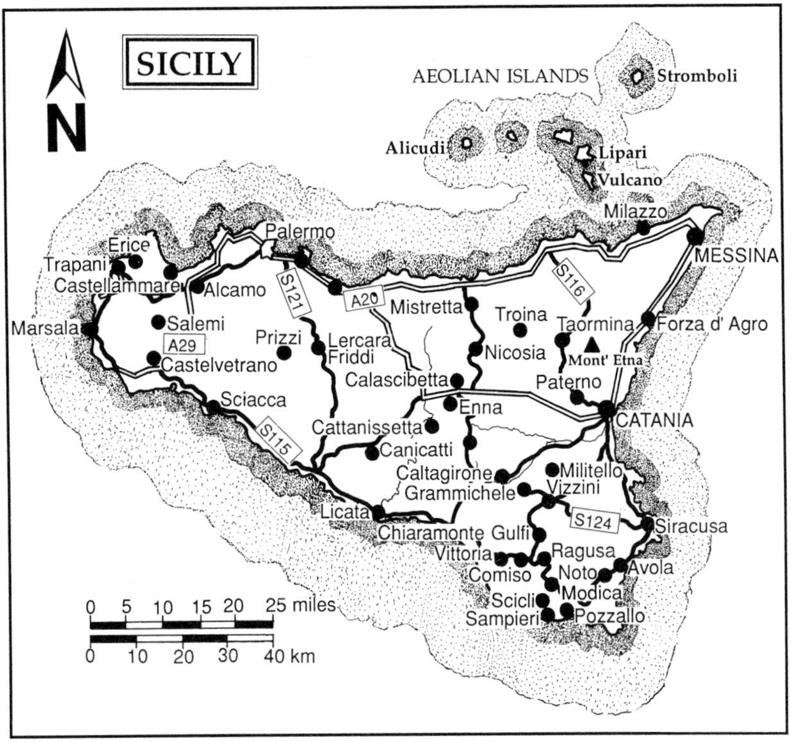

to be the most important Norman building in eastern Sicily. Despite this it is quite difficult to find.

If you are travelling on the motorway take the 'Roccalumera' exit and follow the SS114 southwards. Just outside the town of Santa Teresa di Rive, on the Catania side, the church is signposted. Turn right under a railway bridge and follow the signs until you come to a crossroads. Here the signpost tells you to continue straight on over the bridge, between two armco rails. It is possible to reach the church this way but the road peters out into a bumpy single track through lemon groves and there are no more signposts! If you meet another vehicle you have to reverse miles, seemingly, which is even more hair-raising. An easier route, if the wide river bed is dry, which it usually is, is to turn sharp left at the crossroads and drive inland along the river bed until you see a church on a small hill to your right.

The church itself was built in 1171-2 by Master Gerard the Franck for the Basilian Order of Monks. It is a graceful building, attractively decorated on the outside with mingled brick, buff-coloured limestone and dark lava. The interior was being restored at the time of the writer's visit but even through the scaffolding it was possible to appreciate its beauty.

Forza d'Agro is set on a hilltop and is dominated by a sixteenth-century castle. It commands a magnificent view over the Ionian Sea towards the mountains of Calabria. It is a picturesque place to visit with few if any tourists. The main church contains a beautiful painting by Antonio Guiffre of *Three Angels visiting Abraham*.

Caltagirone

The province of Catania is dominated by Mont' Etna, and is an area popular with tourists. In the south of the region, however, there are several small towns which are interesting to visit and are off the tourist circuit.

Caltagirone, the 'Queen of the Hills', is a centre for ceramics. It was originally inhabited in 2000BC by the Sikels and then came under Greek influence during the Syracusan expansion. The entry of a Ligurian population in 1040 renewed its power and gave it prestige which continued under Norman and Swabian domination.

It is built on three hills, some 2,000ft above sea level and its medieval streets have considerable charm. The local coloured tiles are particularly attractive and enhance the appearance of many of the buildings. The most striking example of this is the stairway above the church of Santa Maria del Monte, built in 1609 to unite the upper and lower parts of the town. It has 142 steps 26ft wide with ceramic tiles of blue, yellow and green design set into the front of each. The whole effect is quite unique. On 25 July, on the feast of San Giacomo, the stairway is lit with lights covered with coloured paper so as to create a luminous arras. In Via Roma is the Museo della Ceramica where one can see examples of the town's ceramics from prehistoric times to the present day.

Nearby **Grammichele** is interesting because of its geometrical shape. After the earthquake of 1693 the town, which had been completely destroyed, was rebuilt following a plan by the Prince of Butera, Carlo Branciforti, reviving the eighth-century Babylonian idea of radioconcentric city planning. The regular streets lead to a central hexagonal square. It is also famous for its dried figs.

Vizzini is probably the site of the ancient *Bidis* mentioned by Cicero. It also claims to be the setting of Mascagni's opera *Cavalleria Rusticana* and Giovanni Verga's *Mastro Don Gesualdo* but these claims are also made by Francofonte just down the road! Vizzini also claims to be the birthplace of Verga though he was, in fact, born in Catania! But whether the operatic claims are believed or not, Vizzini is an attractive and atmospheric town.

Militello

Militello was founded, according to legend, by Roman soldiers from whom the name *militum tellus* (land of soldiers) derives. Over the centuries the town became an important religious and cultural centre with a great number of churches, monasteries and other buildings being constructed, most notable during the Renaissance period. The fifteenth-century Chiesa di Santa Maria la Vetere just outside the city is of particular artistic interest.

Noto

South of Catania province lie the provinces of Siracusa and Ragusa. This south-eastern corner of Sicily is particularly wild, beautiful and unaffected by tourism. There are many beaches south of Syracuse and the countryside is fertile and cultivated with citrus groves.

The town of Noto was completely destroyed by the 1693 earthquake and the prosperous inhabitants built the new town, in pure baroque style, just a few miles from the old one. It was laid out by Giovanni Battista Landolina and the architect Rosario Gagliardi designed the cathedral and other buildings. From the level main street most of the town rises according to set plan. The stone is a warm golden colour and the buildings are surprisingly magnificent for such an out-of-the-way place.

Besides the cathedral one should visit the Palazzo Ducezio built around 1750, the churches of San Francesco and Santa Chiara, the bishop's palace and the Museo Civico. In the museum there is a collection of prehistoric, antique and more modern items from the town of Noto Antica and the surrounding countryside. There are also interesting original architectural drawings for some of the buildings in the town.

There are many delightful back streets in Noto and half the charm of the place is in wandering through them and discovering for oneself the unique atmosphere of this delightful little town.

Ragusa

Ragusa is the main town of the south-eastern corner of Sicily. It has made its money from the thriving industries of oil and asphalt, yet because of its remote position, deep in the wild, hilly countryside and with poor communications it has remained remarkably unexploited.

The old town of Ibla stands on the original Sikel site. After the 1693 earthquake which devastated much of this corner of Sicily, work was begun on the modern town. Its attempt to become an independent community was a source of strife for centuries, but the new part flourished and expanded. The two were united in 1926 when Ragusa became the provincial capital.

The modern town is on a higher level, standing at 1,500ft. Of interest is the baroque cathedral of San Giovanni Battista. The archaeological museum is nearby, and its collection derives mainly from nearby *Camarina*, a Syracusan colony. There are various Greek items from tombs, and reconstructed graves. At the edge of the new town can be found one of the few buildings to have escaped, to any large extent, the 1693 earthquake, the fourteenth-century church of Santa Maria delle Scale, perched on the side of a steep ridge overlooking the old town. Although damaged by the earthquake, and rebuilt in baroque style, the chapels adjoining one of the naves are original, as are a portal and the interior arches with their finely sculptured decoration. From the church terrace there is a beautiful view across to Ibla (the old town which is on the opposite hill) with the rather harsh, rocky hills beyond providing a spectacular setting. There is a lengthy stairway below the church which leads to the old town.

It is a lengthy, tortuous descent from the new town and up again to Ibla but it is well worth making on foot for the views are superb, overlooking the rooftops of the old town. If the journey is made by car it is rather difficult to concentrate on both the views and the narrow streets at the same time. An alternative is to take the local bus, rather a hair-raising experience, but an easy way of capturing some

Siracusa

of the local atmosphere.

Ibla is an attractive place to explore, with narrow medieval streets and small piazzas. The dome of San Georgio dominates the skyline: it is an imposing building, designed by Gagliardi, and standing at the top of a curved stairway above the tree-lined Piazza del Duomo, the social centre of the town, flanked by many bars, shops and cafés.

Modica

The province of Ragusa has a wealth of small towns and villages which are unspoilt by tourism and give the flavour of the 'true' Sicily.

Modica used to be the country town of the area and was particularly influential in the eighteenth century. It was the discovery of asphalt and petroleum at Ragusa that tipped the balance in favour of the latter. Modica's past wealth is reflected in its interesting architecture: San Giorgio is one of the finest baroque churches in the area and many of the town houses have beautiful exterior decorations and carvings.

The town is situated on the site of a former Neolithic settlement where three valleys cross. In 1902 the rivers which pass through the town flooded, causing a landslide, so they have now been covered over. The houses spread up the surrounding hillsides which makes exploration of the town an expedition for the fit. Many of the streets are, in fact, stairways and it is worthwhile taking time to discover delightful views over the roofs of houses crowded almost one on top of the other. From the top of the town you can look across the valley to the houses on the opposite side, the scene looking almost like a Christmas crib.

The church of San Giorgio is situated high up on the east hill, reached by a flight of 250 steps that passes through landscaped gardens. It is reminiscent of the church of the same name in Ragusa, and was probably designed by the same architect, Gagliardi. It dates from 1643, but was damaged by the 1693 earthquake after which it was reconstructed and enlarged. The façade, built in the eighteenth century, is particularly beautiful, as is the interior which is spacious and light. White is the main colour used with a few touches of blue. The altarpiece is made up of ten paintings on a curved frame, showing scenes from the life of St George. It has recently been restored and looks fresh and colourful. One can also visit the cathedral of San Pietro and the church of Santa Maria di Betlem in the lower town, where the highest point of the 1902 flood is marked by a plaque.

A few miles from Modica is **Cava d'Ispica**, a narrow gorge about 8 miles long. Here the visitor can see prehistoric tombs cut into the rock and many other traces of long human habitation, the area also having Christian catacombs and Byzantine chapels. Even today the local peasants use the caves as stores. The gorge is not only interesting archaeologically, but is scenically very spectacular.

Ragusa Province

South of Modica there are two coastal towns which are worth a visit. **Pozzallo** has an attractive terraced park overlooking the wide beach and the sea. In the old part of the town are houses with *ciappette* — the balconies characteristic of the area, with tiled or cemented floors and attractive wrought iron railings. Along the marina one can still see the fishermen spreading their nets out to dry. On the second Sunday in August is the Sagra del Pesce or fish festival, honouring the fish as the source of life. It is worth attending, both as an interesting folk tradition, and as a gastronomic delight.

The old village of **Scicli** stands at the top of San Matteo hill with houses scattered down the sides into three valleys. The setting is quite beautiful, especially when looking up from the coast with the houses basking in the sunlight. In the church of San Bartolomeo is a Christmas crib which dates back to 1535 and is attributed to the Neopolitan artist Pietro Padula. It represents a scene of small farmers grouped around the more static figures of the Nativity. From Scicli the road forks to the beaches of Donnalucata, which has a ruined Norman tower, Cava d'Aliga and Sampieri.

North of Ragusa, **Chiaramonte Gulfi** is a village built on top of a hill named after its founder, Manfredi Chiaramonte. It is known as the Balcony of Sicily because of the beautiful view from the public gardens on the south-west side of the town. To the west one looks down on the small towns of Comiso, Vittoria and Caltagirone, with Gela beach far in the distance; to the north rises the summit of Mont' Etna. Chiaramonte Gulfi is also famous throughout Sicily for its pork and lamb specialities, goat's cheese with peppers, and particularly fine olive oil.

Monterosso Almo, in the extreme north of the region, has a very picturesque old quarter. It too is built on the top of a hill, here descending more gradually to the river valley. Unfortunately the local economy is poor and the lack of employment has caused much emigration. It is a characterful small town nonetheless, dominated by the church of San Giovanni Battista.

Sciacca

Sciacca is the prettiest town in Agrigento province, a town that has been a thermal spa for centuries. It is built in layers down the side of a cliff and the small white buildings, especially those higher up, give an almost North African appearance.

The town is surrounded by a towered wall, built in 1336, while during the sixteenth-century reconstruction work (in late medieval times it was the scene of one of Sicily's greatest family feuds, between the Lunas and the Perollas, which divided the town and caused some damage) the Porta San Salvatore was built and this is still the most spectacular way to enter the town.

North of Sciacca is **Monte San Calogero**, another thermal spa, hot vapour flowing out through a grotto originally hollowed out in prehistoric times, which has stone carved seats but these from a much later period! Legend has it that it was Daedalus who made the baths. Beneath the steam baths are two underground caverns in which Copper Age jars have been discovered together with children's bones. The bones are thought to be from ritual child sacrifice.

Enna

The interior of Sicily is far less lush than the coasts and can indeed be rather bleak. There are, however, a handful of towns which make a trip to the interior an interesting and worthwhile experience.

The centre of the island is already high and Enna clings precipitously to an even higher plateau. At 3,100ft above sea level, it is the highest provincial capital in Italy. It has fine medieval and Aragonese towers and churches as well as magnificent views in all directions. The buses arrive in Piazza Vittorio Emanuele and all the main sights are signposted from there.

The Castello di Lombardia, built by Frederick II, is one of the most important medieval castles in Sicily. It was used as a residence by Frederick III of Aragon, who proclaimed himself 'King of Trinacria' here. Originally it had twenty towers, but only six remain. The Torre Pisano is the best preserved of these and can be climbed, the top offering a wonderful view onto the plain, a view that includes Lago di Pergusa, where the rape of Persephone is said to have occurred. There is a sheer drop from the tower down the rock face below so it is as well to have a head for heights. There is an open-air theatre in the ruins of the castle's chapel where operas are performed during a summer season. Legend has it that King Sikanus and the goddess Demeter are buried together below the castle. From the castle rock the 'Rocca di Cerere' juts out to the north-east and here can be seen a few traces of the Temple of Demeter built by Gelon in 480BC.

Also along the Via Roma (the castle stands at its eastern end) can be found the cathedral, an interesting building incorporating a variety of styles. It was built in the early fourteenth century but a fire in 1446 destroyed all but the apse. The façade is eighteenth-century baroque in a rather strange style, thought to be an attempt to preserve the lines of its Gothic original. The interior is almost all sixteenth

An old lava flow on Mont' Etna

century: the ceiling of the nave and the carved choir stalls are particularly attractive and a remarkable feature is the colonnade of smooth, black alabaster pillars from the sixteenth-century restoration.

Next to the cathedral is the Museo Alessi which houses numerous coins and quantities of weapons dating from the battle for Enna during the slave revolt of 134BC. The rich cathedral treasure which used to be here is now in the custody of the priest.

From the Torre di Frederico II in the public gardens one can see all three corners of Sicily on a clear day. Not surprisingly the tower has acquired the name *Umbilicus Sicilae* as it is meant to be the absolute centre of the island. The entrance to the tower is in Viale IV Novembre, and it is open daily from dawn to dusk. The views from Enna are stunning especially towards Calascibetta on the hill opposite, with rolling mountains in the background.

Saracenic **Calascibetta** is smaller than Enna, its origins being obvious in its old reddish buildings as well as in its name. It is a poor, strange remote place, taking longer to reach from Enna than one would expect, and totally lacking in any sophistication. Yet it has a certain charm and is certainly a 'must' for those wanting to get to know the hard, difficult conditions of the interior.

Enna Province

Nicosia is a pretty, medieval town, dominated by the ruins of a Norman castle which stand on a crag high above the town. A further interesting aspect of the town's history is that its local dialect is said to betray influences of Lombardian and Piemontese settlers. The cathedral of San Nicola has a fine fourteenth-century doorway and inside there are paintings by Velasquez, Pietro Novelli and Salvatore Rosa, together with a crucifix by Fra Umile da Petraglia. The ceiling dates from the thirteenth century. The church of Santa Maria Maggiore, elsewhere in the town, contains a huge marble polyptych showing scenes from the Virgin's life.

Troina is the highest town in Sicily and still shows traces of Greek walls that indicate the antiquity of such a significant site. There is a beautiful view from the Chiesa Madre in the centre of the town, while the church itself is of considerable interest, and dates from the twelfth century.

Erice

Although Erice is visited by tourists and has become a well known international conference centre, it still seems sufficiently unspoilt to merit inclusion. The town lies $8^1/_2$ miles north-east of Trapani in an impregnable position, 2,454ft above sea level. The bus journey takes an hour and it is not much quicker by car. Certainly it is a pity to rush the ride as the views back to Trapani improve by the minute. The sides of the mountain are covered in wild flowers which also make one want to delay the journey.

Mont' Eryx, as it is known in history, has a long association with myth and legend. It is said that Aphrodite snatched Butes the Athenian from the sea into which he had thrown himself, unable to resist the singing of the Sirens, and took him off to her Temple of Eryx to make him her lover. Here, too, Daedalus offered the goddess the golden honeycomb. The misty mountain makes such legends easy to believe.

The towers and most of the walls of the town are medieval, as is the rather romantic castle from which, on a clear day, you can see the coast of North Africa. The atmosphere in the narrow cobbled streets which wind up and down the hills is overwhelmingly medieval. One can glimpse behind the attractive stone façades of the houses to find little courtyards filled with plants.

In the Museo Comunale the visitor finds Antonello Gagnini's *Annunciation*, said to be his best work, a wax nativity scene and a fourth-century BC head of Aphrodite.

The views from all parts of the town are outstanding but particularly so from two towers standing in the public gardens, and from the castle.

Further Information

— Sicily —

Museums and Other Places of Interest

Agrigento
Museo Nazionale Archeologico
Open: Tuesday-Friday 9am-1.30pm, 3-5pm, Saturday and Sunday 9am-12noon.

Calania
Bellini's House
Piazza San Francesco
Open: Monday-Saturday 9am-1pm and Friday 4.30-7.30pm, Sunday 9am-7.30pm.
Admission free.

Castello Ursino & Museo Civico
Piazza Frederico di Svevia
Open: Monday-Saturday 9am-1.30pm, Sunday 9.30am-12.30pm.
Admission free.

Caltagirone
Museum of Ceramics
Via Rima
Open: daily 9am-2pm, Sunday 9am-1pm.
Closed Mondays.

Cefalù
Museo Mandralisca
Via Mandralisca
Open: Monday-Saturday 9am-12noon, 3.30-6pm, Sunday 9.30am-12noon.

Enna
Castello di Lombardia
Open: daily 8.30am-1pm, 3-5pm.

Torre di Frederico II
Entrance in Viale IV Novembre
Open: daily dawn-dusk.

Erice
Museo Comunale Cordici
Open: 9am-2pm, 3-5pm.

Gela
Museo Nazionale

Open: 9am-1.30pm.

Lipari (Aeolian Islands)
Museum
Corso Vittorio Emanuele
Open: daily 9am-1pm, 3.30-6pm.

Messina
Museo Regionale
Viale della Libertà
Open: Tuesday-Friday 9am-1.30pm, Sunday 9am-12.30pm.

Monreale
Cathedral
Open: 7am-12.30pm, 3-6pm.

Noto
Civic Museum
Open: daily
9am-1pm.
Closed Monday.

Palermo
Museo Nazionale Archeologico
Piazza dell' Olivella
Open: Monday-Saturday 9am-2pm, Sunday 9.30am-1pm.

Palazzo Abbatellis
Via Alloro
Open: Tuesday-Saturday 9am-2pm, Sunday 9am-1pm.

Ragusa
Archaeological Museum
Open: daily 9am-2pm, holidays 9am-1pm.
Closed Mondays.

Ribera
Site of Heraclea Minoa Antiquarium
Open: Monday-Saturday 9am-2pm, Sunday 9am-1pm.

Syracuse
Museo Regionale Archeologico
Viale Teocrito
Open: Tuesday-Friday 9am-2pm, Sunday 9am-1pm.

Museo Nazionale del Palazzo Bellomo
Via Capodieci
Open: Tuesday-Saturday 9am-2pm, Sunday 9am-1pm.

Taormina
Greek Theatre
Via Teatro Greco
Open: 9am-1 hour before dusk.

Tyndaris
Archaeological site, see below*.

***NB:** The usual opening times for archaeological sites in Sicily is 9am-1 hour before dusk.

Index